ARMAGEDDON
at the
DOOR

JON PAULIEN

Autumn House® Publishing
www.autumnhousepublishing.com
A Division of **REVIEW AND HERALD**® PUBLISHING
Since 1861

Published by Autumn House® Publishing, a division of Review and Herald® Publishing, Hagerstown, MD 21741-1119

Autumn House® titles may be purchased in bulk for educational, business, fund-raising, or sales promotional use. For information, please e-mail SpecialMarkets@reviewandherald.com.

Autumn House® Publishing publishes biblically based materials for spiritual, physical, and mental growth and Christian discipleship.

The author assumes full responsibility for the accuracy of all facts and quotations as cited in this book.

Texts credited to ESV are from *The Holy Bible, English Standard Version,* copyright © 2001 by Crossway Bibles, a division of Good News Publishers. Used by permission. All rights reserved.

Texts credited to NIV are from the *Holy Bible, New International Version.* Copyright © 1973, 1978, 1984, International Bible Society. Used by permission of Zondervan Bible Publishers.

Texts credited to NKJV are from the New King James Version. Copyright © 1979, 1980, 1982 by Thomas Nelson, Inc. Used by permission. All rights reserved.

Bible texts credited to NRSV are from the New Revised Standard Version of the Bible, copyright © 1989 by the Division of Christian Education of the National Council of the Churches of Christ in the U.S.A. Used by permission.

This book was
Edited by Gerald Wheeler
Copyedited by James Cavil
Cover designed by Trent Truman
Interior designed by Candy Harvey
Typeset: Bembo 11/14

PRINTED IN U.S.A.

12 11 10 09 08   5 4 3 2 1

Library of Congress Cataloging-in-Publication Data
Paulien, Jon, 1949-   .
  Armageddon at the door: an insider's guide to the book of Revelation. / Jon Paulien
    p. cm.
  1. Bible—Prophecies—Armageddon. 2. Armageddon—Biblical teaching. I. Title.
  BS649.A68P38 2008
  236.9—dc22
                              2008005137

ISBN 978-0-8127-0477-8

CONTENTS

Introduction • 5

Chapter 1
The Rise of Islamic "Terrorism" • 9

Chapter 2
The Western Response and the Battle of Armageddon • 27

Chapter 3
Discovering "Armageddon" • 41

Chapter 4
The Meaning of Armageddon • 50

Chapter 5
Going Away to Make War • 61

Chapter 6
The Seven Last Plagues • 82

Chapter 7
All Eyes on the Euphrates • 96

Chapter 8
The Axis of Evil • 116

Chapter 9
The Final Movements (Winners and Losers) • 134

Chapter 10
Dueling Gospels and Worldwide Confederacies • 151

Chapter 11
The Conclusion of the Battle • 168

Chapter 12
Final Reflections on Armageddon • 184

Appendix • 204

INTRODUCTION

One of the more memorable moments in recent history was the plea of American general Douglas MacArthur in the wake of the atomic bombs that fell on Hiroshima and Nagasaki at the close of World War II:

"A new era is upon us. . . . The destructiveness of the war potential, through progressive advances in scientific discovery, has in fact now reached a point which revises the traditional concepts of war.

"Men since the beginning of time have sought peace. . . . Military alliances, balances of power, leagues of nations, all in turn failed, leaving the only path to be by way of the crucible of war.

"We have had our last chance. If we do not now devise some greater and more equitable system, Armageddon will be at our door."[1]

His words illustrate the great power that the book of Revelation and the battle of Armageddon still have in today's world. MacArthur drew the word "Armageddon" from Revelation's account of a final conflict at the end of history that would involve all the nations of the earth. The word is so widely recognized that moviemakers adopted it as the title of a science-fiction film about an asteroid that threatens earth. It was also a mainstay of speeches by President Reagan back in the 1980s, as the final stages of the cold war played out.

The book of Revelation guides us in understanding the successive ages of history and their culmination in a catastrophic struggle between the forces of good and evil. God intended it to help people make sense of the universe and where they stand in it. That is a major reason we are seeing such a great resurgence of interest in Revelation at the beginning of a new millennium.

People today think of themselves as living, at least potentially, in the last generation of earth's history. About three decades ago the Club of Rome (a group of scientists) predicted that by now civilization would have collapsed under the weight of increasing population and the lack of food. Since that time many survival-threatening problems have come to our attention. A major phrase in the current vocabulary is "global warming" (a gradual warming of the earth on account of the effects of human activity). If this condition is not reversed, many scientists feel that it will melt the polar ice caps, inundate coastal areas, and eventually so change the climate of earth that life may no longer be possible on the planet. The destruction of the world's last sizable rain forest (in Brazil) raises questions about the earth's ability to maintain the necessary supply of oxygen in its atmosphere to sustain animal and human life. Alien objects, such as giant meteorites, comets, and asteroids, also endanger our world. The threat of germ and chemical warfare, toxic waste dumps, the destruction of the earth's ozone layer, terrorism, and such new diseases as AIDS, Ebola, and H5N1 have made everyone well aware of human mortality. And recent energy and water shortages raise world consciousness to the fact that natural resources are limited.

As the book of Revelation makes clear, however, our generation is not the first to perceive that it could be the last. The difference is that ours is the first generation that has perceived that the end could come without reference to God. Somehow the idea that God could bring about the end allows for the possibility that He could save as well. But the secular apocalypse looming over us could be the result of an accident of history, even the random madness of a terrorist with a "doomsday machine." Thus we face the end as potentially an "abyss of meaninglessness." We struggle with the terrifying realization that human nature is inherently self-destructive.

Many even perceive our beloved computer technology as a threat to human survival. A warning about the dangers of technology came from none other than Bill Joy, former chief scientist at Sun Microsystems and a creator of Java, a software application that helped make the Internet what it is today. While Joy is at the cutting edge of technological development, he nevertheless argues that technology always leads to "unintended consequences." Just as the widespread use of antibiotics and DDT have had unforeseen and potentially disastrous results, Joy reminds us that Murphy's Law is an inevitable part of technological advances in computing as well.[2]

Building on the work of Ray Kurzweil and Hans Moravec, Joy notes that computer systems are highly complex, involving interaction among and feedback between many parts. Any changes to such a system will cascade in ways difficult to predict. If Moore's Law of hardware advancement (doubling computer performance every two years at no increase in cost) continues to operate, by about 2030 we will be able to build machines that rival human beings in intelligence. Joy argued that when such "robots" exceed human intelligence and become able to self-replicate, the extinction of the human race becomes conceivable, perhaps as early as 2050.

He sees the danger in genetics, nanotechnology, and robotics (GNR) as even greater than that of nuclear, chemical, and biological warfare. The latter are military weapons that remain under human control. The dangers of GNR, on the other hand, arise from their commercial and economic benefits. The marketplace will, therefore, promote and develop them with unintended consequences that will be outside governmental control. "This is the first moment in the history of our planet when any species, by its own voluntary actions, has become a danger to itself—as well as to vast numbers of others," he concludes.[3]

Still, we do find a bit of good news in all this. Jaron Lanier, a specialist in virtual reality systems, argues that Joy and his supporters have confused "ideal" computers with real ones.[4] While we can conceptualize ideal computers, we know how to build only dysfunctional ones. Real computers break down for reasons that are often less than clear, and they seem to resist our efforts to improve them, often because of what we can call legacy and lock-in problems. While Moore's Law continues to work for hardware systems, software seems to be getting worse and worse as systems become more complex.

While in theory, therefore, the hardware could become sophisticated enough to exceed human intelligence, Lanier notes that human beings themselves don't seem able to write software that would make such a superior machine possible (thank God!). If anything, Moore's Law seems to play in reverse when it comes to software. As processors become faster and memory becomes cheaper, software becomes correspondingly slower and more bloated, using up all available resources. So Lanier conceives Joy's eschatological nightmare to end as follows: "Just as some newborn race of superintelligent robots are about to consume all humanity, our dear old species will likely be saved by a Windows crash. The poor robots will linger pathetically, begging us to reboot them, even though they'll know it would do no good." Thus the human race escapes extinction because of "stupid software."

ARMAGEDDON AT THE DOOR

Regardless of the outcome of this debate, it is clear that the book of Revelation speaks to fears and possibilities that are just as real in today's world as they were in the time of John. People today tend to agree with Revelation that society is headed toward catastrophe and chaos unless some extraordinary intervention should occur. They also increasingly agree on the threat facing us: the inhumanity of human beings toward one another. In enslaving or abusing other human beings, we set ourselves up as false gods acting out our own distorted version of reality. The book of Revelation helps us see the self-deception that lurks within.

As we contemplate the potential fate of the world, we will want to get a firm grasp on just how the Bible portrays that end. The book of Revelation depicts the end as preceded by a great final war called the battle of Armageddon. What is the battle of Armageddon and how will everything actually reach its conclusion? To answer these questions is the purpose of this book. The primary data for our journey is the biblical book of Revelation. We will begin, however, with a look at the great battle of our own time, the so-called war on terror, a situation that some have regarded as a precursor to Armageddon. As we examine the forces at work in it, we will gain some insights into what the battle of Armageddon might or might not be.

---

[1] Douglas MacArthur, *Reminiscences* (New York: McGraw-Hill, 1964), p. 276.

[2] Bill Joy, "Why the Future Doesn't Need Us," *Wired*, April 2000, pp. 239-243.

[3] *Ibid.*, p. 248. Joy cites the philosopher John Leslie as estimating the risk of human extinction at 30 percent. Thus Joy believes that the only solution to this danger is consciously to restrict the development of potentially dangerous technologies, "by limiting our pursuit of certain kinds of knowledge" (p. 254). He cites Thoreau as saying that we will be "rich in proportion to the number of things which we can afford to let alone" (p. 258).

[4] Jaron Lanier, "One-Half of a Manifesto: Why Stupid Software Will Save the Future From Neo-Darwinian Machines," *Wired*, December 2000, pp. 158-179.

THE RISE OF ISLAMIC
"TERRORISM"

Seventh-day Adventism rests on a fundamental conviction about history—that sometime during the nineteenth century the world entered the time of the end. Our pioneers, including Ellen White, went so far as to attach dates to that transition, dates such as A.D. 1798 and 1844. But whether or not you feel that such precision is appropriate, virtually all Adventists share the general conviction that we are living very close to the end of history.[1]

Since each Adventist generation has felt that it could be the last one of earth's history, major wars have inevitably led to speculation whether they represented the beginning of the battle of Armageddon. The outbreak of World War I, in which Turkey was one of the major combatants, coincided with the conviction of many that Turkey and the Euphrates River (Rev. 16:12) would play some role in the final conflict. Turkey ended up on the defeated side of that war, losing control of the key part of the Euphrates River, and yet time went on.

The horrific nature of World War II, and the Japanese role in it, likewise attracted the attention of Adventist evangelists. Many suggested that the Japanese were the "kings of the rising sun" (see Rev. 16:12) and would sweep their way along the southern coast of Asia and insert themselves into the Middle East. Their arrival would precipitate the battle of Armageddon. But the Japanese never got that far (their attempts to reach India petered out on the "road to Mandalay" in what was then called Burma and today is Myanmar), and time continued on.

After World War II emerged the cold war, thought by some to be the prelude to World War III. For the first time in human history people had the tools to destroy all life on earth. The nuclear standoff between the United States and the Soviet Union seemed to have all the ingredients of the final battle of earth's history. It was the bulwark of Christian faith in conflict with the forces of atheism. Yet the Soviet Union collapsed, and a "new world disorder" took its place. Only one superpower remains in the world today. But that superpower finds itself almost helpless in the face of a nameless fear, a sense that the very foundation of civilization is in question, not from a governmental system of equal power, but from a handful of religious believers willing to blow themselves up in order to change the world. As was the case with the early church, once again the blood of martyrs is seed, but this time the seed of what?

Is the war on terror World War IV? Is it the beginning of the battle of Armageddon? Have we finally reached the place at which the curtain closes and God plays Taps over the mangled remains of human history? Before we take a careful look at the biblical evidence for the battle of Armageddon, I thought it would be helpful to do a careful analysis of the situation in today's world. Such a thing is not easy to do. History is best written after the events under consideration have finally concluded. While the war on terror is a major part of each day's news, few analysts have been able to step back from those events far enough to see the larger developing picture. But we gain nothing by not trying. The mere attempt at drawing the big picture can stimulate us all to think more carefully and to see more clearly.

The Origin of al-Qaeda

Where did al-Qaeda (the self-appointed leadership of worldwide Islamic terrorism) come from? What is the source of its rage against the West in general and the United States in particular? Is the war on terror destined for success or doomed to failure? Was the war in Iraq a colossal blunder or in some way the key to the whole conflict? The broad perspective of history can help us get a handle on such issues. As we apply that history to the viewpoint of Bible prophecy, I believe that it will prepare us to see more clearly the hand of God in developing events. Although we don't know when Jesus will come, prophecy offers many clues as to the events that will surround His return. This book will attempt to clarify these issues and more.

The Rise of Islam

To understand today's events fully, you have to go far back into history. The story of al-Qaeda begins in the desert sands of the Hijaz, the western part of the Arabian Peninsula, in the seventh century of our era. According to Christian tradition, a conviction shared by the nomadic residents of the Arabian Desert, the 12 disciples of Jesus spread the gospel throughout the then-known world. But there was one exception to this nearly universal growth—the Arabian Peninsula. The people of Arabia did not have an apostle of their own, and they did not have a Scripture in their own language, as the Jews and the Christians did.[2] Distressed by the inconsistencies and confusion they perceived in the two earlier monotheistic faiths, Arabs of the desert developed the conviction that God would one day give them a messenger of their own and a Scripture in their own language.

Their expectation became fulfilled in their minds when a man named Muhammad ibn Abdallah went on a spiritual retreat in A.D. 610 to a cave on Mount Hira, overlooking the city of Mecca (Makkah). Muhammad was one of a handful of Arab seekers longing for a restoration of the pure faith of Abraham (Ibrahim). One night in the cave the sense of an overwhelming divine presence tore him from his sleep. He felt the powerful embrace of an angel who commanded him to recite what God (Allah) was placing in his mind. After a struggle Muhammad found the words of a new scripture pouring from his mouth. The experience repeated itself scores of times during the next 22 years. His followers collected these "recitations" into a book known as the Qur'an.

The teachings of the Qur'an precipitated a powerful spiritual revival that began in Muhammad's lifetime. The Qur'an affirmed that the God of the Bible was the one true God and that the prophets of the Old and New Testaments were His prophets. It called the Arab people to abandon idols and submit fully to this God that the earlier scriptures had proclaimed (the word for God in Arabic is "Allah"). Outlining a society that would transcend tribalism and revenge, the Qur'an called for justice and compassion and forgiveness and for everyone to do battle (jihad) with the forces of evil in their own lives. Thus the Qur'an was a summons to restore the pure faith of Abraham (Ibrahim), which to a large degree had been distorted by the earlier followers of God (a conviction that Adventists share). To a people who had felt left out of the divine plan until then, this was a message of transforming power. And it brought such change into their lives that more and more Arabs became convinced that Muhammad was a true prophet of God, even the preeminent prophet of God.

Whether or not you believe that God had His hand in the rise of Islam, we cannot deny that Muhammad was one of the most significant change agents in the history of the world. The energy unleashed by his recitations turned the Arab people from idolatrous bandits[3] to one of the greatest civilizations that the world had known up until that time. The Islamic empire was the great superpower of the Middle Ages and played a dominant role in world affairs right up to the time of the so-called Enlightenment (the eighteenth century).

Then something went wrong with the Islamic dream. Some scholars trace the beginnings of decline as far back as the Islamic reaction to the Crusades, while others place it in social developments in thirteenth-century Spain. Narrow thinking began to dissipate the energy unleashed by Muhammad's vision. Scholarship that had transformed the arts, the sciences, and literature became focused on maintaining the status quo. The Renaissance, the Enlightenment, and the rebirth of ancient Greek and Roman ideals created the kind of energy in Europe that had characterized the early Islamic empire. The torch of science and learning somehow passed to the West, and the power and wealth of the world went with it. By the eighteenth century of our era the Islamic world had fallen into serious intellectual, political, and economic decline. And by the mid-nineteenth century it was largely "colonized" by the West and has never recovered.

The Rise of Saudi Arabia

In the face of this long-term decline Muhammad ibn Abd al-Wahhab (1703-1792) founded an Islamic "back to the Bible" type of movement. Wanting to restore the pure Islam of the desert, free of all later additions and innovations, he called for careful exegesis (ijtihad) of the sacred texts in order to undo the changes that had led to Islam's decline. In other words, he taught that all the resources needed to restore the greatness of Islam lay in the past.

His is the basic conviction shared by today's Muslim fundamentalists. Much like Fundamentalist Christians and historic Adventists, they seek to restore the faith to its former greatness by careful attention to the teachings of the faith's pioneer(s). The key to Islam's salvation, they say, lies in replicating its past. The Muslim world has deviated from pure Islam, and only a return to its origins will safeguard it from domination and exploitation by the West. It is a conviction strongly exhibited in the Wahabis of Saudi Arabia and the Taliban of Afghanistan. And it was the kind of intellectual atmosphere in which Osama bin Laden and his compatriots grew up.

So the foundation for the development of al-Qaeda was a reaction to the decline in the Islamic world that led to a call to revival of the original fundamentals of the faith. Wahabism became closely entwined with the Saudi royal family (the House of Saud) that came to rule the Arabian Peninsula in the wake of World War I and the decline of the British Empire (the Kingdom of Saudi Arabia was established in 1923).[4]

The second foundation for the development of al-Qaeda occurred in 1938. The king of Saudi Arabia, Abd-al-Aziz ibn Saud, authorized a team of American engineers to explore the trackless desert bordering the Persian Gulf, an arid landscape marked only by the occasional palm-fringed oasis. He hoped they would find water. A tribal leader with precarious finances, Ibn Saud believed the Americans might discover places where he could refresh his warriors' horses and camels.

But the team, from Standard Oil of California, had something else in mind. Geologists had discovered oil in other countries in the region, and the engineers thought they would find more in Saudi Arabia. They drilled more than a half dozen holes without result and could easily have given up in frustration. Instead, they decided to see if going deeper than normal might make a difference. So they set up their equipment again at well 7 and bored deeper than they had ever done before. At a depth of 4,727 feet they finally hit the first sign of what would turn out to be the world's largest supply of crude oil.

Oddly enough, the king did not appear to appreciate the discovery at first. He ignored the news about the oil for an entire year. Finally he and his retinue arrived in a caravan of 400 automobiles at the pumping station of Ras Tanura in time to witness the first tanker hauling away its cargo of Saudi crude. Its discovery would change everything.

Until then the primary source of income in the Saudi kingdom came from servicing pilgrims in Mecca, Islam's holiest city. But even the first shipment of oil produced wealth beyond all expectation.[5] The lives and lifestyles of the Arabian Bedouin would never be the same. An isolated country with no other exportable product now became a major factor in global politics. The Saudi royal family turned into significant players on the world scene. Their wealth became a crucial factor in Middle East politics and the bargaining over global energy supplies.

The First War in Afghanistan

The immediate context for the rise of al-Qaeda was the war in Afghanistan that began in the late 1970s. To understand the motivation of those involved, we need to understand something about the geography of politics. You see, the Eurasian landmass (from Great Britain to Singapore) is the dominant feature in world affairs. Its sheer size and the more than 4 billion people who live there make it so. Any power that can completely control the Eurasian landmass will rule the world. That means it is in the interest of all powers based elsewhere (including the United States) to keep the Eurasian landmass divided politically.[6]

The closest any power has come (at least since the Mongol Empire around the year A.D. 1200) to dominating the entire Eurasian landmass was the Soviet Union. It is no wonder, therefore, that in spite of the inherent weaknesses of the Communist system, Americans rightly feared Soviet power. So a primary focus of American policy in the 1970s was containing Soviet power by encircling it with a system of alliances extending from the northern shore of Norway, across the continent of Europe, through the Middle East, and along the southern coast of Asia all the way north to the Bering Strait. By preventing the Soviets access to warm-water ports, the alliance system limited Soviet power to manageable proportions. The Soviets sought ways to break through this encirclement while the Americans did all they could to keep them boxed in.

But two events threatened this containment. The first was the fall of the shah of Iran in 1979, a key American ally in the encirclement project. If the Soviets could exploit Iran's sudden weakness and punch through to the Persian Gulf, they would break out of their geopolitical confinement and also probably capture the Saudi Arabian oil fields, tipping the balance of world power decisively in their favor. Thus the invasion of Afghanistan less than a year after the fall of the shah seemed like America's greatest nightmare. The Russians were on the move and could potentially drive America completely out of the Eastern Hemisphere.

As the leaders of the American military game-planned for a possible Soviet invasion of Iran, they concluded that they did not have sufficient forces to prevent the conquest of Iran if the Soviets decided on such a course. So the Soviets had to be stopped in Afghanistan. The West needed somehow to turn it into another Vietnam, but this time with the shoe on the other foot. So President Carter authorized the CIA to engage in covert operations in Afghanistan. Agents encouraged and supported Afghan guerrillas to harass Soviet troops in Afghanistan and keep them pinned down there. But how could they accomplish that? Where would the money come from?

Congress was in no mood to appropriate extra funding for the CIA, whose reputation had recently taken a beating. And anyway, going to Congress to fund a covert war would mean it wasn't a secret anymore. But it dawned on President Carter that America was not the only country worried about the Soviet invasion of Afghanistan. Saudi Arabia had even more to lose in Iran and Afghanistan than America did. So the United States approached the Saudis with a proposal. If the Saudis would fund the guerrilla war and recruit Islamic fighters to resist the Soviet occupiers in Afghanistan, the CIA would provide training, coordination, and intelligence.

But the Saudis were not comfortable funding such a war directly from government coffers either. Instead they turned to wealthy, private families, asking them to contribute to the cause of Islamic restoration. Here was an opportunity to reverse centuries of Islamic decline. Many Saudi families contributed vast sums to the project, and the largest and wealthiest of them had come to be known as (can you guess it?) the "bin Laden" family.[7] So President Carter presided over the creation of an international army of Islamic fundamentalists. As has so often happened in history, an ally in one war becomes the enemy in the next. To be fair to Carter, however, his successors, Ronald Reagan and George H. W. Bush, enthusiastically followed his policy. It was a low-cost, low-sacrifice (for Americans) way to keep the Russians bottled up in the vast interior of the Eurasian landmass.

A major element of this situation was the willingness of the American intelligence and military apparatus to pass on their skills to the Islamic fighters. The *mujahedin* learned about covert and special operations. They acquired the skills of stealth and hand-to-hand combat. As they studied what American intelligence knew and how it got such information, they came to understand both the advantages and limitations of military technology. No doubt the Americans thought their Islamic allies ignorant and incapable of using such information against them. But many of Osama bin Laden's fighters were relatively wealthy and highly educated. As they listened they learned well, as the West has come to discover, much to its regret.

The Afghan war was long and brutal. It drained the Soviet Army of strength and credibility and was a decisive factor in the eventual fall of the Soviet Union in 1989. But it also created thousands of hardened and experienced Islamist soldiers, many of them trained by the CIA and American Special Forces. And the fall of the Soviet Union had a powerful impact on those Islamic soldiers. It was the first time in centuries that an Islamic force had defeated a non-Islamic army. And this defeated army belonged to a major world superpower that collapsed in the wake of that war. So it was not just an Afghan victory—it was an Islamic triumph, powered by Islamic fighters and fueled by Islamic money, the fruit of Saudi oil fields (the gift of Allah). In the minds of Islamic fundamentalists it was an Islamic army that gave America its greatest victory over the Soviet menace.

And was the United States suitably grateful for the Islamic sacrifice? To the contrary, America believed that Afghanistan was only a minor factor in the fall of the Soviet Union (no doubt both viewpoints were at least partly right). And America considered itself the driving force behind the resistance. From the American point of view the Islamic world owed America a debt of gratitude. So as America pulled out of Afghanistan after the fall of the Soviet Union, it set the stage for a confrontation between a resurgent Islam and the world's only remaining superpower.

You see, America never entered the Afghan war out of some altruistic motive of defending Islam against atheistic powers. It used the Islamic fervor of Osama bin Laden and others as a tool to keep the Russians encircled in the northern part of the Eurasian landmass. When the Soviets retreated from Afghanistan, the United States completely lost interest in the country and abandoned it, leaving a devastated and impoverished landscape filled with warring tribes and a highly trained, international Islamic army recruited from the entire Islamic world.

What was this army to do now? Just go home? That was not an option.

Such skilled fighters were as much of a threat to their secular governments back home as they had been to the Soviets. So no government in the Islamic world wanted them. They were essentially stranded in Afghanistan, without external support and without purpose. What America and its allies had done in Afghanistan was to train an army of highly diverse people bound together by the common experience of the war against the Soviets, a sense of betrayal by their own governments as well as the Americans, and the awareness that they had the power to change the world. Highly trained people who have lost their designated purpose tend to find one of their own, a purpose that may not be what the trainers had intended. Al-Qaeda was the unintended consequence of short-term American political objectives.

The Gulf War

The trigger point for the war between America and al-Qaeda was Saddam Hussein's invasion of Kuwait in 1990. America regarded it as the action of an isolated rogue state that needed to be put in its place. George H. W. Bush believed that all Muslims would receive his decision to intervene as an act of American solidarity to save an Islamic state from aggression. So the Americans approached the Saudis about basing American troops in their country.

The Saudi ruling family knew that welcoming hundreds of thousands of Western soldiers in their kingdom was a very risky business for them. For many Muslims, the holiness of Mecca and Medina extends over the entire nation containing those cities. The Saudis were caught in a hard place. While Saddam Hussein was an unsavory and dangerous character, inviting Western troops into the land of Mecca and Medina was a fundamental violation of Islamic law. On the other hand, if they didn't extend the invitation, it was likely that Hussein himself would occupy the territory, destroying the wealth and power of the Saudi leadership. So the Saudi leaders opted for the route that best allowed their own political survival. Operation Desert Storm was the result.

In the past, impotent rage would have greeted such "abominations" against Islam. But the war in Afghanistan made it different this time. Those Afghan veterans allowed to return to Saudi Arabia did not feel vulnerable and weak the way the Saudi leaders did. They were ready to defend the kingdom against all comers if need be. Feeling no dependence on the

United States for the "protection" of the holy places, they saw the governments in the Arab countries as corrupt and secular and incapable of leading such a fight. So international, militant, anti-American Islam was born in the wake of the Gulf War, an unintended consequence of what Americans had thought of as a noble action.

Here we see the great philosophical divide between the Islamic world and the West. To the West the militant warriors of resurgent Islam are merely "terrorists," lawless bandits who have no respect for human life and civilized values. Such individuals hate everyone, including most fellow Muslims, and everything that does not agree with their intolerant rantings. But to many in the Muslim world these agents of terror are true patriots, freedom fighters willing to give their lives in the cause of God. They are the only thing standing between the Islamic world and the horrific moral assaults of Hollywood, gay pride, and American cruise missiles.

It is easy in the passion of the moment to overlook that the word "Islam" is closely related to the word "salaam," which means "peace" in Arabic. A careful reading of the Qur'an will reveal far more statements in support of mercy and compassion than in support of jihad. And most of the jihad texts are better read in the context of the battle against sin in one's life than in warfare against others.

We in the West also tend to forget that Christian history is full of fundamentalist extremists who have committed similar acts of terrorism. Adventists should be at the forefront of those willing to acknowledge the terrorist side of the Crusades and the Inquisition, for example. The Crusader conquest of Jerusalem in A.D. 1099 resulted in the slaughter of the entire population of the city—men, women and children. The thousands of civilians included many Muslims and Jews. Some reports even suggest that the Crusaders murdered many of the Orthodox Christian inhabitants of the city along with the rest. The Crusaders were about as indiscriminate in whom they killed as were the followers of Osama bin Laden on September 11.

Because of this great philosophical divide and at the risk of offending many in the West, I will refrain from using the word "terrorists" to describe these Islamic warriors in the rest of this chapter. I will instead follow the lead of George Friedman, who coined the word "jihadists" as a more accurate description.[8] It is my desire here to build bridges of understanding rather than give in to popular prejudices, although I will be the first to confess that it is hard to do. For lack of better terminology, I have retained the overall descriptor of "war on terror" to describe the West's battle to eradicate al-Qaeda and all who live by similar principles.

The Case Against America

Why do the jihadists hate America so? What fueled the destruction of the twin towers and so many other acts of seemingly mindless aggression? Osama bin Laden and those like him are not insane. Not fueled by endless, seething emotion, they have thought through what they are doing, and their sense of purpose is calculated and clear. Osama has articulated five main grievances as the basis for his case against America. We now have enough background to understand his thinking—at least in part.

1. The Decline of Islam

The root grievance has its origin in the overall history we have just reviewed. For at least 1,000 years the Islamic empire and its Turkish successor were superpowers in the world. But during the past couple hundred years the Western powers have divided up the Muslim world among themselves. Since that time the Muslim world has been a backwater in world affairs. Were it not for the fact that the Middle East contains much of the world's oil, the major powers might pay no attention to it at all.

The Western-dominated world seems to humiliate Muslims at every turn. The Israelis (Palestine and the regional wars of 1956, 1967, and 1973), the Serbs (in Bosnia and Kosovo), the Russians (in Chechnya and other Muslim republics of central Asia), and the Indians (in Kashmir and various parts of India) have all found ways to marginalize Muslim interests around the globe. On top of these slights the West has "imposed" Western law codes on Muslim states, enforced Western economic ideas, including the charging of interest (contrary to Islamic law), and exported alcohol, drugs, pornography, and crime. Those who believe that Islamic culture is superior find it frustrating to have to acknowledge that America has vastly greater power and wealth.

2. The Israeli–Palestinian Situation

While securing a homeland for Jews made a lot of sense in the West after the Holocaust, the original partition of Palestine came at the expense of Arabs whose ancestors had dwelled in the land for centuries. The British had promised, during World War I, to support Arab independence in exchange for Arab support against the Turks (remember the movie *Lawrence of Arabia?*). Then during World War II President Roosevelt assured at least one Arab leader that the major powers would not do anything about Palestine after the war without consulting the Arabs first.

Nevertheless, worldwide sympathy for the plight of the Jews during the war resulted in a United Nations partition that ceded more than half of Palestine to the Jews, although only a third of population was Jewish and Jews owned an even smaller percentage of the land. In subsequent fighting the Israelis gained control of the entire territory for decades, despite U.N. resolutions requiring the return of land conquered in 1967. To Arab eyes this looks suspiciously like a revival of the Crusades, with Israel at the forefront and America guiding behind the scenes.

I do not want to be misunderstood here. I know that the Israeli perspective sees the story quite differently. But I think it is important for our purpose to see through Osama's eyes—the eyes of a "terrorist"—as far as that is possible for us to do. Jewish desperation after the Holocaust was real, and for many Jews the homeland in the Middle East was the only spark of hope at the time. But the desperation of the Palestinian refugee camps remains to this day. From the Muslim viewpoint this is a serious injustice that is ongoing and has never been addressed. For bin Laden the injustice is criminal.

3. Secular Corruption in the Middle East

A further major grievance of Osama bin Laden has to do with the corrupt and secular governments ruling most Muslim nations. He and many others view governments of countries such as Egypt, Jordan, Saudi Arabia, and Iraq as unelected, oppressive, pandering to the West, and soft on Islam. It is not surprising that bin Laden, himself a Saudi, is no longer welcome in Saudi Arabia. In fact, he is a greater threat to the sheiks of Saudi Arabia than he is to the United States. He believes that secular Arab leaders are mere tools of the West, using its power to cement their own personal position at the expense of the Muslim masses. While the United States did not directly set up such governments, in the minds of the jihadists they would not stand without continuing American support.

In a real sense Islamists such as bin Laden see the secular corruption of the Middle East as the primary enemy. Afghanistan proved that the great powers could not stand against the faithful if the faithful were resolute and patient. Over time they could deal with the political powers behind Christianity, Judaism, Hinduism, and Communism as needed. For Muslim fundamentalists what really holds Islam back is the corruption and inefficiency in the political and economic realm of the Middle East. The corruption of the secular governments allows the West to exploit Islamic weakness. It is against them that jihadists must fight the decisive battle. The Islamic faithful needed a strategy to destroy the corrupt systems of the Middle East that have been keeping Islam from taking its rightful place in today's world. As long as such systems remain in place, Islam, they feel, will be politically and economically impotent in the larger world.

4. Betrayal in Afghanistan

While the first three grievances are real, they are of long standing and by themselves would not have created the jihadist movement. As we have seen, two trigger points around the year 1990 lit the fuse of Osama bin Laden's anger. The first was the American betrayal in Afghanistan. When the Russians left Afghanistan in 1989, the Americans immediately lost interest, abandoning bin Laden and his *mujahedin* to their own devices. Afghanistan disintegrated into a multitude of factions. Bin Laden felt betrayed. The stage was set.

5. Western Militaries in Saudi Arabia

The final trigger point, as we have seen, was the physical presence of the American military in Saudi Arabia during and after the Gulf War. That has been perhaps the crucial issue for bin Laden. In the 1980s he was not hostile to America, in spite of the Israeli-Palestinian situation. Some evidence even suggests that he may have been on the CIA payroll for a time. While bin Laden also opposed the aggression of Saddam Hussein in Kuwait, he was distressed and then infuriated by the decision of the Saudi government to invite the Americans and other Westerners to "occupy" the holy land. The alcoholism, materialism, immorality, and relative nudity exhibited by Western troops in Saudi Arabia seemed sacrilegious even to moderate Muslims. To bin Laden it bordered on blasphemy.

ARMAGEDDON AT THE DOOR

Why "Terrorism"? Why September 11?

For Osama bin Laden the crucial question became how to restore Islam to a dominant place in the world. Could diplomacy accomplish that? Experience told him that it would not work. The West had been "negotiating" with the Middle East for more than a century, and what was the result? The establishment of Israel, for one thing. Another result was the colonial powers dividing the Middle East into artificial nations with no consideration of tribal borders and local interests. Meanwhile the West grew richer and more powerful, and the Muslim world became increasingly irrelevant.

Should the Muslim world stand up and fight in military terms then? In its present state of weakness that would be foolish. Anyone unconvinced by the dominance of the Israeli attacks in 1967 and 1982 (in Lebanon) should have no further doubts after the Gulf War and the recent conflicts in Afghanistan and Iraq. In an age of information technology both the American and Israeli military are overwhelming and incontestable. Any form of direct frontal assault would be the equivalent of pointless suicide. One would lose thousands of soldiers in exchange for a mere handful of casualties on the stronger side. No one could pursue warfare for long on those terms. So for bin Laden there existed only one alternative to helplessness, and that was what the West calls terrorism.

For jihadist leaders, "terrorism" is nothing more than a negotiating tool. It is a way the weaker party in a disagreement is able to project a sense of power greater than its numbers or its military prowess would otherwise allow. The actual physical damage of terror attacks is not significant in political or economic terms. What is vital is the psychological effect—it is far greater than the sum total of the physical damage or loss of life. Terrorism places those who practice it on the political map. Allowing the weaker party to go on the offensive, it puts powerful nations on the defensive. There exist countless potential targets, and it is so costly to defend them all that the jihadist entity can always find a soft spot somewhere. "If you're throwing enough darts at a board, eventually you're going to get something through," said a Pentagon strategist. "That's the way al-Qaeda looks at it." The secrecy and seclusion of the jihadist makes the attacks extremely difficult to anticipate and defend against.

The only safe defense against what the West calls terrorism is one that anticipates every possible angle of attack, particularly against assets for which adequate defenses are not yet in place, such as water supplies and transportation systems. To make matters worse, every mile of the U.S. coastline is a potential entry point for nuclear, chemical, or biological weapons. In a sense, eradicating such threats is like finding a way to detect and apprehend criminals *before* they commit their crimes.

The ability of the jihadists to attack at will and keep powerful enemies on the defensive gradually wears down even a powerful nation's will to resist. As happened in Spain in 2004, people often prefer peace on jihadist terms to the constant stress of watchfulness and defensive measures. Such a battle expends vast amounts of money, intelligence assets, and personnel to track jihadists at home and abroad. In a sense the United States is attempting to surround itself with a "protective net." But, as *Time* pointed out on March 11, 2002, "all nets have holes." So if the jihadists are patient enough and determined enough, they can wear down and outlast enemies more concerned with personal comfort than with ideological purity.

The Strategy of Osama bin Laden

This gives us some insight into the mind-set of bin Laden when he gave the go-ahead for the attack of September 11, 2001. While the actions of the highjackers were gruesome and incomprehensible to Westerners, they were part of a strategic plan to change the balance of power in the world. The leaders of al-Qaeda see the Islamic world as being occupied by non-Islamic forces. Al-Qaeda, they believe, needs to find a way to end the "occupation" and reunite Islam. Since the United States is the leading power in the world and the patron of many "Islamic" regimes, it is the power behind the "occupation" and, therefore, the great enemy that motivates and controls the anti-Islamic agenda.

Defeating the United States directly is not a realistic option. But the kind of war bin Laden has unleashed now burdens America with billions of dollars of expenses to fight "terrorism" at home and abroad. Distracting Americans with the constant fear of unsuspected attacks, it makes them feel as insecure as Europeans and Israelis have felt for decades. Isolationism looks increasingly attractive. If, in the process, bin Laden could cause the United States to withdraw from the Islamic world, other anti-Islamic powers such as Russia, India, and Israel would be helpless to intervene. Corrupt and secular governments in the Muslim world would then have no base of outside support and would collapse before the Islamic masses.

23

ARMAGEDDON AT THE DOOR

So al-Qaeda does not expect to destroy the United States directly, unless some doomsday weapon comes into its hands. The United States is too powerful and too distant to defeat. Rather, bin Laden's strategy has been to force the United States into a series of actions that destabilize the governments of those Middle Eastern countries dependent on Washington. If he could make the United States look weak and vulnerable in the eyes of the Arab street, the governments of the Middle East would lose their credibility. Should pressure from the United States then force those governments to join it in fighting Islamic militants or to remain silent in the face of Israeli aggression, popular uprisings could easily lead to their destruction. The ultimate goal would be the establishment of an Islamic superpower, a vast Islamic state stretching from Morocco to the island of Mindanao in the Philippines, governed by Islamic law.

Could a bin Laden achieve such goals? He clearly believes that the United States does not have the stomach to suppress a mass, popular uprising. Unlike al-Qaeda, Americans as a rule do their best not to hurt innocents. A military virtually invincible in battle would have a difficult time handling an army of unarmed women and children. Although the United States has important interests in the Islamic world, they are not on a scale sufficient to justify the expense and casualties involved in a long-term occupation. To the degree that further jihadist acts in the U.S. should occur, the American populace could easily sway toward an isolationist stance. And should such isolationism lead to withdrawal from Afghanistan and Saudi Arabia and even the partial abandonment of Israel, the political world would have changed considerably in favor of the Islamic agenda.

So from bin Laden's perspective, war in diplomatic, economic, or military terms would result only in the further humiliation of Islam. But this new kind of war has altered the battlefield odds. Since the targets vastly outnumber the defenders, al-Qaeda has designed a war strategy in which it has significant advantages. U.S. power finds itself weakened in that it must widely disperse defensive action. Suicidal fervor creates a low-tech battlefield that neutralizes superior technology as a weapon.

The goal of the attacks on September 11, 2001, was not to defeat America. America was too powerful and too distant for that to happen. Instead, Osama bin Laden's goal was a very strange one from the Western perspective. He wanted to provoke America against the Islamic world.

More specifically, he wanted to incite America to attack Saudi Arabia. Did you notice that 15 of the 19 hijackers on September 11 were Saudis? While the trained pilots were generally from other countries, the "beef" of the operation (the musclemen who took over the plane) were almost all from Saudi Arabia. Osama wanted it to appear that it was a Saudi raid against America. While he anticipated the attack on Afghanistan in 2001, he was sure that President Bush would not stop there. In order to stop al-Qaeda he would have to control Saudi Arabia as well.

Why provoke an attack on Saudi Arabia? Because that is the holy land of Islam, the site where Allah met the prophet Muhammad, the place of pilgrimage, the territory of Mecca and Medina. If any action could be calculated to inflame the passion of the Islamic masses in the Middle East, it would be a Western occupation of the holy places. Osama bin Laden wanted above all else to arouse the fervor of the people to rise up against the invaders and make life so miserable for them that they would be forced to withdraw, as the Soviets had to in Afghanistan. Yesterday, Afghanistan. Today, Saudi Arabia. Tomorrow? The world! Does it sound like the demented scheme of a madman? To many it does. But when you consider what other options were available to stimulate a global rebirth of Islamic power, bin Laden's scheme doesn't seem so crazy. It was a shrewd calculation that the only way to get rid of corrupt and secular governments in the Middle East was to humiliate the sponsor of those governments—the United States. Once the sponsor proved powerless, these Arab governments would fall, and the Islamic empire would be reborn.

So let me summarize Osama bin Laden's dream scenario. His goal for September 11 was to do something so horrific that the United States would feel forced to invade the Middle East, preferably Saudi Arabia. Osama and his friends could then label it an attack on Islam itself. A guerrilla war against the invaders would incite the Americans to kill and wound many innocent bystanders. The "Arab street"—the common, everyday man and woman in the Middle East—would rise up in righteous anger against the occupiers. The military might of America would prove helpless against an uprising of "people power," unarmed men, women, and children who would be willing to die for their faith.

In the face of such an enemy, America would have little choice but to pull back into bases and leave the streets in the hands of the insurgents, much as had occurred in Vietnam years before. Eventually America would grow tired of the conflict. The media and Congress would unite to force the president to withdraw and abandon the Middle East to its own devices. In the wake of that superpower defeat, the masses in the Middle East would embrace Islam and Sharia law, and the stage would be set for an Islamic superpower that could extend from Morocco to Indonesia. That was Osama's dream, and it will likely outlive him regardless of the outcome in Iraq and the rest of the Middle East.

The question that we cannot avoid is this. Why did President George W. Bush play right into Osama bin Laden's hands with his invasion of Iraq? Was he just stupid, as some of his detractors imply? Or did he know something that bin Laden did not? If Saudi Arabia was the real source of al-Qaeda, why attack Iraq? And what does any of this have to do with Armageddon? Stay tuned.

---

[1] For an analysis of the 1260 days/years of Bible prophecy, see my unpublished paper "The 1260 Days in the Book of Revelation," presented to the Biblical Research Institute Committee of the General Conference on September 29 and 30, 2003, at Loma Linda University. The paper is available upon request from the Biblical Research Institute and can also be obtained in electronic form on a CD from the Web site www.thebattleofarmageddon.com.

[2] For an excellent outline of the events surrounding the rise of Muhammad, see the sympathetic portrait by Karen Armstrong, *Muhammad: A Biography of the Prophet* (New York: HarperSanFrancisco, 1993).

[3] The key to distribution of wealth (social justice) in the Arabian world before Muhammad was the ghazu, or raid, in which a poorer tribe would seize a portion of a richer tribe's wealth by attacking its trade caravans. It was an early "Robin Hood" mentality. One historian has called the raiding party the "national sport" of Arabia in the seventh century.

[4] For a helpful overview of the Wahabi movement and the rise of Saudi Arabia, see Clinton Bennett, *Muslims and Modernity: An Introduction to the Issues and Debates* (London: Continuum, 2005), pp. 18, 53-56.

[5] Adam Zagorin, "Finding the King's Fortune," *Time,* Mar. 31, 2003.

[6] The best analysis of these matters appears in the work of George Friedman, the founder and chair of Stratfor Corporation (Strategic Forecasting), sometimes called a "shadow CIA." George Friedman, *America's Secret War: Inside the Hidden Worldwide Struggle Between America and Its Enemies* (New York: Doubleday, 2004).

[7] I am well aware that "bin Laden" is not a family name in the way that Western names function. It is a patronymic, merely expressing that Osama is one of the sons of a man named Laden (?). Rather than "bin Laden," it would be more accurate simply to call him by his first name, Osama. I have for convenience, however, adopted the common way that the Western press describes him.

[8] See Friedman.

THE WESTERN RESPONSE AND THE BATTLE OF ARMAGEDDON

In his invasion of Iraq in 2003 could President Bush have been doing exactly what Osama bin Laden expected and wanted? Could he have been playing directly into the hands of the jihadists? Did he place young Americans in an impossible situation in which they could be picked off in ones and twos? Was the Iraq adventure doomed from the very start? If so, then why did he go there? Was it simply bad intelligence about weapons of mass destruction? Or was it really all about the oil after all?

The Strategy of George W. Bush

Here I believe that many people have poorly understood the deeper motivations behind the news. The media have hinted at the real geopolitical goals of the Iraq war, but have rarely stated them out loud. The president himself has been careful never to tip his hand publicly, even in the face of just criticism of the goals that were actually stated. Let's briefly go behind the scenes and unravel the deeper actions and motivations that don't always make the news.

What did the invasion of Iraq have to do with the "war on terror"? Why did Bush play bin Laden's game? What was he hoping to gain? The usual reasons make no sense. The invasion was not really about weapons of mass destruction. While it turns out that Saddam Hussein had none of them, everybody, including the Europeans, believed that he did. Yet in spite of that assumption, most did not think that was a reason to invade.

Nor was the invasion really about Saddam Hussein, either. Sure, he was a rather unsavory character. Yes, he gassed the Kurds and massacred the Shiites. His secret police slaughtered people right and left. But such events had been occurring for the previous 25 years and had provoked no American invasion up to that point. Why do so now?

The invasion was also not really about control of Middle Eastern oil. Oil was flowing fine before the war. The war has, in fact, driven up prices and created uncertainty. War hinders trade—it doesn't promote it. So all of the public reasons for the invasion make no real sense.

I believe the real purpose of the invasion was the dismantling of al-Qaeda. Al-Qaeda is not a national government. It is not a definable state with borders and institutions that we can destroy. In order to eliminate al-Qaeda you have to shut off its flow of funds, most of which have been coming from Saudi Arabia. To do that effectively requires cooperation from every nation in which al-Qaeda operates. That demands the free flow of intelligence information. And it calls for people to turn in relatives and friends who are part of the conspiracy. Although al-Qaeda based itself in Afghanistan, it was always rooted in the Arab context. Thus we could not defeat it without projecting power into the Middle East at some point. Osama bin Laden knew that and included that into his calculations of American behavior.

Let me illustrate the problem. Reportedly Osama bin Laden had 52 brothers from a variety of different mothers. Many of them were not sympathetic to the goals and methods of the jihadists. A number of them were living happily in the United States when September 11 occurred. Others, however, were sympathetic. The only way to accurately separate the "jihadists" from the "friends of democracy" in the bin Laden family itself was to be inside the family. In other words, the United States and allied governments needed to be able to penetrate such families intimately and encourage brothers to betray brothers by turning them in to authorities. But the allies also knew that such a thing would be heavily destructive in any close-knit family and would be resisted in most circumstances.

The dilemma for the rulers of Saudi Arabia after September 11 was that they had to choose between pleasing the United States, who wanted to root out every potential jihadist in Saudi Arabia, and satisfying their own people, who disliked such disruptive activities occurring in their own country and in their own families. Why would they choose to please the United States over their own people? After all, if they offended their own people, it would motivate their own people to overthrow them. So there was no way the Saudi rulers would fully cooperate with the United States in the war on terror unless they were more afraid of the United States than they were of their own people.

In a desperate attempt to distract the United States, the Saudi leadership began floating exciting proposals for a resolution of the Israeli-Palestinian conflict. Although such proposals had no chance of being accepted by those who would be most affected by them, offering them set conditions for Saudi cooperation in the war on terror that the United States could never fulfill. What the United States heard in these proposals was that the Saudis had no intention of helping to destroy al-Qaeda.

So how could the United States get at al-Qaeda in Saudi Arabia? One option was to invade Saudi Arabia and do the job themselves. But that is exactly what bin Laden was hoping for, and it would likely have resulted in a mass uprising against the United States. The other option was to raise the threat of invasion to such a high level that the Saudi leadership would become more afraid of the United States than they were of their own people. To do that, the United States had to find a way to project power effectively into the Middle East without inflaming the opposition of the Arab masses. The American government had to convince the average Middle Eastern Arab that it was overwhelmingly powerful and much to be feared. Al-Qaeda could put on a big show, but it was essentially weak and could not protect its own. In other words, the United States had to create the perception that the jihadist project was doomed to failure and that casting one's lot with the United States was the more effective way to create positive change in the Middle East.

Enter Saddam Hussein. If there existed one ruler in the Middle East widely despised in the Arab world and whose demise would cause few tears to be shed, it was Hussein, the oppressive, secular president of Iraq. President Bush gambled that taking him out would not inflame the Arab street. There would be anger at the presence of foreign occupiers, but it would be a manageable reaction. And if Saddam could be replaced by a government "of the people" there might even be some gratitude for American intervention.

The Invasion of Iraq

What did the invasion of Iraq have to do with the war on terror? At least three things. 1. It enabled America to project power into the very heart of the Middle East. 2. It exploited the fundamental fault line in the

Islamic world, the division between Sunni and Shiite. 3. Finally, it distracted the jihadists away from direct action against the United States. And there was a high likelihood that all three things would occur without the specter of mass uprisings across the Middle East. As with September 11, the real reasons for the invasion of Iraq were quite different than those generally given in the news media. The "liberation" of Iraq was not the primary goal, but the consequences of that liberation would deeply impact the war on terror. Let me unpack each of these three reasons briefly, because they may not make sense on the surface.

1. *Projecting American power.* When it comes to the Islamic world, the United States has had more military failures on its record than successes (the failed hostage rescue in 1980, incidents in Lebanon and Somalia, and weak responses to earlier al-Qaeda attacks). As impressive as the 2001 defeat of the Taliban was, it still required the help of others and left the country relatively unpacified. So the United States, in spite of its massive power, had the reputation of a military and political weakling in the Middle East. It had to find a way to convince all players that this time it really meant business.

In order for a nation to truly project power, it cannot simply threaten from afar. It has to be able to put troops on the ground and directly challenge a nation's intimate interests. The invasion of Iraq put massive American power in the very heart of the Middle East. From the center of the Middle East, that power could intimidate Syria, Iran, and Saudi Arabia, three absolutely critical players in the battle against al-Qaeda. The neighboring nations would have to keep in mind the "elephant next door" in every word and action they took from then on. In actual fact, shortly after the invasion in March 2003 all three neighboring countries began to cooperate with the United States in back channel ways. The cooperation was usually covert; the public rhetoric (for the people's consumption) remained opposed to American interests.

This is why Germany, France, and Russia opposed the Iraq war. They too disliked Saddam and believed that he had weapons of mass destruction and could pose a threat to civilization. But the Middle East had been their backyard for 200 years. The last thing they wanted was the American elephant in it! So they resisted the invasion in public ways that seemed inexplicable, but it was all about power and who would wield it where. Everyone knew that the real issue was projection of American power into the Middle East, and no one wanted to talk about it. That is why the whole debate over the Iraq war was so surreal.

2. The differences between Sunni and Shiite. The biggest barrier to Osama bin Laden's dream of an Islamic empire is not American power, but a fundamental fault line in the Islamic world itself, the differences between the Sunni and Shiite branches of Islam. This division between Sunni and Shiite makes little sense to the average Westerner. It basically has to do with which of Muhammad's original followers he intended would succeed him after his death. But the issue is very real to Muslims and can raise even greater passions at times than the divide between Catholics and Protestants in the Christian world. The Sunni side of the debate is by far the stronger. In fact, the only two Islamic countries in which Shiites are in the majority are Iraq and Iran.

Osama bin Laden is a Sunni, so the Shiites would naturally oppose his agenda. Saddam Hussein was a Sunni (although we have little evidence that he took his "faith" seriously), so he had seized power in Iraq against the will of the majority of his people (Shiites). A major war strategy of the United States has always been to divide and conquer. In 1941 it succeeded in separating Stalin from Hitler in order to win World War II. Then in 1974 President Nixon fragmented the Communist world by befriending China at the expense of the Soviet Union. By invading Iraq, the United States exploited Shiite opposition to Sunni ambitions, thus splitting the Islamic world in two and securing Iran's back-channel cooperation in the war on terror. It also terrified the Saudis, who have always feared Iraq and Iran, in part because of a restive Shiite minority of their own.

Unfortunately, President Bush's Iraqi invasion has created an unintended consequence for both him and Osama bin Laden. By enabling a Shiite majority government in Iraq, the American intervention has empowered the Shia and made Iran the leading beacon of jihadist opposition to American power. Bin Laden's actions and the nature of Bush's response have unintentionally succeeded in marginalizing bin Laden's role within the worldwide jihadist network. As a result Iran has positioned itself as the primary obstacle to the American and Israeli agendas in the Middle East.

3. Distracting jihadists away from the homeland. By projecting American power into the Middle East, the invasion of Iraq presented the jihadists with a multitude of Western targets close to home. Attacking the American homeland from hideouts in southwestern Asia is a highly difficult and expensive business. Sending a lone suicide bomber into a crowded restaurant next door is a lot less tricky and still makes a statement, especially if an American soldier or two gets killed in the process. So an almost perverse goal of the invasion was to take the war on terror to the enemy, thereby distracting jihadists from the more difficult yet more effective approach of threatening the American homeland. As President Bush said more than once, "I'd rather fight them over there than in our homes and communities here."

The invasion of Iraq was like a magnet, drawing jihadists and their sympathizers from all over the Middle East (and even Europe and Africa) to the "decisive battle." From both Osama bin Laden's viewpoint and that of the American government, it centered the war on terror in the Middle East instead of New York. That war would be won or lost on Iraqi soil, a location both sides preferred.

And from the American perspective, this shift occurred without the collateral result of a general uprising of the Arab street. While a significant insurgency has occurred in Iraq, it has largely limited itself to the Sunni sectors of the country. The vast majority of the Iraqi people have opposed the insurgency from the beginning. So in terms of Osama bin Laden's grand strategy, the Iraq war started out as a victory for the American president, who gambled that the Arab street would tolerate the action, and on the whole, that turned out to be the case.

President Bush did not seem to have anticipated a number of things about Iraq, however. He did not anticipate that Saddam Hussein would hold back his most skilled troops in order to wage a long-term guerrilla war in the streets of central and western Iraq and that such a tactic would be successful enough to be a major drain on American energy. He did not anticipate that Iraq would become a drawing card for jihadist "volunteers" from all over the Islamic world and that they would become the formidable opponents they have been. He did not anticipate that democracy would be so challenging in an environment in which everyone's first loyalty is to the local tribe, not the country as a whole. He did not anticipate that Sunnis would use bombings and suicide missions as negotiating tools to gain a stronger place at the democratic table. And he did not anticipate that the average Iraqi would be more resentful of occupation than grateful for "liberation."

THE WESTERN RESPONSE AND THE BATTLE OF ARMAGEDDON

What Americans and the American government do not seem to understand is that any time you intervene in the sovereign affairs of another country, you upset the balance of that society. After the fall of the Soviet Union George H. W. Bush proclaimed a new world order, in which politics would take a back seat to economic prosperity. Under the Bushes and Bill Clinton, America has seemed to think that Middle Eastern peoples wouldn't mind a little American intervention as long as their lives were freer and more prosperous. But in fact such involvement always advantages one political group over another. In Iraq the Shiites and Kurds benefited more than the Sunnis. It helped Afghanistan's minorities more than the majority Pashtuns. And in Kosovo, American action aided the majority Albanians more than the minority Serbs. Therefore, while well intended, American intervention inevitably tended to destabilize the local situation, creating unintended consequences in every case.

So the invasion of Iraq did not prove to be the clean, overwhelming victory that President Bush and his advisors had hoped. While American troops in Iraq have certainly gotten the attention of the Saudis, the Syrians, and the Iranians, they have been so occupied with the insurgency in Iraq that they have not been the truly effective threat intended. In fact, the Saudis themselves have covertly supported the Sunni insurgency in Iraq to keep the Americans occupied and to undercut the Shiites politically. The American media and the Congress have also provided a constant negative drumbeat in the background, which has unintentionally encouraged the jihadist movement just when everything seemed to be lost for them.

On the other hand, we have had no immediate repeat of September 11 on American soil. While a number of smaller bombings occurred in places such as Indonesia, Saudi Arabia, and Spain, the American homeland itself has seemed increasingly secure. The power of al-Qaeda to launch brilliant and complicated attacks anywhere in the world appears to have seriously lessened. Al-Qaeda's leadership has become more obsessed with survival than with planning for future attacks.

At the time of writing this, I sense that America's power has generally succeeded in diverting al-Qaeda from major attacks on American soil. While the United States and allied countries have taken serious casualties in Iraq, they are nowhere near the level of Vietnam, and the bombings are not a serious military threat to overthrow the occupation. In military terms the insurgency is an annoyance but not a threat. The Arab street is also annoyed at the occupation, but a long way from rising up to provide a serious obstacle to it. If such an analysis is anywhere close to correct, the greatest danger to the American strategy could well be war-weariness at home rather than the actual course of the conflict on the ground.

Projecting the Outcome

As I write, the outcome of the war on terror is still in doubt. America remains mired in the Middle East. Various factions in Iraq are still more divided than united. The insurgency continues. Al-Qaeda remains on the run, but is still alive in some fashion. Young men (and sometimes women) continue to line up in large numbers to blow themselves up for the cause. The world has become accustomed to intrusive security measures at airports and hotels. Everyone is more on edge than they used to be. The war on terror is far from over, and its final outcome is hard to predict. But I would like to close with some indicators by which you can measure the war on terror's condition in the future.

Signs of American Success

Which way are things heading in the war on terror and how can you know? It is difficult to project, but the following signs would indicate that the war on terror is going better for the West than the negative drumbeat of the media might indicate.

1. *More years go by without a significant jihadist attack on the American homeland.* The longer the time without a significant attack, the more certain it becomes that al-Qaeda and related organizations have been disrupted to the point of strategic ineffectiveness. Small attacks in Europe and the Middle East are becoming almost business as usual, but they do not threaten the world political order to a significant degree. If al-Qaeda cannot produce a repeat of September 11, its goals are in danger of nonfulfillment.

Al-Qaeda's method of operation is to stage infrequent but spectacular attacks. Nevertheless, a total absence of attacks in the U.S. mainland for six years or more is out of character. It raises doubts whether the terrorist operation is capable anymore of a September 11-size attack on America. The longer that period continues, the greater the likelihood that the lull is not by choice on al-Qaeda's part.

THE WESTERN RESPONSE AND THE BATTLE OF ARMAGEDDON

I remember someone asking me on September 11, as we were watching CNN coverage of the Trade Towers disaster, "Do you think there will be more attacks like this?" I responded, "No, I think they just blew up 20 years of assets." In other words, the kind of covert operation that can assembled 20 people willing to die, yet smart enough to get into the U.S. and elude American security for as long as necessary, might take 20 years to put together. My sense then was that it was a one-shot event that would not soon be duplicated. Subsequent events seem to support that gut feeling.

Having said this, however, it might not be necessary to coordinate 20 people in order to sneak a rudimentary nuclear device into the United States. A satchel-sized nuclear bomb could kill tens of thousands without the operational complexity of September 11. So even if al-Qaeda's operational capabilities are severely degraded, it may still retain the capability of significantly hurting the United States.

2. *The Arab street remains generally quiet and accepting of the American presence in the Middle East.* Osama bin Laden's strategy centered on provoking a massive popular reaction against American empire building all over the Islamic world. That has clearly not happened up to this point and seems increasingly unlikely, barring some additional provocation beyond the current wars in Iraq and Afghanistan. Ability to "manage the news" in the Middle East and to win hearts and minds on the street will probably be a crucial factor, although America has never been very good at that. As of this writing, al-Qaeda has not yet found a way to incite the Arab street. As long as that continues, al-Qaeda's ultimate goals remain only dreams.

3. *Iraq is able to form a unity government in which all major sides play a role and minority rights are protected.* Such a government would divide the Iraqi insurgency, bringing the secular insurgents to see politics rather than violence as the way to benefit their constituency best. The foreign jihadists sent in by al-Qaeda would then be marginalized and exposed to capture and would probably leave the country, looking for easier pickings. This would be Bush's best-case scenario.

But developing a unity government will require a deft hand. The American challenge in Iraq is to find a way to please all the warring factions to the place at which a central government can keep the peace and allow the American forces to go home or to do what they were placed there to accomplish in the first place: be a strategic threat to al-Qaeda sympathizers in Saudi

Arabia, Syria, and Iran. But this is a nearly impossible balancing act. Iraq has four main political groups. The Shiite religious parties want Islamic law (their style), while the Sunni religious parties seek a different form of Islamic law. The Kurds are Sunni in profession but generally secular in orientation. And the Sunni and Shiite secularists regard a religious government as anathema.

In a Western setting it would seem that there is plenty of room for compromise and team-building. Why can't Sunni and Shiite religious parties get along? Shouldn't the Sunni Kurds and the Sunni Arabs be able to find common cause? And shouldn't the Kurds and the secular Arabs be able to work together? Yet a history of oppression and revenge killings leaves all sides taking the position of "My way or no way!" So the idea of an Iraqi unity government would be nearly impossible to create and extremely challenging to maintain.

4. *Some or all of the remaining "big four" jihadist leaders (Osama bin Laden, Ayman al-Zawahiti, Mullah Omar, and Abu Musab al-Zarqawiti [Zarqawi was killed in 2006], are killed or captured.* These individuals have great symbolic value to jihadists around the world. Networks of sympathizers protect them in the places where they hide. To be able to capture or kill them signals a breakdown in their sympathy and support network, a further indication that their organizations have seriously degraded. It would lead to a perception of weakness in the jihadist movement, which could cause young people to choose other outlets for excitement besides resistance to the world order.

5. *Democracy takes full root in the Middle East.* This would mean that many Islamic fundamentalists have decided that the ballot box is better than the bomb to achieve political and religious goals in the Islamic world. Islamic fundamentalism does not have to be at war with the West. Guerrilla wars do not usually cease through military means. They tend to end when everyone decides that the fighting is counterproductive and goes back to negotiation and diplomacy as the best ways to safeguard people's various interests.

Signs of Jihadist Success

The following developments, on the other hand, would indicate that the war on terror is going badly for America and its allies.

1. *Al-Qaeda and/or related organizations demonstrate that they still have the ability to stage a major attack like that of September 11 in America or in the heart of Europe.* An escalating level of attacks around the world, not just in the Middle East,

would be a sign of increasing jihadist strength and success. But it is also possible that the relentless Western assault on all levels of the jihadist movement has caused the jihadists to go underground and take a longer-range view of the conflict. Jihadists and their sympathizers have long memories and a lot of patience. The war on terror will likely outlast the presidencies of George Bush and at least one or two of his successors. But al-Qaeda will attack America again if it is able to and if such an action would serve a strategic purpose.

Although jihadists look for soft targets, such things are becoming harder and harder to find in a world of obsessive security. But people cannot put up with stringent security forever. At some point, people and their governments will relax their vigil, and life will attempt to return to something a bit more "normal." Then we will see whether the jihadists have been able to maintain their focus in hiding and whether they will be able to rebuild the networks that seem to have been shattered during the years following September 11.

Oddly enough, the softest American target may be the border with Mexico. Individuals from countries that harbor or even sponsor terrorists have been captured along the southern U.S. boundary. Many are likely to have passed through. On the other hand, it is extremely difficult for people of Middle Eastern appearance to get hold of explosives in the United States, so Iraqi-style bombings would be hard to pull off, even if "sleeper" agents are already in the country.

My guess right now is that the war on terror will go on for decades (if time should last that long), but at a lower level of hostilities than was the case in 2007. Since the goal of the jihadists was political change in the Islamic world, many jihadists may follow the lead of some Sunnis in Iraq and give the political process a try. The jihadists may find that a rising level of democracy in the Middle East is an excellent way to achieve at least some of their political and religious goals.

2. *The Arab street becomes increasingly anti-American and anti-Western.* If the average Muslim begins to think like the jihadists, it would be an ominous sign. Should women and children and ordinary Iraqis begin confronting American soldiers in large numbers (people power), you can know that the Vietnam syndrome is kicking in and that the Western militaries will soon be withdrawing from the streets into bases. This will result in a more unstable situation.

The reality is that while the Americans were blindsided by the insurgency in Iraq, the situation in the first years after the invasion was not nearly as serious in military terms as it sounded in the media. Things would have to get worse than 2007 before the war would be in serious trouble from a purely military perspective. Internal memos among the jihadists about Iraq have been largely pessimistic. In terms of the big picture, the Iraq war, painful as it has been for the Americans, has not been a plus for the jihadist side.

An outside power, however, cannot shut down a guerrilla war by itself. It needs significant allies in the local situation. Total loss of Iraqi support, for any reason, would signal that the American project in Iraq is doomed. The cause of the loss of support (whether prisoner abuse, the killing of women and children, offensive cartoons) wouldn't matter—only the outcome. At the time of writing, Iraqis seem more concerned with internal differences than with the presence of "occupiers." But it could change rapidly. Here is a key area that bears watching as time goes on.

3. *Attempts to create a stable government in Iraq completely fail.* Should Iraq break into several de facto pieces (the Kurdish north, the Shiite south, the Sunni northwest), things could quickly get out of control. In that situation it would be very hard for the Americans to know whom to fight. Turkey, concerned about an independent Kurdish state, would feel under pressure to intervene, which would put the Americans at odds with a close and vital ally. Iran would feel threatened by the ascendancy of either the jihadists or a rebirth of Saddam's Baath Party and would likely intervene covertly in the south and middle of Iraq. The Syrians would take advantage of the instability to upset the situation further and get the heat off themselves. The Saudis would no longer feel the need to support the war on terror, and jihadists everywhere could hide out in an unstable Middle East. All sides would be tempted to use oil as a hostage to their own ambitions, which would unbalance the world economy. So a destabilized Iraq and Middle East is not in the interests of a calm and peaceful civilization.

A particular element to keep an eye on is America's relationship with Iran. The Iranians have many agents in the Shiite south and a great deal of influence. If they wanted to, they could turn the south of Iraq into an insurgent war zone overnight. The Iraqi insurgency of 2003-2007 confined itself almost entirely to Baghdad and areas to the north and west, the so-called Sunni Triangle. The insurgency affected no more than 20 percent of the country. The relative quiet of the Shiite south suggested a strong back-channel relationship between the United States and Iran. Iran would keep the Shiites quiet in exchange for Shiite religious dominance of the resulting Iraqi democracy. This would still seem to be the best path to resolution.

Except that the Saudis also have a stake in the situation. The last thing they want is a Shiite Iraq allied with Iran. They have been covertly supplying jihadists in Iraq with money and turning a blind eye to the large number of Saudis who have gone to Iraq to join the fight against the Americans and their Shiite allies. On one thing the Saudis and the Americans agree in Iraq. They do not want to leave Iraq in the hands of the Iranians. So any kind of settlement in Iraq would be complicated, and things could further disintegrate at any time.

4. *The American heartland turns against the war.* No American president has ever had 100 percent support for any war. For example, a significant minority of the people, called Tories, opposed the American Revolution. It is not even necessary for a majority of the people to endorse a war that the administration feels is vital to the national interest. Vigorous debate is part of the democratic process. And while congressional debate over a war can be discouraging to troops in the field and somewhat encouraging to the enemy, it does not have a massively negative effect on the outcome on the conflict.

No president, however, can prosecute a war after losing his own base of support. So even if a pro-war Republican is elected to replace President Bush, he can only continue the war as long as the vast majority of the Republican base accepts it. Significant defections from "red state" Republicans would be an ominous sign for a Republican president. At the time of writing the national consensus was teetering on the brink of a move toward withdrawal from Iraq. Osama bin Laden knew from the beginning that the American public has little patience for drawn-out and inconclusive wars. Whether withdrawal from Iraq would play directly into his hands would need to be carefully considered. While America's power to continue is great, its will is in question.

5. *The implosion of Pakistan.* One scenario in the war on terror raises perhaps the greatest nightmare of all for American leaders. And that would be the disintegration of Pakistan along the lines of what has happened in Iraq. Large parts of the country are relatively lawless already. Many feel that al-Qaeda's leadership is hiding in those ungovernable regions along the

Afghan border. As I write, stability seems to be breaking down elsewhere in the country as well.

What makes Pakistan vital to watch is the fact that it is a nuclear power. The government there controls a considerable arsenal of weapons of mass destruction. To my knowledge, such an arsenal has never, in the history of the world, ever gotten out of the hands of stable, governmental control. But what happens to those weapons if Pakistan disintegrates into civil war? What if allies of al-Qaeda take over the government and some of those weapons fall into jihadist hands? The civilized world would then be in a position far more precarious than anything we know now. Pakistan definitely demands our attention as the future unfolds.

Conclusion

My sense at the time of writing is that the jihadists' political goals are likely to fail in the short run in the face of massive Western security measures. This will result in a lower level of jihadist activity but not its total disappearance. What the West calls terrorism will be an ongoing reality for the rest of our lives to some degree, and perhaps also the lives of our children, should time last that long.

At some point, worldwide weariness could cause disillusionment with democracy and a rebirth of autocratic governments. Such governments would gain their legitimacy from the public need for peace and safety. Saddam Hussein was an evil man in many ways, but he did succeed in keeping a lid on Iraq's many warring factions. People may eventually feel nostalgia for the "good old days," when strong leaders kept evil at bay and people were able to walk the streets in safety. Such a scenario echoes the kind of situation described in the biblical depiction of the battle of Armageddon.

We turn now to a careful study of what Revelation has to say about the final conflict of earth's history. When we have completed this study, we will take a brief look at the scenario in *The Great Controversy*, by Ellen G. White, which is based to a large degree on the same evidence. Then in the last chapter of this book we will revisit the war on terror and the above projections in light of what we have learned about the battle of Armageddon in Bible prophecy. So fasten your seat belts, put your tray tables in the locked and upright position, and join me in this journey through the end-time scenario of Revelation.

DISCOVERING "ARMAGEDDON"

I was new to the Seventh-day Adventist Theological Seminary when I first got seriously interested in the battle of Armageddon. I was living in an old dormitory at Andrews University (old Burman Hall) that my father had also occupied at one time. All the seminarians were placed on the top floor, where things would occasionally get out of control. I remember that one night a couple of budding preachers got into an argument and ended up spraying each other with fire extinguishers in the hallway. So much for maturity arriving automatically at the age of 21!

Anyway, in that dorm situation I had the opportunity to rekindle an old friendship with a young man named Don. Don had been blind from birth, which led to many interesting situations back in college (Atlantic Union College), where he had lived near my roommate and me. Knowing that Don needed transportation from time to time, I decided to include him in whatever Sabbath activities I was involved in. One Sabbath he asked if we could attend worship services at a small African-American church about 15 miles away. Someone there had asked him to teach the Sabbath school lesson. I didn't have anything else I had to do, so I agreed to drive him over. The highlight of the drive to church was a small hump in an otherwise flat road. Since Don couldn't see, I sped up as we approached the hump and gave him a roller-coaster-type surprise. It was the kind of thing that I often did just to let him know he was a regular guy and wasn't going to be coddled because of what others might perceive as a limitation.

Don had barely gotten around to forgiving me when we arrived at the little church. After he presented the Sabbath school lesson, we sat with the congregation of about 25, waiting for a guest speaker to arrive and hoping one of us wouldn't get drafted at the last minute. Just in time a large African-American pastor hurried in. He quickly let us know that in spite of the small crowd, he had come to "preach!" And preach he did!

The sermon was on the battle of Armageddon. He moved from text to text with confidence. The story he told about the end-time battle was fascinating, I had never heard anything quite like it before. Working particularly from some Hebrew words in Ezekiel, he painted a scenario in which the people of God would gather in the Middle East at the end of time. They would be at peace with God and humanity, and all would seem to be well. But suddenly from the far north would come a massive attack. In the Hebrew of Ezekiel he found references to Russia (Hebrew *rosh*, translated "chief prince" in Ezekiel 38:2), Moscow (Hebrew *Meshech*) and Tobolsk (Hebrew *Tubal*), explaining that the army that would attack the Middle East was the forces of the Soviet Union, joined by the Iranians and others.

The conflict would focus on the land of Israel as we know it today. The invading army was of such large numbers that they appeared like clouds covering the land. In the middle of the struggle God would intervene with a large earthquake, which would so frighten the army that they would begin to fight each other. God then would cause what was left of the Soviet army to be devastated with nuclear missiles (see Eze. 38:22), presumably with the assistance of the United States. The missiles would destroy 85 percent of the attackers. It would take seven months to bury the Soviet dead.

Needless to say, his scenario blew my young pastoral mind away. I was really excited to get into the text for myself and see if these things were so. In the car on the way home I shared my excitement with Don. A year ahead of me at the seminary, he immediately called the sermon "a bunch of baloney." He accused the preacher of being completely oblivious to sound principles of interpretation. Somewhat deflated, I nevertheless determined to study and think for myself. When one preacher says the opposite of another, the only sensible response is to go back to the Word of God for yourself. That Sabbath morning experience launched me into a lifelong study of the battle of Armageddon. If it were not for that sermon, the book you hold in your hand might never have been written. So God can use any circumstance He wishes to bring us to the place where He wants us to be.

Returning to my dorm room that afternoon, I grabbed the fourth volume of my *Seventh-day Adventist Bible Commentary* and looked up Ezekiel 38. Sure enough, the scenario outlined in the sermon did appear there, although the author listed it as one of several options, and a fairly unlikely one at that. I pulled out the text of Ezekiel 38, looking for references to the battle of Armageddon. To my great surprise, the word "Armageddon" did not occur anywhere in Ezekiel 38. In fact, I could not find it in the book of Ezekiel at all. I was shocked! Someone had preached a sermon on the battle of Armageddon based largely on Ezekiel 38, yet the chapter had nothing to say about any battle of Armageddon! How did the preacher know that Ezekiel 38 had anything to do with Armageddon?

I decided it was time to get serious about my research. Taking my Bible concordance, I determined to check out every reference to Armageddon no matter where it might be located in Scripture. I wanted to be sure I didn't leave out any text that might be helpful in understanding the end-time battle.

Soon I couldn't believe my eyes. No matter what concordance I used, I could not find the word "Armageddon" anywhere in the Bible except Revelation 16:16. Only one single reference! Here is my own translation of that text: "And he gathered them together at the place which is called in the Hebrew language Harmagedon." The Bible has no other reference to the word Armageddon (or Harmagedon). Whatever we can know about the battle of Armageddon must emerge from the context of this verse in the book of Revelation.

As you may remember, if you have read my previous book *The Deep Things of God*, the larger context of Revelation includes the other 65 books of the Bible. The visions of Revelation often build on the words and ideas of the Old Testament, either by alluding to it directly or echoing its language. In addition, Revelation is firmly related to the New Testament, in which the gospel of Jesus Christ provides the foundation for its end-time message. We will explore this larger context in the following chapters of this book, but in this chapter we want to focus on the meaning of the word "Armageddon" itself.

Where did the H in Harmagedon come from? I wondered. I soon learned in Greek class (I was taking intermediate Greek that quarter) that the answer involved a small mark on top of the *a* in Armageddon. It is called a breathing mark. The breathing mark I found at the beginning of "Armageddon" is the kind of breath you take when you pronounce the letter *h*. In many ancient manuscripts the breathing marks don't appear, and even when they do, it is sometimes easy to miss them. So the translators of the King James Bible just wrote out the letters and ignored the breathing mark at the beginning of the word. So "Harmagedon" in Greek was translated as "Armageddon" in English. And Armageddon has become a word we all recognize.

The two *d*'s in Armageddon are harder to explain, since there is only one *d* in the Greek. But modern translators seem to have kept the two *d*'s because people are familiar with the spelling.

After discovering that Revelation 16:16 is the only place in the Bible that the word Harmagedon appears, I studied the immediate context in verses 12-16. The name Harmagedon is the location of the final battle of earth's history (verse 16). In that battle three demonic frogs gather the kings of the whole earth to the great battle of God Almighty (verses 13, 14). Without question this is the closing battle of earth's history. According to the text, the struggle has several other players. Verse 12 mentions the great river Euphrates and the kings from the rising of the sun, and verse 13 speaks of the dragon, the beast, and the false prophet. And verse 15 indicates that the people of God are somehow involved as well. Only one thing seemed obvious at this point—the battle of Armageddon was truly the final conflict of earth's history. The meaning of the word itself, however, was still a mystery.

The text of Revelation 16:16 is perfectly clear on one thing. The word "Harmagedon" is in some way Hebrew in origin. So I decided to see if "Harmagedon" or something like it appeared in the Hebrew Old Testament, but it wasn't there. No wonder this text has frustrated students of the Bible for centuries! The word translated "Armageddon" occurs only one time—Revelation 16:16.

At this point I remembered that many words in Greek and Hebrew are compounds. In other words, they are combinations of two or more smaller words. For example, the English word "understand" is made up of two smaller words, the word "under" and the word "stand." When you "stand under" someone else you can more clearly perceive the world from their perspective. So we can often clarify the meaning of a compound word by breaking it up into its component parts.

After examining the various possibilities, I made my first breakthrough. In Hebrew *har* means "mountain." Harmagedon makes some sort of reference to a mountain. In fact, one could translate the word as "Mountain of Magedon." Finally I was getting somewhere! If I could only find a mountain named Magedon, I might be able to pinpoint the location of the final battle of earth's history! So I began looking through atlases of the ancient world for a mountain named Magedon, but I didn't find one. A quick look at a Hebrew concordance also indicated that *magedon* was not a word in the Hebrew vocabulary. So I was stumped once more. All I knew was that *Harmagedon* represented some sort of mountain.

One day in class a New Testament teacher began discussing the ancient world into which Jesus was born and in which the early church grew and developed. As he mentioned various developments in the time of Jesus he repeatedly talked about "the Septuagint." I had never heard this word before, so after several repetitions I raised my hand and asked, "What is the Septuagint?"

"Oh, I'm sorry," the teacher said. "I thought everyone was familiar with that."

I know he didn't mean it that way, but the comment sure made me feel dumb.

"In the centuries before Jesus was born," he went on, "more and more Jews began moving to other parts of the Mediterranean world. Many settled in Egypt and Asia Minor, others in Syria and Greece. Some even went as far as Rome and Spain. In most of these areas Greek had become a common unifying language, so the children of these Jews learned the Greek language and through time gradually lost their ability to understand Hebrew. That meant that if they were to be able to study what we call the Old Testament, they would need to have a translation of the Hebrew Old Testament into the Greek language."

Another student interrupted. "But what did they do for these people in the synagogue before such a translation was made?"

"They continued to recite the Hebrew Bible from the front," the professor replied, "just as Jews still do today. But they followed the reading with what they called a 'targum,' an oral translation of the Hebrew into the local language of the people. We know that the oral Aramaic targums eventually were written down, and the oral Greek targums no doubt formed the basis of the written translation that came together during a couple hundred years in the city of Alexandria.

"According to Jewish tradition, 70 scholars assembled in Alexandria, and each of them made his own independent translation of the five books of Moses from Hebrew into Greek. When they got together and compared the 70 translations with each other, they discovered that all 70 were identical! According to the story, this was how the Septuagint came into being, the Greek translation of the Torah."

"But what does the word 'Septuagint' mean?" another student asked.

"Oh, sorry. I probably should have explained that right off. The word 'Septuagint' comes from the Greek word for 'seventy.' It reflects the story about the 70 translators. Obviously, scholars today don't think it happened exactly that way, but somehow the Septuagint translation got put together in the centuries just before Jesus came to earth. What is important to Christians is that the Septuagint became the first Bible of the Christian church. It helps us understand how early Christians understood the Old Testament."

I jumped into the discussion again. "Is that why New Testament quotations of the Old Testament often read quite differently from our own versions of the Old Testament?" In my mind I hoped it wasn't another dumb question.

"Right!" the teacher stated. "New Testament writers often quote the Septuagint rather than translating directly from the Hebrew text. It is clear that there are significant variants between the Septuagint and the Hebrew text that has been passed down to us. Scholars have long debated whether the Septuagint or our current Hebrew text is more true to the original. But the differences can be seen in the quotations of the Old within the New Testament itself."

Wow, was that class ever an eye-opener! I went up to the teacher afterward and asked where I could find a Septuagint and whether or not there was any concordance I could use to look up words in it. He told me how to find such tools in the library. I couldn't wait for some free time to see if the Septuagint would be any help in my quest to understand the meaning of Har-magedon. Today you could do the following study on many computer Bible programs.

I had a free hour a couple days later and went to the seminary's reference library. Pulling down a printed copy of the Septuagint, I then located the concordance to the Septuagint. I found myself holding my breath as I opened the concordance looking for "harmagedon," but I was disappointed. It wasn't in the Septuagint, either. For a moment I slumped back in my chair. *No wonder everybody but that preacher thinks this is a complicated topic,* I thought. But then I remembered that "Harmagedon" was a compound word!

So I paged over to the *m* section, looking for *magedon*. It had three references! Yes! At last I was getting somewhere! The references were Joshua 12:21; Judges 1:27; and 2 Chronicles 35:22. When I let out a quick yelp, I immediately flushed with embarrassment as several sets of eyes glared at me out of the tomblike silence of the reference room. Mouthing a quick apology, I grabbed my Bible and began looking up the three passages. I started with Joshua 12:21. It was part of a list of all the kings of city-states that Joshua had killed in the conquest of Canaan after Israel crossed the Jordan River: "The king of Taanach, one; the king of *Megiddo*, one" (Joshua 12:21, ESV).

A quick glance at the Greek of the Septuagint showed me that *magedon* was a translation of Megiddo! An ancient Canaanite city at the edge of the Valley of Jezreel, Megiddo was part of the inheritance given to the tribe of Manasseh after the conquest. The Valley of Jezreel lay between Samaria and Galilee. So it was a pretty strategic location. It was also clear that the reference here was to the city of Megiddo and not something else, since the list included the kings of a whole series of major cities all over Canaan: Jerusalem, Hazor, Lachish, Arad, Libnah, Hebron, Gezer, and Jericho. So *magedon* here was a reference, not to a mountain, but to a city! And it was a list, not of cities conquered, but of ones whose king had been killed in battle. Not sure what to do with this information, I went on to the next text in my list: "But Manasseh did not drive out the people of Beth Shan or Taanach or Dor or Ibleam or *Megiddo* and their surrounding settlements, for the Canaanites were determined to live in that land" (Judges 1:27, NIV).

Once again we have a list of cities, this time from the territory of

Manasseh, which the members of the tribe did not conquer. Evidently Israelites slew the kings of those cities but did not occupy the cities themselves. Once again *magedon* is the Greek word used to translate Megiddo, the name of one of the cities. So for my purposes, the text yielded the same basic information as the previous one.

The third text I looked up was 2 Chronicles 35:22: "Josiah, however, would not turn away from him, but disguised himself to engage him in battle. He would not listen to what Neco had said at God's command but went to fight him on the plain of Megiddo" (NIV).

The passage sounded real interesting, so I looked up this battle in a Bible history book. I found out that about 609 B.C. Pharaoh Necho (Neco) II of Egypt wanted to prevent the destruction of the Assyrian Empire by Babylon. So he took his army and planned to pass through King Josiah's territory to join the remaining Assyrians at Carchemish in what is modern-day Iraq. Josiah intervened with his army and perished near the city of Megiddo in a futile attempt to stop Necho. What I found especially intriguing in 2 Chronicles 35:22 was the phrase "plain of Megiddo." From the perspective of the biblical author one could apply the name Megiddo to the whole valley as well as the city. So I learned that the name of a city could also refer to the geographical area around the city. Not knowing whether that was an important insight, I filed it away in the back of my mind.

One thing I noticed in all of these texts. The Greek *Magedon*, with one *d,* consistently translated the Hebrew Megiddo, with two *d*'s. In the Hebrew a double letter is usually signified by a little dot, but the dot is not always there in the text since the native speaker can just sense it based on how the particular letter is related to the other letters in the word. Perhaps the translators of the Septuagint worked from Hebrew texts that didn't have the dot. That might explain why translators of the English Bible render *Harmagedon* with two *d's*: Armageddon. The original translators must have understood *harmagedon* to mean "mountain of Megiddo," and Megiddo has two *d*'s.

Then I discovered something even more interesting. When I glanced back to the Septuagint concordance I noticed just above *magedon* a reference to *mageddon*. Evidently, in 2 Kings 9:27 the Septuagint translates Megiddo with a double "d," as *mageddon*! So the English term Armageddon definitely seemed to be based on the concept "mountain of Megiddo." I wasn't sure where the *n* in *mageddon* came from, but the word clearly seemed based on the Hebrew word Megiddo. The English translation goes as follows: "When Ahaziah king of Judah saw what had happened, he fled up the road to Beth Haggan. Jehu chased him, shouting, 'Kill him too!' They wounded him in his chariot on the way up to Gur near Ibleam, but he escaped to *Megiddo* and died there" (2 Kings 9:27, NIV).

So in three of the four cases of *magedon/mageddon* in the Greek Old Testament we have a clear reference to the city. In the fourth case the name's reference expands to the whole plain in which the city of Megiddo was located. As I looked up Megiddo in a number of Bible dictionaries I found that the region of Megiddo was often an ancient battleground. It was near Megiddo that the armies of Israel under Deborah and Barak defeated Sisera and his Canaanite army (Judges 5:19). The scene of the fatal struggle between Josiah and Pharaoh Neco (2 Kings 23:29, 30; 2 Chron. 35:22) was such a memorable event in Israel's history that the Bible recalled the mourning for Josiah 100 years later in Zechariah 12:11. Thus if John was alluding to this ancient battleground, Megiddo's significance for ancient Israel made it an appropriate background to his description of the final struggle between the forces of good and evil.

When I combined the conclusions of my study, it seemed clear that the most natural understanding of *harmagedon* in Revelation 16:16 is "mountain of Megiddo," a compound word derived from the Greek transliteration of the Hebrew word *har,* which means "mountain," and the Greek transliteration of the Hebrew for Megiddo. But I was still troubled about one thing. While the Bible can talk about the Valley of Megiddo and the city of Megiddo, nowhere in the Bible do we find any mention of a mountain of Megiddo. And no matter which atlas you use, you won't find a mountain of Megiddo anywhere on earth! So while I seemed to have discovered the meaning of Armageddon, it didn't tell me anything important. I still had no idea what "mountain of Megiddo" had to do with the sixth plague of Revelation 16.

THE MEANING OF
ARMAGEDDON

I decided it was time to get some expert help. I heard that one of the teachers in the seminary had published an article on Armageddon, so I decided to visit him and find out what mountain of Megiddo was all about. I made an appointment for the following week and was on pins and needles to see what I would learn from the interview.

"So I hear you're really interested in the word 'Armageddon'!" the teacher said. "I published an article on that in a scholarly journal just a couple years ago. So what do you think it means?"

"Well, I'm not really sure yet," I replied, "but I've been looking at parallels in the Septuagint, and it appears as if the word 'Armageddon' means 'mountain of Megiddo.'"

"You think so?" the teacher said skeptically. "I've found a lot of problems with that idea."

"Really?" I said, trying to sound respectful. "But what else could it possibly mean?"

"Well, first you have to determine whether what seems like the obvious reading is really correct," he replied. "If that cannot be correct, then you have to look at whatever other possibilities there may be."

"OK, so I guess I need to know why you don't think mountain of Megiddo is the correct meaning of Armageddon."

"Here's what I've found," he said, pulling a copy of his article out of one of the drawers in his desk and handing it to me. Red markings indicated the places he had made his argument against the concept of "mountain of Megiddo." "For one thing, while the Old Testament knows of a city of Megiddo (Joshua 17:11; Judges 1:27; 1 Kings 4:12; 9:15; 2 Kings

50

9:27; 23:29, 30), a king of Megiddo (Joshua 12:21), a valley of Megiddo (2 Chron. 35:22; Zech. 12:11), and waters of Megiddo (Judges 5:19), it knows of no Mountain of Megiddo." During the next half hour we looked at all the above texts together. He did seem to have a point. Nowhere does the Old Testament mention any mountain of Megiddo.

"But I already knew that," I protested cautiously, having already been burned more than once by the stating of a hasty opinion in the matter. "Can't John take a number of different Old Testament pieces and put them together in a new way? After all, the word 'Armageddon' begins with *Har*, which means 'mountain.'"

"True," the teacher replied patiently. "But that is not all. Not only does mountain of Megiddo not appear anywhere in the Old Testament— it is not found anywhere in all of the ancient world before the reference in Revelation. Not only that, the fathers of the church during the two or three centuries after Revelation was written didn't interpret it as mountain of Megiddo either. So if John understood Armageddon as mountain of Megiddo, he was taking it to mean something no one before or after him understood. That seems pretty unlikely to me.

"Many scholars in the past have explored this issue," he went on, "and nearly all of them disagreed with the mountain of Megiddo interpretation. If you look at ancient writings outside the Jewish world they often speak of a mythical mountain at the end of the world. But that mythical mountain is never called Megiddo. There is, however, something even more decisive in my mind."

"What is that?" I asked, not sure that I wanted to know.

"If you go to the Old Testament passages related to the end of the world, they never describe the final battle of earth's history as happening at Megiddo. Rather, it always takes place around Jerusalem. Zechariah 12 depicts a future battle in which all the nations gather against Jerusalem, but God delivers the city by making it like an immovable rock [Zech. 12:1-9]. In Zechariah 14 all the nations assemble against Jerusalem and conquer it, with half the people going into exile. But at that point God intervenes with a plague on Jerusalem's enemies and restores the city [Zech. 14:1-15]. Joel 3:12-16 has all the nations advance into the Valley of Jehoshaphat, just outside Jerusalem. Once again God intervenes to destroy the armies. Finally, in Daniel 11 the king of the north pitches his tents near the 'glorious holy mountain,' a reference to the site of the Temple. Then Michael stands up to defend his people [Dan. 11:40-45; 12:1]. You will even find echoes of the final battle around Jerusalem in Revelation 14, just two chapters before Armageddon [Rev. 14:19, 20]. So nowhere in the Bible do we have any evidence that the end-time battle will occur in relation to Megiddo, much less to a mountain of Megiddo."

Just then the bell rang out in the hall. The teacher looked at his watch, and an expression of horror crossed his face. "It's already 11:30," he exclaimed. "I'm late for class! I have to go."

"I'm so sorry," I responded. "I'm sorry to take so much of your time." Hastily I backed out of the teacher's office, overwhelmed with the force of his arguments against what I had found in my own Bible study.

A few days later I checked back with the teacher's secretary to see if I could make another appointment to learn what he actually thought Armageddon meant.

"Oh, that won't be possible," she said in a voice that allowed for no protest.

"Why not?" I protested anyway.

"He's teaching an extension class in Africa and won't be back in the office for at least a month."

Well, so much for that, I thought. *I guess I'm on my own.* Where to go from here? I contacted another teacher who hadn't done a study of Armageddon but might be able to help me with my search. He suggested I examine the references to Armageddon in a number of Bible dictionaries and encyclopedias. Perhaps if I looked at enough of them I would probably get a pretty good idea of the various ideas on Armageddon that people held.

That sounded like a good idea, since the other teacher wouldn't be back for a month. Free Sunday afternoon, I decided to spend it in seminary reference, looking at the dozen or so Bible dictionaries available there. I was anticipating my wedding in a couple months, but at the time I was single and my wife-to-be was almost 1,000 miles away, so I didn't have a lot things going on that would distract me from my study interests (everyone knew better than to have me responsible for any of the wedding arrangements!).

After lunch on Sunday I gathered all the Bible dictionaries and encyclopedias I could find in the reference room, including one or two in German, which I could work through with the help of a German-English dictionary. As I examined the various dictionaries, I discovered that seven major views on the meaning of Armageddon had developed during 1,900 years of interpretation. While my journey through these dictionaries would probably not be of interest to you, I think it would be helpful for me to list the seven major options for you here. (For a more detailed description of them, see "What is Armageddon?" on the following Web site: www.thebattleofarmageddon.com.)

1. A geographical location in Palestine, such as the Valley of Jehoshaphat or Mount Tabor.

2. The "mountain of slaughter" based on Zechariah 12:11.

3. The "mountain places" of Megiddo, including Mount Carmel.

The first three explanations of Armageddon derive from how the translators of the Septuagint understood the Hebrew Bible. The next three attempts suggest that the text we have is corrupted or changed. They show how the shift of a letter or two would alter the meaning of the word.

4. The city of Megiddo.

5. The "fruitful mountain" or "fruitful city."

6. The "mountain of assembly."

And finally:

7. A mythical mountain at the end of the world. This last view derives, not from the grammar of Revelation 16:16, but from ancient legends.

One thing seemed clear from those hours of reading through Bible dictionaries and encyclopedias: barring the discovery of additional evidence, the word studies done on *harmagedon* have brought us about as far as they can. All the major ideas on the subject have been around for more than 50 years. While many of the ideas were new to me, they were not so to the scholars who had invested their lives in the book of Revelation. If a breakthrough was going to occur in the study of Armageddon, it would have to come from some direction other than the exploration of the word and its component parts.

Weary from a whole raft of new-to-me ideas, I leaned back in my library chair, reached back with my hand, and rubbed a sore spot on my back. *Was this really worth it? Yes*, I thought, *it's fun to wrestle with deep biblical concepts, even if the way out of a problem isn't obvious along the way.* But I was starting to get hungry again, and if anything, I seemed further from a solution to my problem than when I began. The abundance of solutions and the great creativity with which people have developed them certainly suggested that it is unwise to be dogmatic about the meaning of the word "Armageddon." Yet I wasn't satisfied to settle for a nonanswer. There had to be some key to the problem.

What simplified things a little for me was the realization that most scholars basically settled on one of two interpretations. 1. Many agreed that "mountain of Megiddo" must be a reference to some sort of geographical location in Palestine, whether literal or spiritual. Five or six of the seven options were variations on this basic idea. 2. The rest of the scholars went with some form of the "mountain of assembly" interpretation. In that view, Har-Magedon describes the heavenly throne room as the object of Satan's final attempt to put himself on God's throne (cf. Isa. 14:12-15; 2 Thess. 2:4). So the bottom line was to figure out which of the two basic options was more likely.

I gathered up my notes, put all the reference books on the reshelving cart, and headed for my dorm room to get ready for supper. I was thinking about how stupid I felt when talking to the teacher the week before. It turned out after all that many scholars agreed with me in seeing mountain of Megiddo as the most likely meaning, so I was not really as dumb as I had felt that day. I decided to go over the teacher's arguments against mountain of Megiddo once more. Did they really hold up?

What had he said? "There is no such thing as a mountain of Megiddo in the Old Testament or anywhere in the ancient world, for that matter." That sure sounded convincing at first blush, but the more I thought about it, the more I realized it was an argument from silence. Just because the scattered literature we have from the ancient world doesn't mention an idea, that doesn't demand that the ancients didn't know about it. And even if they didn't make that connection, it doesn't mean John could not have made the association on the basis of his vision and his previous study of the Old Testament. If the connection made sense to me on the basis of Scripture, it could have made sense to him as well. But how could one know for sure?

The teacher's next argument was more troubling: "None of the early fathers of the church interpreted Armageddon as mountain of Megiddo either. This is true throughout the second, third, and fourth centuries after New Testament times." The implication was serious. You would think that if the meaning of Armageddon was that obvious, those closest to the time of John would have known about it. But none of them did. Deep in thought, I hardly noticed the falling leaves of autumn around me.

Then my head popped up from my reverie. What had the New Testament teacher said about Paul in class the other day? He had commented that the early church was so puzzled by Paul that his theology went completely unnoticed for the same 200-300 years. We know that the apostle's writings existed during those centuries, yet his theology made essentially no impact on the church during those times. It was not until Augustine, around the year 400, that Paul's theology began to have an effect. It dawned on me that if the early fathers of the church could completely ignore the theology of Paul, which covered half the books of the New Testament, why should we be surprised if they did not have a clue about Armageddon either?

It was like the sun breaking through the clouds. Mountain of Megiddo didn't sound that far-fetched after all! While the Old Testament normally locates the final battle around Jerusalem, it wouldn't be impossible for a New Testament writer to use the Josiah encounter or Deborah and Barak's struggle against the Canaanites as an example of the battle at the end of the world. It seemed to me that my teacher's arguments could not be the end of the discussion.

Arriving back at the room, I ran into a fellow student I had known growing up in New York City. "What are you doing for supper?" he asked.

"What else?" I said. "Good old Andrews cafeteria." (Back then we had no options such as Subway, Taco Bell, and Pizza Hut in Berrien Springs.)

Although he made a face, he didn't offer to drive us to South Bend for something more exotic. "Give me a couple of minutes to put these notes away and wash up, and we can go together," I said.

"Sounds great," he replied.

Going to my room, I carefully organized my notes on the desk. Then I headed down the hall to the bathroom and washed my hands. As I reached for a paper towel I realized that it would be hard to shake the research I had done that afternoon. I might talk about all kinds of other stuff, but in the back of my mind I'd still be working on the mystery of Armageddon. Stopping by Bill's door, I knocked, and we headed off to the cafeteria for supper.

"What have you been up to lately?" he asked as we headed through line, collecting our food.

"Oh, I've been studying the meaning of the word 'Armageddon' in the book of Revelation. I spent the whole afternoon on it, and I think I'm more confused than I was when I started!"

"Well, that's what you get for going where even angels fear to tread," Bill quipped. Although he was considering ministry as an occupation, he was definitely not traditional ministerial material. At times he seemed a bit flippant about spiritual things. But he did have a keen mind, and it was fun to discuss issues such as Armageddon with him. It dawned on me that he had visited Israel the previous summer, so I asked him about his trip.

"It was pretty cool. We went to Jerusalem, the Dead Sea, Galilee, Tel Aviv, Haifa, and even Eilat, on the Red Sea's Gulf of Aqaba."

"What was your favorite part of the trip?" I asked. We put our trays down at a table some distance from most of the students.

"Oh, the Old City of Jerusalem is really cool, of course. They've got all these little alleys with shops selling food and souvenirs, such as sandals, candlesticks, and wooden Nativities. But I think my favorite spot was En-gedi."

"En-gedi? Where's that?"

"It's the place where David hid out from Saul. It's a really dry place near the Dead Sea, but every so often you come around the bend and there's a waterfall, right in the middle of the desert! It must have been 110 degrees, and it felt good to stand under the waterfall and cool down. The water must have been close to freezing! Then we went from there and floated in the Dead Sea for a while. Really cool!"

I tried to imagine what those places looked like. It would be 20 years before I would get to see them for myself. Then it hit me that Bill might be able to help me with my little project on Armageddon.

"Hey, Bill! Did you ever get to Megiddo?"

"The ruins of the city of Megiddo?"

"Is there any other kind of Megiddo?" I retorted.

"Well, people sometimes talk about the Valley of Megiddo, but Megiddo was actually an ancient city, guarding the pass that led across Mount Carmel. That's why a lot of battles were fought there . . ."

"Did you say Mount Carmel?" I exploded, almost spraying food in his face.

"Whoa!" he shrieked. "Get a muzzle on that food cannon! You almost knocked me out with that one."

I laughed a bit, but refused to be deterred. "Did you say Megiddo is near Mount Carmel?"

"Of course. Mount Carmel is actually a ridge along the southern edge of the Valley of Jezreel. It starts right on the coast in Haifa and runs sort of southeast for a dozen miles toward the Jordan Valley. The best way to cross it is a pass that feeds right into Megiddo at the base of the mountain. In fact, we visited the site where they think Elijah defeated the prophets of Baal. It is the highest point on the ridge, just overlooking Megiddo."

In a state of shock, I quickly forgot anything else Bill said or anything that happened that evening. All I remember is that I was captured by the thought that Elijah defeated the prophets of Baal by calling fire down to earth from heaven. The fire demonstrated that the God of Israel was the true God. The fact that the prophets of Baal could not bring fire down from heaven proved that they were not worshipping the true God. It reminded me of one of the key elements of the final events in the book of Revelation: "[The land beast] performs great signs, even making fire come down from heaven to earth in front of people, and by the signs that it is allowed to work in the presence of the beast it deceives those who dwell on earth, telling them to make an image for the beast that was wounded by the sword and yet lived" (Rev. 13:13, 14, ESV).

Could it be that "mountain of Megiddo" was a cryptic way of recalling the Old Testament story of Elijah's showdown with the prophets of Baal? On Mount Carmel there took place an encounter between Yahweh and Baal, between Elijah and Baal's prophets. There were competing claims as to who was the true God, and the showdown on the mountain settled the issue by fire. It sounded greatly like the scenario in Revelation 13-17! What if Armageddon was a symbol of Mount Carmel and the decisive events that happened there? At that moment the solution to the whole problem seemed to open itself up to me.

The various word studies had taken me as far as they would likely go. All of the various suggestions I had read were possible, but only the mountain of Megiddo interpretation was based on a straightforward reading of the Greek text of both Revelation and the Old Testament. Still, by itself that was not good enough. The key would be to examine the larger context of the battle of Armageddon in Revelation 13-17. Whatever reading fit best with that overall context was most likely the correct one.

The next day as I was walking down the hall on the third floor of the seminary building I saw one of the Hebrew teachers standing in front of his office. He greeted me and asked whether I had learned anything interesting lately.

"Well, I'm studying the meaning of the word 'Armageddon' in Revelation 16:16. The text says that it is based on a Hebrew word, but no such word occurs in the Old Testament. I've drawn the conclusion that *har-magedon* probably means 'mountain of Megiddo,' but many scholars think it should be 'mountain of assembly.'"

"Actually," he replied, "I've done a little study on the meaning of Armageddon myself. And I share some of your concerns about the 'mountain of assembly' interpretation.

"What do *you* think Armageddon means?" I asked, putting him on the spot.

"Actually, I think it is a reference to Mount Carmel."

"No way," I exclaimed. "I just came to that same conclusion yesterday!"

"Great minds think alike!" he grinned. "You see, the name Megiddo is not limited to the city of that name. The ancients often used it to speak of something else in the geographical area. For example, the phrase 'waters of Megiddo' is a reference to the Kishon River in Judges 5:19. And while Megiddo is not the name of a mountain, it isn't really a valley, either. The ruins of the ancient city perch on an elevation overlooking the Plain of Jezreel. Since the city was located at the foot of the Carmel range, 'mountain of Megiddo' could easily be a reference to Mount Carmel [see 1 Kings 18:19, 20; 2 Kings 2:25; 4:25]."

"This is so exciting," I said. "That's just what I was thinking!"

"The different possibilities for the word Armageddon kind of leave us at an impasse," he went on. "So the best way to decide how Revelation is using Armageddon is to see how each of the options plays out in the rest of the book. It seems to me that the Mount Carmel interpretation best explains the final battle in Revelation. The narrative of Elijah on Mount Carmel is like a background story to the whole account from Revelation 13 to Revelation 19. It functions a lot like the fall of Babylon account does in the same texts. To understand Revelation fully, you need to be familiar with the story of Babylon's fall as told in Isaiah, Jeremiah, and Daniel."

"That gives me a lot to work with," I said with some excitement.

"You'll have to take it from here, because I don't have time right now to fully investigate the ideas I've just shared with you. But if you study the last half of Revelation carefully, I think you'll find that the Mount Carmel theme lies behind a lot of the descriptions in the second half of the book."

"Thanks so much for your time," I said as I began to back out of his office. I didn't want to seem rude, but I couldn't wait to get back to my room and get my Bible out to investigate for myself. Fortunately, I had no classes on Monday, so I hurried to the dorm, closed myself in my room, dug out my Bible, and began carefully to examine Revelation 12-20, looking for hints of the Mount Carmel story there. Although my Greek was still pretty basic, I kept the Greek text handy, along with a Greek-English lexicon.

The first clear reference to the Carmel episode in these chapters was the one that first triggered my imagination: Revelation 13:13, 14. There the land beast calls fire down from heaven in the sight of humanity. It was part of a series of allusions to such Old Testament events as the deceptive magicians of Pharaoh, the creation of Adam and Eve, and the death decree of Nebuchadnezzar in Daniel 3. All four incidents were Old Testament challenges to God. Satan challenged the words of God in Genesis 3, as did Pharaoh's magicians the words that Moses and Aaron spoke for God just before the Exodus. Nebuchadnezzar challenged the vision he had received from God in Daniel 2 by setting up the image of Daniel 3. And of course Elijah faced the challenge of Baal on Mount Carmel.

It was on Mount Carmel that the prophet called fire down from heaven to prove that Yahweh was the true God. But in the case of Revelation 13 it is the land beast who commands fire from heaven. Like the magicians of Pharaoh, the land beast seeks to prove that the counterfeit god is really the true one. And in the end-time showdown, we find the outcome of Mount Carmel reversed. In Revelation the fire strikes the wrong altar. Thus the battle of Armageddon will include a major deceptive action on the part of Satan and his earthly supporters.

Reading on, I found a further reference to Mount Carmel in the immediate context of the word "Armageddon" itself (Rev. 16:12-16). As part of the sixth bowl plague, the mention of *harmagedōn* comes at a pivotal point in the book of Revelation. The drying up of the Euphrates River in verse 12 is a central issue in Revelation 17, as we will see in future chapters. Revelation 16:13 mentions a deceptive trinity called the dragon, the beast, and the false prophet. The beast here points back to the sea beast of Revelation 13, so the false prophet must be a reference to the land beast. On the original Mount Carmel the priests of Baal played the role of false prophets. The land beast of chapter 13 fills that role in the battle of Armageddon.

The reference to the demonic trinity in verse 13 connects this passage with chapters 13 and 19, in which we observe the same characters at work. On Mount Carmel many false prophets tried to bring fire down from heaven. It is on *harmagedôn* that the dragon, beast, and false prophet of Revelation 16:13 meet their end.

Reading on, I noticed that the fate of the beast and the false prophet is the same as that of prophets of Baal in the Old Testament account. As in the original instance, we find the issue settled in Revelation 19:20, 21 by fire and by sword. The outcome is the same in both cases.

Revelation's series of allusions to the Mount Carmel story provided the assurance that the most obvious reading of *har-magedon* is also the one that best fits the overall story of the battle of Armageddon. This will become even clearer after our detailed study of Revelation 13-18 in the chapters to come. The larger context becomes the place in which the Mount Carmel interpretation of Armageddon finds its clearest support.

Having said this, however, I must point out that the sixth bowl plague itself is not the battle of Armageddon—rather, it is the gathering of forces for that conflict. We find the battle itself outlined in the seventh bowl plague, described in Revelation 16:17-21 and elaborated in Revelation 17:12-17 and chapter 18 as a whole. The outcome of the struggle is the fall of Babylon. So Revelation mingles two important stories of the Old Testament: the fall of Babylon and the fall of the prophets of Baal. Images of both events lie behind the narrative of Revelation.

The gathering of the kings of the world by the three unclean spirits (Rev. 16:13, 14) is the demonic counterpart to the gathering call of the three angels of Revelation 14:6-11, who represent the followers of the Lamb. Therefore, the battle of Armageddon serves as the climax of the spiritual war over worship outlined in chapters 13 and 14 (Rev. 13:4, 8, 12, 15; 14:7, 9, 11), a conflict that brings the whole world to a fateful decision with permanent results. As in the original instance, fire and sword settles the issue in Revelation 19:20, 21. A closer look at chapters 13-17 of Revelation will unpack the details of the battle of Armageddon. Get your Bibles ready for an adventure!

GOING AWAY TO MAKE WAR

Things are not always what they seem. One of the best places to get away around Andrews University is the shore of Lake Michigan. For those who have never visited Michigan, the Lake (which is what the locals call it) looks just like an ocean. You cannot see the other shore, and on stormy days the waves can reach six to eight feet in height. It is the fifth-largest lake in the world. The main difference between Lake Michigan and an ocean is the lack of saltiness in the water.

A string of seashore parks in the area run from the city of St. Joseph right down to the border of Indiana. The beaches in those parks have a beautiful white sand that squeaks when you walk on it because of the high quartz content. Prevailing winds from the west have piled up the sand into enormous dunes, more than 100 feet high in places. Green beach grass covers them, so they look like hills with sand patches from a distance. But in winter the sledding is awesome! Without rocks and trees in the way and soft sand under the snow one can reach exhilarating speeds down the steep lee slopes of the dunes without endangering life and limb.

On a brisk Sabbath afternoon in the fall it is delightful to stand on top of one of the dunes and look across Lake Michigan toward Chicago. In fact, on an exceptionally clear day one can see the top half of the Sears Tower (110 floors) peeking up out of the water! But there is one thing that stands out above all others—the overwhelming impression that the lake is flat and that, therefore, the earth must also be flat! You see, things are not always what they seem. In actual fact the surface of Lake Michigan has a faint curvature to it, but it is undetectable to the eye. It underlines the point that the things that the eyes see and the ears hear are not always accurate. Our senses are limited and can easily be deceived. This truth is of major importance to the study outlined in this chapter. We turn now to the text of Revelation itself.

While the word "Armageddon" occurs only in Revelation 16:16, the final battle of earth's history is the major concern of the second half of the book, running from Revelation 12:17 all the way through chapters 19 and 20. So in order for us to gain a clear picture of the battle of Armageddon it is important to begin our study in the foundation text, the one that sets the big picture for everything that follows: Revelation 12:17. The last verse of chapter 12, it sets the stage directly for chapters 13 and 14 and indirectly for chapters 15-19.

An Angry Dragon

Revelation 12 takes us from the original war in heaven on through decisive events of the birth, death, ascension, and enthronement of Christ (Rev. 12:1-5, 7-12). It goes on to describe the persecution of the church (by a dragon who could no longer continue the war in heaven) through the intervening period (verses 6, 13-16), and concludes with an introduction to the final battle of the dragon against the remnant of the woman's seed (verse 17).

From verse 17 onward the book of Revelation focuses almost entirely on the final events of earth's history. The same dragon who fought the heavenly Christ (Michael—see verse 7) also battled the earthly Christ (the male child of the woman—verse 5). He then sought to destroy the woman (who represents those who overcome by the blood of Christ—verses 11-16). After this he mounts his final attack on the remnant of her seed (Christ's last-day people). So the actions of the dragon mark the different stages of Revelation 12 and show that chapter 12 portrays a sequence of events running from before the cross all the way to the final showdown of earth's history.

"And the dragon was wroth with the woman, and went to make war with the remnant of her seed, which keep the commandments of God, and have the testimony of Jesus" (Rev. 12:17).

Why is the dragon angry? Actually he stays angry, since he was already that way when cast out of heaven in verse 12. His repeated failures have left him frustrated. He was not able to devour the male child of the woman in verse 5. Nor was he strong enough to win the war in heaven (verse 8), and thus God cast him out (verses 9-12). The earth helped the woman in the desert, preventing the dragon from destroying her (verse 16). Then the dragon went off to make war with the remnant of her seed (verse 17). This reference to the seed of the woman reminds us of God's promise to Eve in the Garden of Eden (Gen. 3:15). The Lord promised that her seed would crush the serpent's head. Revelation 12:5 also reminds us of the child of the woman. Both seeds allude to Jesus. It is He and He alone who can defeat the dragon (Satan). Jesus' people are safe only when they stay close to Him.

Who are Jesus' people in this text? The passage calls them "the remnant of her seed." This concept of remnant is very familiar to Adventists and has a long history in the Old Testament and the Jewish literature of the century before the composition of Revelation. It is so important that I plan to write a whole book on it soon. The focus of the present book is a bit more on the dark side of the final conflict.

We need to notice one more thing about Revelation 12:17. The dragon does not attack the remnant directly. Instead he "went to make war." He retreats from the remnant to stand on "the sand of the sea" (verse 18 in Greek, usually found in Revelation 13:1 in English translation). Instead of attacking the remnant, he heads for the beach! It seems a rather strange way to make war. What is going on here?

Apparently the dragon's repeated failures have made him cautious (paying attention to the story line of Revelation). He realizes he doesn't have the strength to defeat the purposes of God on his own, so he decides to go to the beach and summon a couple of allies to his support in the final conflict. He calls up two beasts, one from out of the sea and the other up from the earth. With the addition of these two allies the remnant now faces three opponents instead of one: (1) the dragon; (2) the beast from the sea; and (3) the beast from the land.

Now, at this point I want to offer a word of caution for all my Adventist readers. Adventists have a tendency to relate all of these beasts and the other symbols of the book directly to history. The dragon represents one power, the beast from the sea stands for another, and the beast from the earth depicts a third. And it is not a bad thing to try to understand the implications of Revelation for Christian history. But what often happens is that we get so absorbed in history that we fail to follow the *story* of Revelation itself. In the process we may miss important information that would be vital to our understanding not only of history but also of the text of Revelation. The book is a narrative, and the story is worth exploring in its own right. I will have much to say about history and its meaning in the book on the remnant that will follow this one. But for now I want to concentrate on the narrative of chapter 13. I believe that when I do that, you will be amazed at the kinds of things that are easy to miss.

An Unholy Trinity

It doesn't take a math genius to notice that the dragon, plus the beasts from the sea and from the land, make up a group of three. What immediately comes to mind is that the book of Revelation often speaks of God in threes. He is, for example, the one "which is, which was, and which is to come" (Rev. 1:4; cf. 4:8). What we seem to have here in Revelation 13 is a counterfeit of the holy three, Father, Son, and Holy Spirit. But don't just accept my word for it. Let's take a closer look at these three and see if that is what is actually going on.

We'll start with the dragon. Of the unholy three, the dragon appears first and has the fundamental authority over them. He is associated with the serpent in the Garden of Eden, and Scripture calls him the devil and Satan (Rev. 12:9). So the dragon represents the great counterpart to the position of God, thus serving as the leader of all the forces of evil in the universe. The dragon is the source of all evil, and he happily shares his authority with the land beast and the sea beast. So it should not surprise us that he plays the role of counterfeit to the position of God the Father in the universe.

The parallel becomes even more interesting when we examine the features of the sea beast (Rev. 13:1-10). It seems that Revelation portrays the sea beast as a parody or counterfeit of Jesus Christ. Let's look at the text. "And I saw a beast coming out of the sea. He had ten horns and seven heads, with ten crowns on his horns, and on each head a blasphemous name. The beast I saw resembled a leopard, but had feet like those of a bear and a mouth like that of a lion" (verses 1, 2, NIV).

If you were walking around in the forest and saw an animal with seven heads and 10 horns, what would you know? That you had been drinking! No such animal exists. But if you saw two animals with seven heads and 10 horns, what would you conclude? That you have found a species—two of a kind. That is what is happening here. The dragon looks really strange, different from any animal in the real world. But as strange as the dragon appears, the sea beast looks just like him, with seven heads and 10 horns. And here is where the counterfeit comes in. In the Gospel of John, Jesus said, "Anyone who has seen me has seen the Father" (John 14:9, NIV). In other words, Jesus looks just like His Father. In the counterfeit, the sea beast resembles the dragon, who is the counterfeit of the Father.

"Now the beast which I saw was like a leopard, his feet were like the feet of a bear, and his mouth was like the mouth of a lion. The dragon gave him his power and his throne, and great authority" (Rev. 13:2, NKJV).

This text tells us that the sea beast gets his authority from the dragon. He does not have it on his own. The passage also reminds us of a saying of Jesus: "All authority in heaven and on earth has been given to me" (Matt. 28:18, NKJV). Just as Jesus received His authority from His Father, so the sea beast obtains his from the dragon. Once again the sea beast relates to the dragon in the same way that Jesus does to His Father.

"And one of [the beast's] heads was, as it were, slaughtered to death, but the wound of his death was healed. And the whole world was amazed on account of the beast" (see Rev. 13:3).

What does it involve to have one's head slaughtered to death? It means to be killed. If the seven heads of the beast are actually consecutive (as is the case with the beast of Revelation 17:9—sort of like the "nine lives" of a cat) then the slaughter of one of the heads kills the whole beast. And if the beast is dead and a healing takes place, what do we call that? A resurrection! So the sea beast counterfeits the death and resurrection of Jesus!

The author of Revelation does not want the reader to miss this point. He repeats the key word in Revelation 13:8: "The Lamb *slaughtered* from the foundation of the world." The word translated "slaughtered" in verse 8 is the exact same word applied to the sea beast in verse 3. Because the Greek language has several words for death and killing, the repetition of the unusual word "slaughter," therefore, is very significant. Since verse 8 is a clear reference to the death of Jesus, verse 3 points to a deliberate counterfeit of the cross. The sea beast has a death and a resurrection just like Jesus!

Verse 4 of chapter 13 tells us that those who admire the sea beast do so with the phrases "Who is like the beast? who is able to make war with him?" What is interesting here is that the Hebrew name Michael means

"Who is like God?" It is roughly the same question asked about the beast in Revelation 13:4. Since Michael is probably another name for Christ in the book of Revelation (see Rev. 12:7), we have a further indication that the sea beast is a deliberate counterfeit of Jesus Christ.

The beast from the sea also has a ministry that lasts for 42 months: "It was allowed to exercise authority for forty-two months" (Rev. 13:5, NRSV). Why 42 months? How long was the ministry of Jesus? Three and a half years. And how long is 42 months? Three and a half years! So the sea beast not only mimics the position of Jesus within the godhead, but also counterfeits His life, death, and resurrection. In a multitude of ways the beast from the sea masquerades as Jesus Christ.

One thing you can't miss about Revelation is all the animals in the book, but it is not really an animal story, is it? It reminds me of the animated film *The Lion King*. On the surface *Lion* King was an animal story centered on the African plains. But it quickly becomes clear that *Lion King* is not really an animal narrative. Rather, it is about people and their character, about how groups of human beings interact with each other. In fact, it is an African Apocalypse in which animals symbolize human interactions. The film teaches lessons about real life in the human dimension.

The book of Revelation is like that. To use today's language, it is like a cartoon fantasy, in which the animals represent kingdoms and institutions and the way they relate to each other under God's ultimate control (Rev. 17:17, 18). A key part of it is the sea beast, a counterfeit of Jesus Christ. The sea beast in the story walks, looks, and talks like Jesus Christ, but is really a perversion of everything Christ stands for. Revelation is truly a symbolic book (Rev. 1:1). Nothing is exactly what it may seem on the surface.

Now, if the dragon counterfeits God the Father and the sea beast God the Son, then it would make sense for the land beast to be a counterfeit of the Holy Spirit. And a careful look at Revelation 13:11-14 indicates that it is. Notice verse 11: "Then I saw another beast coming up out of the earth, and he had two horns like a lamb and spoke like a dragon" (NKJV). The beast that rises from the earth has "two horns like a lamb." The word "lamb" occurs 29 times in the book of Revelation, and 28 of them refer to Jesus Himself. The only other occurrence of the word is here. So this beast is also a lot like Christ. How does that fit into a masquerade of the Holy Spirit? Go a little deeper with me.

GOING AWAY TO MAKE WAR

Do you remember what the Gospel of John calls the Holy Spirit? Most people would respond, "The Comforter." And that is true, up to a point, but it is not the whole story. Actually, John 14:16 describes the Holy Spirit as *"another* Comforter." That means He is not the original Comforter— that is Someone else. Who is *the* Comforter? It is Jesus.

Picture the scene. It is the upper room, just before the crucifixion of Jesus. The disciples are quite depressed. Jesus has announced that He is going away, and they don't know what they will do without Him. But He says, "Don't worry; if I go away, I will send you *another* Comforter. Someone who will comfort you the same way I do." Jesus promises the disciples that He will not leave them in the position of orphans (John 14:18). The work of the Holy Spirit is to replace the activity of Jesus in the disciples' lives. His work is modeled on that of Jesus, and He does it in behalf of Jesus. So it is consistent with the role of the Holy Spirit to say that He is "like the Lamb." So the land beast of Revelation 13 is similar to the Holy Spirit in that he is "like a lamb." But that is not all.

"And [the land beast] exercises all the authority of the first beast on his behalf, and he causes the earth and everyone who lives in it to worship the first beast, whose deadly wound was healed" (see verse 12).

Notice that the land beast is uninterested in promoting himself. His role and purpose is to advance the power and the interests of the sea beast. This also reminds us of what Jesus said in the upper room. The Holy Spirit does not push Himself (John 16:13). Instead He is always pointing to Christ and reminding of His words (verses 13, 14). So the land beast relates to the sea beast in the same way that the Holy Spirit does to Jesus Christ.

That brings us to the next verse. "And he performed great signs, so much so that he even caused fire to come down from heaven to earth in full view of men" (see verse 13). Did the Holy Spirit in the New Testament ever bring fire down from heaven? Yes, on the day of Pentecost in Acts 2! On that occasion the Holy Spirit brought fire from heaven to earth to anoint the original disciples. It was the greatest and most powerful act of the Holy Spirit up until that time. So the land beast performs another act reminiscent of the Holy Spirit. The land beast not only counterfeits the general function of the Holy Spirit—but he specifically counterfeits Pentecost itself. The activity of the land beast at the end of time precipitates a powerful spiritual revival that counters the work of

God. Why does the land beast bring fire down from heaven? "And he deceives those who live on the earth because of the signs he was given power to do on behalf of the first beast, saying to those who live on the earth that they should make an image to the beast who had the wound of the sword and yet came to life" (see verse 14).

These texts predict a great final worldwide deception in which a counterfeit trinity stands in the place of God. The counterfeit Pentecost confuses people about the true God and His purposes for the last days of earth's history. But the land beast's strategy includes an additional step, and this becomes crystal clear in the next verse: "And [the Land Beast] was permitted to give *breath* to the image of the beast, in order that the image of the beast might speak and cause everyone who does not worship the image of the beast to be killed" (see verse 15). The word "breath" here is the same word in Greek as "spirit." The land beast gives "spiritual" life to the image of the beast. But instead of a spiritual appeal to the world, the land beast gets ugly and demands worship of the image under the threat of death.

The devil (who operates behind the scenes through the dragon and the beasts) has two primary methods of dealing with human beings. 1. On the one hand, he counterfeits the work of God in order to deceive people and persuade them to give allegiance willingly to him rather than to God. 2. On the other hand, he uses force, persuading people by intimidation to do what they otherwise would not do. We see both forms of persuasion illustrated in the mark of the beast passage (Rev. 13:17). Some will follow his unholy trinity because they genuinely believe that in so doing they are worshipping God. The ones marked on the forehead are the truly deceived. Others follow the beast, not because they really believe in him, but because they want to live and eat and have jobs. Going along out of fear, they are the ones marked on the hand.

Through the course of history force has had its limits, and persecution has often backfired. When a person's faith comes under threat, it often grows stronger. In the face of violent opposition, prayers become charged with fervency. So in the last days of earth's history Satan does not limit his attacks to frontal assaults and intimidation, but brings in deception refined almost to perfection so that people will not be able to tell which side is right. They will not be sure whether they are dealing with Christ or Satan. The counterfeit Holy Spirit will use a counterfeit Pentecost to confuse people about the workings of God and to deceive them regarding his intentions for humanity at the end of time. *During the last days things will not be as they seem.*

The Spiritual Implications of Deception

As we encounter the deceptions of the last days, what difference will it make in our lives? I think at least three things. I think we will pray as we have never prayed before. I think we will search the Scriptures as we have never searched them before. And I think we will exercise more self-distrust when it comes to our knowledge of God. Often, when we learn a little about the Bible, we feel confident that we have a handle on the divine. It is as if we can put God in a box in which we know what He is like and what He will and will not do. But the Bible warns us that God's thoughts are not our thoughts, nor His ways ours (Isa. 55:6, 7). When we have a true sense of how vulnerable we are to deception, we will recognize our deep need for His guidance every moment of every day.

I have a little strategy that helps to keep me humble (as much as that is possible in my broken condition). I call it the ladder of humility. I first heard a version of it from Fritz Guy, a teacher at the seminary during my doctoral program. The ladder starts with me. I am at level one when it comes to knowledge. Having a Ph.D. in New Testament, I know quite a bit. After all, I've studied the Bible carefully for decades and have written a lot of books about it. Also I've learned a lot about terrorism and world affairs and about relationships and how people grow emotionally. So level one is not a bad place to be. Level one is everything that I know.

But level two is infinitely higher. It is what everyone on earth knows, something so much bigger than my knowledge that I wouldn't know how to compare them. If you ever get a chance to visit Andrews University, go to the library. Have a look at the stacks and stacks of books that seem to go on forever. Yet that library contains only a fraction of the knowledge that everyone on earth has. What everyone on earth knows is even bigger than all the knowledge you can access on Google, and even that is so huge that I can hardly comprehend it. So knowledge at level two is infinitely bigger than what I know.

But that doesn't even come close to level three. Level three is what everyone in the universe knows. Human knowledge right now is limited to what is available on earth. We know next to nothing about the endless procession of galaxies, filled with unimaginable wonders. When we consider all the combined knowledge of every creature in the universe, it is infinitely larger than what even all of humanity can grasp.

But then comes level four of the ladder of humility. Level four is what everyone in the universe could know, given an infinite amount of time and opportunity. That dwarfs all the knowledge current in the universe by an infinite amount. But even level four still pales in significance compared with level five.

What is level five? It is what God knows. How big is the gap between level four and level five? As vast as that between Creator and creature, between infinite and finite. Each step in the ladder of humility is so large as to be almost unimaginable. And I am four levels below God. Can you see why it is sheer stupidity to think that we can ever have a complete handle on Him? No matter how much I study, no matter how much I learn, my knowledge is as minuscule as dust in comparison with what God knows.

But let me take it the other way for a moment. What is the difference between what I know and what a 2-year-old does? Again, this is almost infinitely vast! Can you, as an adult, talk to a 2-year-old? Yes, you can. You can get down on one knee, look into his or her eyes, and talk 2-year-old talk! Can you discuss quantum physics or the seven trumpets of Revelation? No. Of course you can communicate with a child, but only at his or her limited level.

Now, think about what that means for the Bible. Consider the challenge God faced when He chose to reveal Himself in Scripture. Can we learn about Him from the Bible? Yes. We can gain a basic understanding of Him and His ways. But that understanding will always be limited by our own situation. When God talks to us through the Bible, it is like an adult trying to reach out to a 2-year-old, except that the gap between Him and us is infinitely greater than that between adults and small children.

The ladder of humility keeps me from getting overconfident in my knowledge of God as we approach the end of history. Deception works because our knowledge is so limited in the first place. Put on top of that our tendency to take the easiest way out of any situation, and we are all vulnerable. So as we approach the end we need to pray and study as we have never done before. And we must do so in full awareness of our limitations and of our deep necessity for daily divine guidance.

I know that some Adventists will say, "Come on, I know that my knowledge is limited to some degree, but we Adventists have the end-time scenario down. No end-time deception will fool us! We know where we stand, and we will be on the right side when the end comes." I wish that were 100 percent true, but I fear that the Bible teaches us otherwise. Let me draw the scenario of deception a little more tightly. To do that, I would like to have you read Revelation 13:13, 14 one more time: "And he performed great signs, so much so that he even caused fire to come down from heaven to earth in full view of men. And he deceives those who live on the earth because of the signs he was given power to do on behalf of the first beast, saying to those who live on the earth that they should make an image to the beast who had the wound of the sword and yet came to life."

Miraculous, powerful signs! Things will not be what they seem. When the end-time comes, you will not be able to believe what you see, hear, or touch. Unlike any time ever before, it will get truly scary. If you take a broad read through the New Testament, you will discover that Revelation 13:13, 14 is one of four passages that explicitly discuss an end-time deception. The other three are 2 Thessalonians 2:8-12, Matthew 24:24-27, and Revelation 16:13, 14. If we want to get the full picture of what the Bible has to say about the end-time deception, we need to go to all the passages that directly address the subject.

Deception in the New Testament

Let's start with 2 Thessalonians: "And then the Lawless One will be revealed, whom the Lord Jesus will slay with the breath of His mouth and destroy by the brightness of His coming, whose coming is according to the working of Satan in all kinds of miracles and signs and lying wonders, and in every deception of unrighteousness among those who are being destroyed" (see verses 8-10).

Notice right off that the subject of the passage is the same as that of Revelation 13:13, 14. It is all about the great deception that will occur on earth just before the second coming of Jesus. Observe also that it uses the same language as Revelation 13, warning about great signs that Satan does

71

to trick humanity. So the signs and wonders put forth to mislead the inhabitants of the earth here parallel the last deception of earth's history in Revelation 13.

At this point I want you to see something unusual in the translation above. The last word of verse 8 is "coming"—"the brightness of His *coming.*" The first major word of verse 9 is also "coming"—"whose *coming* is according to the working of Satan." The Greek word for "coming" in both cases is *parousia,* the typical Greek word to describe the return of Christ. But that creates a problem. Is this text saying that the second coming of Jesus will be according to the working of Satan? That would be hard to believe. So what other possibility is there? That the "coming according to the working of Satan" is a coming of the lawless one (an end-time enemy power in service of Satan—for more detail, see my book *What the Bible Says About the End-time* [pp. 95-101]).

In other words, at the end of time there will take place a counterfeit of the second coming of Jesus. The lawless one will have his own *parousia.* But that raises another question. Which of the two comings will happen first? Go back to verse 8. There it tells us that the arrival of Jesus will destroy the lawless one. So if the coming of Jesus annihilates the lawless one, that of the lawless one must be first. So a major part of the miraculous signs that Satan will perform at the end includes a counterfeit return of Jesus.

But the end-time deception is even more severe than a counterfeit return of Christ. Take a look at Acts 2:22. That text contains the same three words as 2 Thessalonians 2:9 and will help us understand something more about the end-time deception. The speaker is the apostle Peter on the day of Pentecost. He is addressing the Sanhedrin, the same body that had condemned Jesus to death less than two months before.

"Men of Israel, hear these words, Jesus of Nazareth, a man commended to you by God through *miracles, wonders and signs,* which God did among you through Him, as you yourselves know" (see Acts 2:22).

Did you notice that "miracles, wonders, and signs" are the same words used to describe the satanic deception at the end of time? In Acts 2:22 they portray the earthly ministry of Jesus, when He went about doing good in first-century Galilee and Judea. They are activities that the members of the Sanhedrin would have known about. So "miracles, wonders, and signs" are like a summary statement of Jesus' earthly ministry. According to 2

Thessalonians 2:9, at the end of time Satan will do the very kinds of things that Jesus did when He was here on earth in human form. In other words, Satan will counterfeit the earthly ministry of Jesus in some form just before the end. Just consider the following scenario.

Your neighbor knocks on the door and says, "Have you heard that Jesus has returned to earth?"

"No! How could that be?"

"Check out the news!"

You turn on your TV. It shows a video of a man who resembles the pictures of Jesus you saw growing up. His voice is gentle as He chides the leaders of the earth for their self-centeredness. He calls on all nations to put aside their differences and unite for the common good of humanity. If you didn't know the Scriptures, you would swear this *had* to be Jesus. But the Bible tells us it will be a deception. It is one thing to think about end-time deception from a safe distance, but are you ready to actually encounter it? to set aside the impressions of your eyes and ears and apply the truths of Scripture to what you experience?

The only way to handle such a deception is to know the Word of God in such a way that you will recognize the deception when it arrives. And we still have two New Testament texts to look at. Let's go to Matthew 24, which expands on what we have just explored: "Then, if anyone should say to you, 'Look, here is the Messiah,' or 'there!' do not believe it! For false messiahs and false prophets will arise, and they will do great *signs and wonders* so as to deceive, if it were possible, even the elect. See, I have told you ahead of time. Therefore, if anyone says to you, 'Look, he is in the desert!' do not go out. 'Look, he is in the inner rooms!' do not believe it. For as lightning comes out of the east and shines all the way to the west, so will the coming of the Son of Man be" (see verses 24-27).

Notice how the language of Matthew 24 resembles that of Revelation 13 and 2 Thessalonians 2. The sea beast of Revelation 13 is a false messiah (christ), and the land beast is a false prophet. They, along with the lawless one of 2 Thessalonians, do signs and wonders in order to deceive those alive on the earth at the end of time. And this deception will be so severe that even the elect of God will tremble! The severity of the end-time deception should concern all interested in the teachings of Scripture.

Perhaps this is a good time for me to reflect on a major teaching in evangelical Christianity that could feed right into this deception. I want to make it clear right from the start that I respect the sincerity and the Christian spirit of those I disagree with on this, but I believe that this popular concept could be setting many Christians up to believe the lies of Satan at the end of time. Many evangelicals teach two separate comings of Christ. The first will be a secret coming, in which He "raptures" only the Christians from the earth. Seven years later is the visible appearing, in which He sets up His kingdom on the earth.

Such teaching rests on an external construct imposed on the Bible. Nowhere in the Bible can you find any text that speaks of two comings of Christ. You can reach that conclusion only if you arbitrarily say that one statement applies to His secret coming and another applies to the visible one. But no text in the Bible explicitly presents this rapture theology. In order to find it in the Bible, you have to approach Scripture with that conclusion already in mind.

Let me in a way take one thing back. Actually one text in the Bible— and only one—does speak of two comings of Jesus, and that text is 2 Thessalonians 2:8, 9. But as we have already seen, it does not support the rapture theology. According to 2 Thessalonians, the first of these comings of "Jesus" will actually be a counterfeit. It will be the appearance of the lawless one. When Jesus does return, there will be nothing secret about it. You won't have to travel to see it, because it will be spectacular, visible, public, and experienced by all—like lightning searing across the sky. As I said, it is possible, by applying an external construct to the Bible, to make Scripture say the opposite of what it actually teaches. And all this plays into the hands of the deceiver.

Deception and the Battle of Armageddon

Having looked at the two texts outside of Revelation that discuss the end-time deception, we will want to look at the other passage in Revelation that speaks to this issue: Revelation 16:13-16, the famous battle of Armageddon passage. "And I saw, out of the mouth of the dragon and out of the mouth of the beast and out of the mouth of the false prophet, three unclean spirits like frogs" (see verse 13).

Who are the dragon, the beast, and the false prophet? They are the same three characters we saw in Revelation 13. The "beast" refers to the sea beast and the "false prophet" refers to the land beast (see also Rev. 19:20). The text takes up the story that we left in Revelation 13. It treats the same subject as Revelation 13—end-time deception—and describes the same characters that we met there. But it adds something extra. Out of the mouths of each of the characters emerges an evil spirit that resembles a frog.

Why frogs of all things? The key to the answer lies in the Old Testament background to this chapter. The language of Revelation 16 is thoroughly grounded in the plagues against ancient Egypt just before the Exodus. One of those plagues consisted of an overabundance of frogs. But of all the Exodus plagues that Revelation could mention at this point, why choose the one of frogs?

When Moses first approached Pharaoh in the narrative of the Exodus, his God-given authority received its authentication when his brother Aaron threw down his walking stick and it became a snake (see Ex. 7:8-10). If Pharaoh was anything like many of us, he probably jumped three feet in the air, stood on the arms of his throne with his knees shaking, and said, "Get that thing out of here!" But Pharaoh's magicians weren't nearly as worried. They threw down their own walking sticks, and the rods became snakes also (verses 11, 12).

So Pharaoh relaxed about the threat (verse 13). Moses and Aaron had magical powers, but his side did too. It seemed to be a manageable challenge to his authority. Then Moses and Aaron went out and turned the waters of the Nile into blood (verses 14-21). Again the Egyptian ruler was upset. But once again his magicians counterfeited the divine miracle (verses 22, 23).

Next Moses and Aaron struck Egypt with a plague of frogs (see Ex. 8:1-6). Once more Pharaoh's magicians duplicated the feat (verse 7). Although God's plagues were always more impressive than the magical arts of Pharaoh's court, the various counterfeits gave the king excuses to reject God's appeals to him. It turned out, however, that the plague of frogs was the last one that Pharaoh's magicians managed to duplicate (verses 18, 19). The frogs, therefore, were the last deception of the Exodus. That is why we find frogs in Revelation 16:13. They signal that the message of Revelation 16 has to do with the last deception of earth's history. "For they are spirits of demons, doing signs, which go out to the kings of the whole inhabited world to gather them to the battle of the great day of God Almighty" (see verse 14).

Revelation 16:14 says that these frogs are "spirits of demons" (NIV). What is a demon? An evil angel. So the three frogs are the demonic counterparts of the three good angels of Revelation 14:6-12. Both groups of angels have a mission to the whole world (Rev. 14:6; 16:14). One trio calls the world to worship God while the other trio seeks to gather the people of the world into the service of the unholy trinity. In the end it will be Trinity against trinity, and three angels against three angels. So the counterfeit does not cease with Revelation 13—a counterfeit of the Godhead and of Pentecost. Nor does it conclude with 2 Thessalonians—a counterfeit of the Second Coming and the ministry of Jesus. We find also a counterfeit of the gospel—God's end-time message in Revelation 14:6-12. This counterfeit is what the battle of Armageddon is all about. "And he gathered them to the place that in Hebrew is called Harmagedon" (see Rev. 16:16).

As you remember from the previous chapter, Harmagedon is the Greek form of a couple Hebrew words that mean "mountain of Megiddo." But no mountain in all the world has the name Megiddo. Rather, Megiddo was a city on a small elevation at the edge of the Plain of Jezreel. Looming over the place where the city of Megiddo was, however, is a range of mountains called Carmel. Carmel is the mountain of Megiddo in the same sense that Mount Rainier is the mountain of Seattle and Table Mountain is the mountain of Capetown. Mount Carmel is the mountain you could see from all over town, even though Megiddo itself was not on a mountain.

Mount Carmel was the site where the great Old Testament showdown between Elijah and the prophets of Baal took place (1 Kings 18:16-46). On that occasion Elijah's prayer brought fire down from heaven onto an altar to prove that Yahweh was the true God. According to Revelation, the Mount Carmel experience will be repeated at the end. Once again a showdown will take place between the true God and a devious counterfeit. But one thing will now be different. The fire that flashes from heaven will fall on the wrong altar! It will be the counterfeit Elijah and the counterfeit three angels who bring fire down from heaven to earth (Rev. 13:13, 14). On that day your eyes and your ears will tell you that the counterfeit trinity is the true God. Your five senses will deceive you.

Secular people are set up for such a deception. Their beliefs focus on what can be seen, heard, tasted, touched, or smelled. "Reality" rests on what the five senses are capable of perceiving. But Scripture says that in the final crisis of earth's history, those who trust in their five senses will be deceived. It will be a battle between two truth systems. One will appear established scientifically while the other will be confirmed only by Scripture. To quote the words of Jesus, "I have told you now before it happens, so that when it does happen you will believe" (John 14:29, NIV).

That is why the message of Adventism is so important for today. Things are not always what they seem. People need to know that those who trust primarily in their senses will succumb to deception. Beyond the five senses is a higher reality that can be tasted in Christ. The higher reality of faith is perceived with the help of Scripture and is not normally accessed by the senses alone. The Mount Carmel experience will be repeated at the end—in support of the counterfeit trinity. On that occasion all the evidence of your eyes and your ears will tell you that you've been wrong to follow the Bible.

Scripture portrays the end-time as a period of great deception. Reason will then lead us astray as our eyes, our ears, and our total experience will seem to be telling us that the prophecies of Scripture are wrong. Revelation portrays the end-time in terms of a battle between the Scriptures and perception, between reality as grasped by the five senses and ultimate reality as revealed by God Himself. This is at the heart of the message that Adventists have to bring to the world. In a secular age, one that trusts in reason and perception, it will never be a popular message, because it will go against the grain.

It is probably pointless to conjecture exactly what the end-time deception is or how it will affect people. Prophecy provides us with the core events of the future but leaves many of the details open. The description comes to us in John's language. He projects the future from the context of his time and place (God meets people where they are). So we cannot know exactly how the deception will take place. But consider how someone would react if the following scenario ever took place. It is one based on what many people think they see the New Testament as teaching about the great battle at the end of the world.

Early one morning you get up from a restless sleep vaguely disturbed by things that went thump in the night. Peering past the living room curtain into the street, you recoil with horror. A silver Toyota Camry has jumped the curb across the street, skidded across the lawn, and wiped out most of your neighbor Charlie's prize peonies before embedding itself into the retaining wall between his driveway and Homer's. Homer is out inspecting the wreck and the damage to the retaining wall. But you see no sign of Charlie or of any occupants of the Camry, which is too heavily damaged for anyone to have extricated themselves from its remains.

A glance up and down the street indicates that it is only one of several such mishaps on your block. As more and more neighbors cluster around the wrecks, you notice with some concern that none of the "born-again" types seem to be around. Then you remember Charlie talking about a "rapture" in which all the born-again Christians vanish, leaving chaos behind. You remember him telling you to read the *Left Behind* books and watch Christian television, but you never got around to it.

Now it is a different story. Flipping on the TV, you turn to the Christian Broadcasting Network. It is immediately clear that something is seriously wrong. Chaos fills the screen as people mill back and forth, stopping occasionally to chat with one another. Finally one of them comes to the anchor desk to inform you with a trembling voice that apparently the "Rapture" has come. Christian singers have vanished in midconcert. Evangelical preachers have disappeared in midsermon. Airplanes have crashed in midflight, minus pilot and copilot. The entire world has come to a standstill!

Would such an event get your attention? Would it make you wonder if everything you've believed was a big mistake? Would you wish that you had spent a little more time studying your Bible and a little less time on soap operas and the latest game and reality shows? The above scenario was only an illustration—the end-time deception will probably be much more subtle and severe than the kind of thing we imagined here—but I hope you can sense the disorienting power that the end-time Mount Carmel experience will exert. A world full of people who trust in the five senses will experience miracles, signs, and wonders designed to persuade everyone to accept a counterfeit of the true God.

What kind of God would allow a deception so severe that even His own people will tremble in anxiety over it? The answer lies in 2 Thessalonians 2: "[The lawless one's] coming is according to the working of Satan in all kinds of miracles and signs and lying wonders, and in every deception of unrighteousness among those who are being destroyed, because they did not receive the love of the truth, in order that they might be saved" (see verses 9-12).

Who are the people being deceived? According to the text, not just anybody, but specifically those who did not receive the love of the truth. At this point we learn something that is very startling. "And for this reason God sends them the working of deception in order that they might believe the lie" (see verse 11).

That's an incredible statement. If I had made that up, no one would believe me. But it's in the Bible. God sends the delusion—the working of Satan (according to verse 9)—in order that they may believe the lie. What kind of God are we dealing with here?

"In order that everyone might be judged who has not believed the truth but has delighted in unrighteousness" (see verse 12). The word "judged" here is often translated "condemned." The purpose of the end-time deception (from God's perspective) is to clarify where everyone stands in relation to the truth about God. To be specific, three classes of people exist on earth today. One group consists of those who love the truth, and they will not be deceived no matter what. The second class of people is made up of those who hate the truth. Both segments are in the minority in today's world. Most people belong to the third class: those who neither love nor hate the truth. Instead, they prefer to avoid commitment—to sit on the fence.

This helps us understand why God takes responsibility for the end-time deception, even though it has Satan's fingerprints all over it. God's purpose is to say, "It is time to get off the fence. You must commit yourself one way or the other." The great end-time deception forces a decision. To stay neutral is not an option anymore. Everybody ends up on one side or the other. When the end does come, everyone on earth will have made a firm decision either to love the truth or to love unrighteousness.

Ellen White describes this end-time deception in *The Great Controversy*:

"As the crowning act in the great drama of deception, Satan himself will personate Christ. The church has long professed to look to the Savior's advent as the consummation of her hopes. Now the great deceiver will make it appear that Christ has come. In different parts of the earth, Satan will manifest himself among men as a majestic being of dazzling brightness, resembling the description of the Son of God given by John in the Revelation. Revelation 1:13-15" (p. 624).

"Only those who have been diligent students of the Scriptures and *who have received the love of the truth* will be shielded from the *powerful delusion* that takes the world captive" (p. 625; italics supplied).

If we took Paul, John, and Matthew seriously regarding the great deception at the end, would it make any difference in the way we live today? I believe that it would. For one thing, we would study the Bible as we've never done before. Our busy and fragmented lives often prevent us from knowing the Book the way we could. We would also stop being satisfied with what we have been taught. Instead, we would feel an increasing need to understand the Bible for ourselves. When the deception comes, it will not be enough to have read this Book—you will need to know the Bible for yourself.

Those who take the Bible's picture of the end seriously will also combine Bible study with prayer as they've never done before. In a time of deception I have to be very careful about trusting my own perceptions, even when I'm studying the Bible. It is possible to put Bible texts together to prove almost anything one wants. When we study, we need to pray for a spirit of self-distrust, so that we will not be too quick to think that our personal perception is *the* way to read a particular passage. The great deceptions that lie ahead should lead us to be cautious about any "truth" that sounds a whole lot like the way that we normally think.

Fortunately, the Bible's description of the end-time deception does contain good news. Verse 10 tells us that the lost are destroyed because "they did not receive the love of the truth, that they might be saved" (NKJV). I think that's good news. If I were to say, "You had better learn to love the truth, or you will be deceived," it would leave you terribly discouraged. You might think you had to work up a love for the truth. But what if it took two weeks, or two months, or two years before you could create in yourself even a little love for the truth? What if you never succeeded?

But that is not what 2 Thessalonians 2:10 says. It declares that those who are deceived at the end refuse to *receive* the love of the truth. The love of the truth is something you can obtain as a gift. If you want the love of the truth, you can have it—it's free, right now. And that's good news. You can be ready for the end now. And you don't need to know "when," because you can have a love for the truth now. You can pray a prayer like this: "Lord, give me a love for the truth no matter what the cost."

That's a difficult prayer, because if you pray that prayer, you will not only receive a love for the truth but also pay the cost. Love for the truth can demand your job, your family, your reputation, even your life. I don't know what that cost might be in your life, but it's not a prayer to offer lightly. But if you offer that kind of prayer, you will receive what you have asked for, because God will not ignore such a prayer. And when you receive His gift of love for the truth—when you have a wholehearted desire to know God and to do His will—you can know that the deception at the end will have no power over you. In the words of Ellen White once more: "Only those who have been diligent students of the Scriptures and *who have received the love of the truth* will be shielded from the *powerful delusion* that takes the world captive" (*ibid.*; italics supplied).

"The time is at hand when Satan will work miracles to confirm minds in the belief that he is God. All the people of God are now to stand on the platform of truth as it has been given in the third angel's message. All the pleasant pictures, all the miracles wrought, will be presented in order that, if possible, the very elect shall be deceived. The only hope for anyone is to hold fast the evidences that have confirmed the truth in righteousness" (Ellen G. White, in *Review and Herald,* Aug. 9, 1906).

Though they may be severe, her words are encouraging to me. If I invite God to build a love for the truth into my life, I need not fear the deceptions of the end. And if I make the Scriptures my foundation and stand on the platform of truth that God has revealed to His people, I will not be deceived by the "evidence" of my senses in the final crisis. The experience will be challenging, but the path of safety is clear—and it is sure.

But is this what the battle of Armageddon is really about? Isn't that about planes and tanks and fighter aircraft? How do we reconcile images of spiritual conflict with the popular picture of a great war (like that on terror) that centers on the Middle East? The book of Revelation has much more to say about the battle of Armageddon.

6

THE SEVEN LAST PLAGUES

We have noticed in earlier chapters that the Bible names the battle of Armageddon only once (Rev. 16). Chapter 16 discusses it as part of the sixth and seventh bowl plagues. So before we take a closer look at the battle itself, I want to spend a little time examining the overall context of the bowl plagues in which Armageddon occurs. We have noticed in the previous chapter that the unholy trinity of Revelation 13 surfaces again in the context of Armageddon (Rev. 16:13-16). But Armageddon appears in a new section of Revelation. Revelation 15 first introduces the vision of the bowl plagues: "And I saw another great and amazing sign in heaven, seven angels having the seven last plagues, because in them the wrath of God is brought to its full completion" (see verse 1).

The Setting of the Seven Last Plagues

This text recalls the phrase "your wrath has come" in Revelation 11:18 (I outline the following in considerable detail in my earlier book *What the Bible Says About the End-time*). Verse 18 offers a summary in advance of the major events of the second half of the book of Revelation. The "wrath of the nations" is depicted in the actions of the unholy trinity in Revelation 13. In response, God pours out His wrath in chapter 15 and the chapters that follow. So we find a natural thematic development in the second half of Revelation. The nations display their anger by attacking the remnant (Rev. 12-14). God responds by afflicting the nations (Rev. 15-18). Then the focus moves to the final events in the great controversy (Rev. 19-22). Revelation 11:18 summarizes this final part of Revelation through the "judgment of the dead" and the "reward of the saints." The primary focus of chapter 16, then, is on the actions of God rather than on those of Satan or of the nations that follow him.

The bowls themselves strikingly parallel the seven trumpets. The main difference is that most of the trumpets affect thirds of the earth while most of the bowls impact the entire earth. As we see in the chart of Revelation's structure below, the seven bowls follow the final crisis scenes of Revelation 12-14, but they also parallel the trumpets. As is the case with the other visions of Revelation, the seven bowl plagues begin with a sanctuary introduction (see chapter 6 of the introductory volume to this series: *The Deep Things of God*).

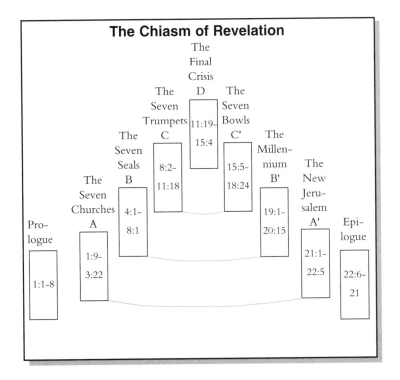

The Chiasm of Revelation

"After this I looked and in heaven the temple, that is, the tabernacle of the Testimony, was opened. Out of the temple came the seven angels with the seven plagues. They were dressed in clean, shining linen and wore golden sashes around their chests. Then one of the four living creatures gave to the seven angels seven golden bowls filled with the wrath of God, who lives for ever and ever. And the temple was filled with smoke from the glory of God and from his power, and no one could enter the temple until the seven plagues of the seven angels were completed" (Rev. 15:5-8, NIV).

In this sanctuary introduction to the seven bowl plagues we see the heavenly temple, also called the tabernacle of the Testimony. The language of the passage combines the image of the Mosaic tabernacle with that of Solomon's Temple in Jerusalem. The Mosaic tabernacle was a portable tent sanctuary that traveled with the Israelites when they wandered for 40 years in the wilderness of Sinai. It was smaller and much simpler than the Temple of Solomon, which was a permanent building. The Greek word translated "temple" here (*naos*) Revelation 11:19 used to describe the most holy place of the heavenly temple. It is the place where God's throne appears. So the introduction to the bowl plagues of Revelation 16 parallels the introduction to the previous section (Rev. 12-14).

The temple in heaven was opened previously (in Rev. 11:19 and, possibly, in Rev. 4:1, although the language of "temple" [*naos*] is not used there). It seems that the heavenly temple is consistently one of the main sources of plagues on the earth in the book of Revelation (Rev. 8:5; 14:15-17; 16:1, 17). The bowl plagues, the trumpets, and the seals all originate from the heavenly temple. But God's mercy also originates from the temple (Rev. 8:3, 4), so the heavenly temple seems to be another way of speaking about the governing center of the universe. In other words, in heaven there is a place in which the essential business of the universe takes place. It is also the place worship occurs. The heavenly sanctuary and the heavenly throne room are one and the same. But why is the temple in heaven opened now?

"Out of the temple came the seven angels with the seven plagues. They were dressed in clean, shining linen and wore golden sashes around their chests" (Rev. 15:6, NIV). The seven angels seem to be commissioned agents with a job description. They are to carry out punishments against those who have persecuted God's people and blasphemed His character. But the punishing angels wear golden sashes around their chest, like the "son of man" who tenderly cares for the churches (see Rev. 1:13). We find no contradiction here. The same uniform is worn for both actions. Both mercy and judgment are qualities of the same God. So the temple is the source of both judgment and mercy. What makes the difference in God's response is the attitude and disposition of those He is dealing with.

84

In the Old Testament God set up the covenant in order to regulate and safeguard His relationship with Israel. The concept of covenant was all about relationship. The covenant regulated the way relationships were supposed to go. The beauty of the Old Testament covenant was that Israel knew exactly what kind of God they were dealing with. Not only did He require things of them—He subjected Himself to the same rules of relationship for Israel's sake (see Deut. 7:9). Yahweh was not arbitrary and capricious the way the pagan deities were. The covenant provided security for Israel. The people knew how God would respond in any situation. It was all spelled out in the covenant. Yahweh was consistent and Israel was secure in its relationship with Him because of the covenant.

But the covenant had two sides to it. The covenant between Israel and God specified the behavior of both parties. Since God is always faithful to His covenant, the "wild card," or variable, in the relationship of Israel with God was the human side of the equation. Israelites who treasured their relationship with God found the guidelines for maintaining that relationship in the covenant. As they responded appropriately to God, they would receive blessings, or positive consequences, in response.

On the other hand, when they disobeyed the covenant, they suffered the results of a broken relationship with God. This process began in the Garden of Eden when Adam and Eve disobeyed Him and reaped the consequences. We see it clearly spelled out in the "curses" of the covenant (Lev. 26:14-39; Deut. 28:15-68) and experienced in the desert wanderings under Moses. The process drew to a close in the book of Revelation.

It was from the "curses" of the covenant that the concept of "plagues" in Revelation got its start. Plagues were the consequences of disobedience to the covenant. In Leviticus 26 and in the Old Testament prophets they included war, famine, pestilence, and wild beasts (Lev. 26:21-26; Eze. 14:12-21). These plagues lurk behind the description of the four horsemen in Revelation 6. "Then one of the four living creatures gave to the seven angels seven golden bowls filled with the wrath of God, who lives for ever and ever. And the temple was filled with smoke from the glory of God and from his power, and no one could enter the temple until the seven plagues of the seven angels were completed" (Rev. 15:7, 8, NIV).

The four "living creatures" of Revelation are the agents of God closest to the throne. They lead the songs of praise that ring through the heavenly throne room (Rev. 4:8-11; 5:8-14). Also they are closely involved with the breaking of the seals and with the four horsemen of Revelation 6. In Revelation 6 all of humanity is subject to the plagues unleashed by the horsemen, but the seven last plagues poured out in the bowls of Revelation 16 strike only the wicked.

The seven golden bowls remind us of the cup of God's wrath (Rev. 14:9-11 and Isa. 51:17-23). According to the third angel's message (Rev. 14:9-11), those who worship the beast and his image (cf. Rev. 13:14, 15) and receive the beast's mark (cf. verses 16, 17) drink the wine of God's fury from the "cup of his wrath" (Rev. 14:10, NIV). In the Aramaic translation of Isaiah 51:17-23 the word for "cup" could mean either "cup" or "bowl." The same word can be used for both. It means that the "cup of wrath" of Revelation 14 and the "bowls of wrath" of Revelation 15 are one and the same. So the bowls of wrath in Revelation 15 and 16 are a further extension of the cup of wrath in Revelation 14. Thus the seven bowls are actually an outgrowth of the third angel's message of Revelation 14.

According to Revelation 15:7, one of the four living creatures around the throne of God gives each of the seven angels a bowl of wrath to pour out on the earth. The bowls recall not only Isaiah 51 but also the bowls used in the Old Testament for drink offerings in the tabernacle and Temple (Ex. 27:3; Num. 4:14; 1 Kings 7:40, 45, 50; and 2 Kings 12:13; 25:15). The drink offerings in the sanctuary were part of the ongoing relationship between God and His people in the Old Testament. But in Revelation this positive image becomes negative. The pouring out of these bowls onto the earth demonstrates that mercy has ceased and human probation has now closed.

This becomes even clearer from Revelation 15:8. Smoke from the glory of God fills the temple in heaven. As a result no one is able to enter the temple throughout the time when the bowls of wrath are being poured out. Intercession no longer goes on. The services that keep people in relationship with God are suspended. Once again what was originally a positive image taken from the inauguration of the wilderness tabernacle and the dedication of Solomon's Temple has been turned upon its head.

"Then the cloud covered the Tent of Meeting, and the glory of the Lord filled the tabernacle. Moses could not enter the Tent of Meeting because the cloud had settled upon it, and the glory of the Lord filled the tabernacle" (Ex. 40:34, 35, NIV).

"When the priests withdrew from the Holy Place, the cloud filled the temple of the Lord. And the priests could not perform their service because of the cloud, for the glory of the Lord filled his temple" (1 Kings 8:10, 11, NIV). During each of these dedication services such glory blazed inside the tabernacle and the Temple that the services had to stop. Revelation 15:8 reverses this inauguration imagery. In the context of the seven bowls the glory of God doesn't celebrate the opening of the temple in heaven but instead enforces its close. The emptiness of the temple reflects a time that no one will be performing intercession from inside the temple. Mercy has ceased, and probation has closed. The seven bowl plagues pour out the wrath of God unmitigated by any trace of mercy (Rev. 15:1). The consequences of disobedience now fully manifest themselves.

This scene seems to be parallel to the one near the close of the seven trumpets. In Revelation 10:7, when the seventh angel is about to sound his trumpet, the "mystery of God" is finished. The "mystery of God" represents the gospel, which will be proclaimed throughout the earth until just before the second coming of Jesus (Matt. 24:14). The sounding of the seventh trumpet, therefore, occurs at the same time as the emptying of the temple in Revelation 15. This means that *all seven bowls are part of the seventh trumpet.* They are located within the final period of earth's history, after the close of probation. Let's take a look at what happens on earth when the bowls are poured out.

The First Four Bowl Plagues

"Then I heard a loud voice from the temple saying to the seven angels, 'Go, pour out the seven bowls of God's wrath on the earth'" (Rev. 16:1, NIV).

Scripture frequently uses the term *poured out* with reference to the blood of the sacrifices in Leviticus. When the priest slaughtered an animal at the bronze altar, he caught the spurting blood in a bowl for dipping and sprinkling. The leftover blood he then poured out at the base of the altar. The same Greek word appears in verse 6, but is usually translated as "shed" instead of "poured out," masking the connection: "For they have shed ["poured out" in Greek] the blood of your saints and prophets, and you have given them blood to drink as they deserve" (verse 6, NIV). John chooses the language of sacrifice and persecution to describe God's response to the persecution of His saints.

The pouring out of the bowls in Revelation 16 is in response to the anger of the nations. The bowls get poured out because the nations have poured out the blood of God's people. There is an immediate and direct correspondence between the two. The seven bowls are God's just reaction to the oppression of His people.

"The first angel went and poured out his bowl on the land, and ugly and painful sores broke out on the people who had the mark of the beast and worshiped his image" (verse 2, NIV).

As we have stated above, the seven bowls of Revelation parallel the seven trumpets. The first bowl is poured out on the "land," in other words, the earth. It is the same word used in the first trumpet. The second trumpet and bowl both fall on the sea, the third on the rivers and springs, and the fourth involves darkness in each case. But the parallels are not complete. The first four trumpet plagues all strike the natural world, at least in terms of the surface imagery. But this first bowl plague and also the fourth affect humanity directly.

In the first bowl plague ugly painful sores break out on human beings. In the Greek "sores" is the same word as the one used for the "boils" that afflict people during the plagues of the Exodus (Ex. 9:8-12). The Old Testament also employs the same word for leprosy (Lev. 13:18-27). As such, it came to be seen as a punishment for sin (2 Kings 5:25-27 and 2 Chron. 26:16-21), a curse of the covenant (Deut. 28:27, 35). Perhaps that is why Job's friends thought he was under God's curse when he broke out in boils (Job 4:7-9; 15:20-26).

In the story of Revelation, therefore, one of the consequences of rebellion against God in the last days is tremendously painful skin sores. They fall on those who have the mark of the beast and worship the image of the beast. Such individuals are the oppressors of God's people and not just people at random. Their sores distract them from implementing the death decree of Revelation 13:15. In chapter 16 God carries out what He stated in Revelation 14:9-11.

"The second angel poured out his bowl on the sea, and it turned into blood like that of a dead man, and every living thing in the sea died" (Rev. 16:3, NIV).

As with the second trumpet (Rev. 8:8, 9), this bowl falls on the sea and causes water to turn into blood. In the second trumpet only a third of the sea turned to blood and a third of the living creatures died. But in the second bowl the plague is intensified to include the entire earth. All the waters in the sea transform into blood, and every living thing in the sea dies.

Once again the question arises whether the plague is literal or symbolic. It is based on one of the 10 plagues that struck ancient Egypt during the time of Moses and the Exodus. According to Exodus the literal water of the Nile literally turned into blood (Ex. 7:14-24). So the plague of Revelation 16 may be equally literal. Some have suggested that this could refer to a "red tide" in which the red color is not literally blood, but a change in the water's microscopic life. Be that as it may, the result of this plague is quite deadly for the fish in the sea and would cause huge disruption for the world's human population as well.

"The third angel poured out his bowl on the rivers and springs of water, and they became blood" (Rev. 16:4, NIV).

The third bowl parallels the third trumpet as well. In the third trumpet a plague poisons a third of the rivers and springs of the world. This embittering results in the death of everyone who tries to drink the water. But in the third bowl all the rivers and springs in the world turn to blood without any reference to death. Once again the language of the bowl plague appears to be quite literal and universal. But we notice a difference between this bowl and the two previous ones. In this one a song follows the plague, praising the justice and fairness of God for executing judgment appropriate to the crime.

"Then I heard the angel in charge of the waters say: 'You are just in these judgments, you who are and who were, the Holy One, because you have so judged; for they have shed the blood of your saints and prophets, and you have given them blood to drink as they deserve.'

"And I heard the altar respond: 'Yes, Lord God Almighty, true and just are your judgments'" (verses 5-7, NIV).

This song picks up on the themes of the one sung in the previous chapter, that of Moses and of the Lamb (Rev. 15:3, 4). Both songs assert that the outcome of the conflict at the end of time will demonstrate that God's ways are just and fair. You see, the saints and prophets had been tried in earthly courts simply for serving God and rejecting the counterfeit. But the determination of such earthly courts runs counter to the final judgment of God. At the close of earth's history He reverses the decisions of the earthly courts and carries out His own judgment on the very ones who falsely accused His people.

"The fourth angel poured out his bowl on the sun, and the sun was given power to scorch people with fire" (Rev. 16:8, NIV).

Here the parallel between the trumpets and the bowls ends up as a direct contrast. The fourth trumpet smites the sun, as well as the moon and the stars, with partial darkness. So one might expect the fourth bowl to produce total darkness. But that is not what happens. Instead, the intensity of the sun's light and heat increases to unbearable levels. Instead of darkening the sun, its strength grows, and the pain of the fourth plague is one of excessive heat.

When I was a child, I thought I had experienced this plague! July days in New Jersey can be almost unbearably hot and humid. And at that time people were just beginning to hear about air-conditioning. I can distinctly remember the first time I rode in an air-conditioned bus and the great relief from the heat I experienced. But we had no air-conditioning at home or in the family car. I can remember lying in my bed at night with pillow and sheet drenched with sweat. Repeatedly I would wake up because drops of sweat slid down my side or from my forehead onto my eyelids.

Since that time I have learned that the heat and humidity I experienced as a child was only the "tip of the iceberg"! I have since been to Singapore, where people essentially dash from air-conditioned apartment to air-conditioned car to air-conditioned office to air-conditioned store to air-conditioned restaurant. Even a short walk at 6:00 in the morning will leave one's clothes completely soaked with sweat. On one occasion I remember taking off a shirt and wringing several ounces of moisture into the hotel tub! It's hard to think straight under that level of heat and humidity. But the wicked who experience the fourth bowl plague focus their minds on God as a result of this plague. Notice the remarkable verse that follows:

"They were seared by the intense heat and they cursed the name of God, who had control over these plagues, but they refused to repent and glorify him" (verse 9, NIV).

The crucial point in this text is that the plague serves as a call for repentance to the wicked, but they reject it. The plagues fail to change their mind, and they absolutely refuse to glorify God. This points back to the first angel's message in Revelation 14:6, 7. The angel there calls on every nation, tribe, language, and people to fear God, give Him glory, and worship Him. The Lord provides opportunity for everyone to turn away from the worship of the beast and his image and to give glory to the true God of heaven. According to Revelation 11:13 some people *do* repent just before the close of probation (verse 15, cf. Rev. 10:7), but most of humanity does not. The close of probation is not some arbitrary decree on God's part, but a settled disposition for good or for evil on the part of the human beings to which He has appealed through the three angels of Revelation 14. The close of probation results from people settling into a life commitment either positively or negatively.

Nevertheless, God takes responsibility for His actions in relation to the lost. He has "control over these plagues" (Rev. 16:9, NIV). As we have already seen, He participates in the deception at the end of time, almost to the point of claiming to be its author (2 Thess. 2:11). The unity of the nations against His people at the end of time is all part of His controlling plan (Rev. 17:17). But while God takes responsibility for His own actions, the wicked do not accept responsibility for theirs. Instead, they try to blame Him for the consequences of their own decisions.

It is hard for Westerners to understand the tension between the sovereignty and control of God on one hand and the responsibility of human beings for their own actions on the other. People often find the extreme viewpoints more comfortable than the tension in the middle. Some people doubt His sovereignty over our universe. They believe that the universe is essentially out of control, and that life is impossible to manage. If God is "dead," then the universe must be managing itself, a scary concept. Others feel that God is so in control that they have no freedom or responsibility at all. At either extreme, life has no meaning. We are either the result of random processes or we are prisoners in a cage of divine making.

The Bible, however, is not a Western book. It is grounded in Hebrew thought and philosophy. Hebrew thought finds no contradiction between the idea that God is fully in control and the concept that human beings are nevertheless responsible for their actions. The beauty in this Hebrew tension is that we can trust that everything will turn out all right in the end and still do everything in our power to help everything turn out all right. God is fully in control of the plagues, yet they are fully the consequence of human actions. While that strains Western logic, God's thoughts are not our thoughts (Isa. 55:6-8).

The Meaning of the Plagues

Let me reflect on the first four plagues for a little bit. Are the bowl plagues literal or symbolic? It is difficult to know from the language of the text. On the one hand, the book of Revelation normally prefers a figurative reading. The very first verse of the book tells us that the vision upon which Revelation is based was "signified." God placed it in symbolic language to express the deeper meaning of His purposes for the end of human history. So the seals and trumpets (Rev. 6-9) should probably be read in a symbolic way because they contain language that points to a figurative approach (Rev. 8:8; 9:7, 17). But what about the bowl plagues? Could one take them symbolically?

When I look at the first four bowls symbolically, I see the following. Figuratively, the plagues could represent the consequences that come as a result of sin—the curses of the covenant, much like the seven seals. The boils could symbolize the suffering caused by sin. The waters turning to blood could be like the shedding of the blood of those that the wicked have oppressed. The scorching sun could stand for the intensified glare of God's Word as it points out sin and calls for judgment on those who oppose God.

But when reading these texts in the Greek, you get the impression that something more direct and literal is in view. If a symbolic reading does not bring convincing clarity to the meaning of the text and a literal reading does, the literal reading can be preferred, but this would be the exception in Revelation, not the rule.

If you take the first four bowl plagues literally, they represent the terrible physical and emotional experience of the last generation of the wicked. God has removed His restraining hand on Satan's actions. Wars increase. Crime and instability are rampant. Diseases get out of control, and no amount of medical or pharmaceutical remedy seems able to stem the tide. The weather goes haywire, producing extremes of heat, wind, and rain. Strange chemical changes create corrosive and undrinkable water.

It is not certain, on the basis of the text, whether the author intended the literal or the symbolic reading. The symbolic reading is not particularly fruitful theologically. On the other hand, a truly literal reading has its challenges as well. Even if some sort of universal war played a part in the destruction of the wicked, the casualties of such a war would have to be enormous beyond imagination to turn all the waters of the ocean bloody red.

But either way there is a theological issue that we need to address as we approach the part of the chapter that mentions Armageddon (Rev. 16:16). According to the text of Revelation, the bowl plagues occur after the close of probation, when intercession no longer takes place in the heavenly temple (Rev. 15:5-8). They fall exclusively on the wicked, who have totally ceased to repent.

So what is the point of such plagues? If people can no longer repent, it seems vengeful and capricious to torment them further. It is one thing to remove oppressors and abusers from the universe and quite another to drag them from torment to torment along the way. That sounds like cutting off a cat's tail inch by inch. Even if the job needs doing, you can accomplish it with a lot less suffering than that.

The answer may lie in the major underlying theme of the seven bowls: the justice (fairness) of God. The actions of the seven bowls are not arbitrary. God is not some celestial sadist who enjoys the suffering of His creation. Everything He does has its ultimate purpose. The crucial passage is Revelation 16:5, 6: "You are just in these judgments, you who are and who were, the Holy One, because you have so judged; for they have shed the blood of your saints and prophets, and you have given them blood to drink as they deserve" (NIV). As the objects of God's executive judgment, the wicked receive in kind what they have done to others. The punishment of the plagues is appropriate to the crime.

You see, the justice (fairness) of God is the ultimate issue. How can He judge people for all eternity on the basis of a few years of up-and-down behavior? How do we know the wicked wouldn't change if they knew God better or had the opportunities that the righteous had? Can we really trust the end-time judgment of God?

The plagues demonstrate that those counted wicked continue to oppose God no matter the circumstances. Sufferings that have led millions to cry out to God through the centuries only cause their opposition to become even more pronounced and severe (verses 8-11). Earlier plagues had brought people to repentance (Rev. 11:13), but now the wicked have turned away so long and so completely that they are no longer capable of opening themselves to divine salvation. At the same time, the sufferings of the righteous in the last days do not separate them away from God. Instead their loyalty to Him intensifies. The same sufferings have a solidifying and intensifying effect on all. The righteous become more righteous and the wicked become more wicked.

The close of probation is not an arbitrary decree on God's part. It is simply a time that world affairs are so arranged that everyone makes a settled decision for or against Him at the very same time. The plagues also are not arbitrary, even though they strike after the close of probation. They also serve God's purposes. The plagues of Revelation 16 demonstrate the truth of Revelation 15:3: "Just and true are your ways" (NIV). In other words, even though God's judgment is based on what to us is inconclusive evidence, it is completely fair and completely accurate. The pouring out of the bowl plagues demonstrates to the universe that the Lord knows what He is doing, whether or not we fully understand it or accept it.

The fifth bowl continues describing plagues along the lines of the disasters that struck Egypt at the time of the Exodus.

"The fifth angel poured out his bowl on the throne of the beast, and his kingdom was plunged into darkness. Men gnawed their tongues in agony and cursed the God of heaven because of their pains and their sores, but they refused to repent of what they had done" (Rev. 16:10, 11, NIV).

Thus the fifth bowl plunges the beast's entire kingdom, presumably the world (Rev. 13:4, 8), into darkness. In contrast to the throne of the beast, other parts of Revelation mention the throne of God (Rev. 12:5; 14:3; 16:17, etc.). Is such darkness literal or figurative? Literal darkness would certainly be annoying, but would probably not, in and of itself, be the kind of threat that the earlier plagues were. Darkness does not cause pain of itself unless the pain results from a fear of the dark.

So it is not normal darkness. It represents some kind of challenge to the beast's authority over the earth. A throne is a place from which authority and power flow. It may be through literal darkness or perhaps a revelation of some kind that brings the sea beast's authority into question before the world. The sense of "wondering after the beast" is gone (Rev. 13:3-8). As was the case with the fourth plague, the "darkness" fails to elicit repentance from those who have made up their minds against God.

The first four bowl plagues are poured out on individuals, and people begin to realize that something terrible is happening. But the fifth plague is different. It strikes the seat of the beast. God is now specifically targeting the systems and institutions that have opposed Him and oppressed His people. While up to this point people may have been unsure that decisive events were occurring, these events are now fully in the international news media. The pouring out of the fifth bowl is like the overture to the battle of Armageddon. It is the beginning of God's full and final action on those who have opposed Him and His people.

ALL EYES ON THE EUPHRATES

For most of my life I have associated family trips with Interstate 80, the major east-west highway that runs from New York City to San Francisco. I grew up in New York City, and my aunt and uncle lived in Lincoln, Nebraska. So my earliest memories of childhood include traveling Interstate 80 and its predecessors from New Jersey through Pennsylvania and Ohio, on through Indiana, Illinois, and Iowa, and eventually through Omaha, Nebraska, the final stretch to Lincoln. The Great Plains with their enormous skies always fascinated me as a child, and they continue to do so to this day.

But my favorite part of the Great Plains is even further west than Lincoln, Nebraska. In early adulthood my wife and I moved to Andrews University in Michigan, not too far from Interstate 80 in northern Indiana. Through the years much of the rest of both my family and my wife's family moved to the Denver, Colorado, area. So family vacations increasingly included trips down Interstate 80 past Lincoln to the turnoff in central Nebraska where Interstate 76 spurs off from I-80 to connect Nebraska with the Denver area. This stretch goes through my favorite part of the Great Plains, 100 miles of rolling treeless hills to the east of Denver. The sky is huge, with hardly a trace of human habitation in sight (except, of course, the concrete ribbon of Interstate 76), and there is the sweet anticipation of the Rocky Mountains soon to come. As the car crests each of the rolling hills, my eyes search the horizon for the first trace of the great mountain wall known as the Front Range.

On a clear day, and there are many of those on the Great Plains, you can get the first glimpse of the high mountains around mile 100 (100 miles from Denver and perhaps 100 more to the snowcapped peaks of the Front Range). Their breathtaking vastness creeps up the horizon, becoming clearer and clearer, larger and larger, as the miles go by. Even in summer the top third of the mountain wall has the sparkling whiteness of eternal snow. The rest of the mountain wall is dark gray to black in contrast. I love the mountains, and as I drive through eastern Colorado I can't wait to get close to them.

Seeing the Big Picture

The New Testament is a lot like traveling through eastern Colorado. While one finds many beautiful things, yet there is the sense that the best is yet to come. Every so often you catch a brief glimpse of something way in the future. Second Thessalonians 2 is one of those places. Some people call it the Little Apocalypse, because so much information about the end of the world is stuffed into such a small space (we visited there briefly in chapter 5). While Revelation gives us the big picture, it has so much fascinating detail that we may miss the forest for the trees. So before we explore the battle of Armageddon, let's catch a glimpse of the big picture by reading 2 Thessalonians 2:7, 8.

"For the mystery of lawlessness is already at work. Only he who now restrains it will do so until he is out of the way. And then the lawless one will be revealed, whom the Lord Jesus will kill with the breath of his mouth and bring to nothing by the appearance of his coming" (ESV).

This text tells us that there are two basic types of knowing in the time between the first and second advents of Jesus. And they come in sequence—in two historical phases. First of all, there is the present time, which is a one of mystery and restraint—in other words, a period of ambiguity. Things are not as clear as we would like. In the words of Paul: "We know in part . . . we prophesy in part. . . . We see through a glass, darkly" (1 Cor. 13:9-12). During such ambiguity there is no clear distinction, for example, between good and evil. Good people do bad things, often unintentionally, while evil people from time to time do things that are amazingly good or beneficial to many. And there is no ideal nation. While some nations may have a more positive influence than others, we discover a lot of shades of gray when we get away from the bright colors of uncritical patriotism.

An example of this was Iraq under Saddam Hussein. Few would argue that the man was essentially evil in the cold-blooded way he dispatched family, friends, and large numbers of people in rival ethnic groups and political factions. He self-servingly built huge palaces for himself while millions of his people went hungry. And he sacrificed millions of lives in Iraq, Iran, and Kuwait in pursuit of his unbridled military and political ambitions. Yet his reign kept the seething hatreds among Sunni and Shiite, Arab and Kurd, under control. Children could freely play in the streets, and everyday life was largely calm and peaceful. Is Iraq better off now that Hussein is no longer in control? The answer to that question is more ambiguous than Westerners, or even most Iraqis, would like. That is what life in the present age is like.

I recently met a leader of the Adventist Church in Iraq under Saddam Hussein. He told me that Hussein was very favorable and kind to the church and its members. At one point they were suffering a great deal because all crucial exams took place on Sabbath, with no exceptions allowed. It meant that members of the Adventist Church could not advance in school, could not qualify for the best jobs, and ultimately could not participate in government. Hussein himself ordered with his own signature that special accommodations be made for Adventists and others who worshipped on the Sabbath. His public persona was evil, yet he was capable in some circumstances of acts of concern and compassion for the disadvantaged. That is what life is like in the present age. It is an age of mystery and ambiguity.

During such times we need to avoid the temptation to believe that we have everything perfectly clear. A certain amount of humility is needed. But this can be difficult for many. Whenever I have question-and-answer sessions with church groups certain people always want to know all about the difficult and obscure texts of the Bible. They desire clues on how to interpret the seals and the trumpets or seek clarity out of Daniel 11. And if I can't give it to them, they are determined to provide it for themselves. They ask such questions as "According to the Bible, the secret things belong to God [Deut. 29:29]. What are those secret things?" What are they? I have no idea! That's why the Bible calls them secret things! And I suspect that some of those secret things will always belong to God, simply because God is infinite and we are limited in what we can ultimately understand.

But there is some hope for curiosity seekers. According to 2 Thessalonians 2:7, 8 a time of revelation, in which we will be able to clearly distinguish good and evil, will come. That is what the battle of Armageddon is all about. Revelation 16 and 17 unpack the period of "revelation" in 2 Thessalonians 2. It describes as clearly as we can understand ahead of time just what the final events will be like. The drama of the battle of Armageddon breaks through the ambiguity, disclosing many of the secret things. To the degree that human beings can understand the future, the picture comes into focus in the chapters we are about to explore together.

Beginning with Revelation 16:12, we get into the heart of the end-time battle. We will gain a considerable amount of insight into the consummation of all things. These texts seek to show how the powers that oppose God and His people at the end of time will meet their fate. They also help us understand how to stay true to God in the final tests to come. In order to comprehend the battle of Armageddon, we begin with the sixth angel in a pivotal verse (verse 12). It introduces a brief summary of Armageddon (verses 12-21), expanded by a more detailed elaboration in the chapters that follow (Rev. 17-19).

Before I begin, let me say a word about one of my favorite professors, Han LaRondelle. Professor LaRondelle was the teacher who most strongly inspired me to study Revelation and to investigate particularly the role of the Old Testament in the book. He also encouraged me to read the work of Louis Were, an Adventist evangelist and mentor of his. Although much of what follows in this chapter comes from my own textual work, I know that my debt to LaRondelle, in particular, is deep beyond measure. May he continue to live long and prosper!

How to See Deeply

While the battle of Armageddon chapters bring a basic clarity to the mysteries of the end, such truths do not lie on the surface. These are extremely challenging texts that have been subject to a wide variety of interpretations in the past. So before we get deeply into them it would be helpful to review quickly the basic steps of interpretation laid out in the opening book of this series, *The Deep Things of God*. If you have not read this volume, you will want to do so. It provides, in considerable detail, the tools and processes that allow the teachings of Revelation to emerge naturally from the text. The goal is to understand God's intent for the book rather than read our own ideas and concerns into the puzzling imagery of the text. I will summarize the interpretive strategy of the book briefly here.

Four major steps help us unpack the symbolic visions of the Apocalypse. The first is like the strategy used in any other passage of the New Testament. I called it "basic exegesis." That means to examine carefully the words, the phrases, the grammar, and the syntax of every verse in which you are interested. You use dictionaries, concordances, and commentaries to assemble as much information about the text in its original setting as you can. Then you carefully compare all that can be learned about the history, culture, and setting of first-century Asia Minor, the place to which John wrote his book.

But in Revelation you can understand perfectly well what the text is saying and still have no idea what it means. For example, it is clear that the first trumpet (Rev. 8:7) portrays an angel in heaven blowing a trumpet with the consequence that hail and fire, mixed with blood, strike the earth, burning up a third of the earth, a third of the trees, and all the green grass. We have no question as to what the text is saying. The issue is What does it mean?

That is where careful study of Revelation has exposed three further strategies for understanding passages such as that about the first trumpet. You examine the text in light of the overall structure of the book, explore the allusions and echoes to the Old Testament in the text, and then seek to discover the impact that the gospel has had in transforming Old Testament images in the light of what Christ has done for us. We will need all three of these extended strategies in order to understand what is going on in Revelation 16:12:

"The sixth angel poured out his bowl on the great river Euphrates, and its water was dried up in order that the way of the kings from the rising of the sun might be prepared" (author's translation).

The Euphrates River

As with the first trumpet, the images are fairly plain on the surface. It is not hard to recognize what the text says, but much more difficult to know what it intends. So we need to apply the more extensive four-step method summarized above.

As we have seen in the previous chapter, the "bowl" in this text is probably a sanctuary image drawn from the Old Testament. But while the image originates in the sanctuary service, in Revelation the bowls cause major destruction to the earth and its people: sores, water turning to blood, rivers and springs transforming into blood, and the sun scorching people with intense heat. By comparison with the previous plagues, the sixth plague seems like nothing. It is merely the drying up of one of the world's thousands of rivers. And the Euphrates River historically has been something of a seasonal river that ceases flowing from time to time. But first impressions in Revelation are often far from the mark. Much more lurks below the surface of this text.

One of the distinguishing marks of the Euphrates River in ancient times was that it passed right through the center of Babylon, an ancient city that was the capital of an ancient empire. Babylon was something like Kansas City. The latter consists of two cities in two different states, divided only by the Missouri River. Although separated by the river and political barriers, Kansas City is one unified city for all practical purposes. So the mention of the Euphrates River in this text probably sets the table for the many citations of Babylon in the passages to follow (Rev. 16:19; 17:5; 18:2, 10, 21). And whatever the Euphrates River means in this verse, its drying up prepares the way for the kings who come from the rising of the sun, whoever they are.

Three crucial questions spring to mind as one strives to unpack the deeper implications of Revelation 16:12. 1. What does the Euphrates River mean in this text? Is it literally the Euphrates River in ancient Mesopotamia? Or is it a symbol of something else? 2. What is the drying up all about? Is that literal or symbolic? 3. Who are the kings from the rising of the sun? Are they specific world powers or something else?

We will be able to answer our three questions by applying the three extended strategies noted above. 1. John explains the meaning of the Euphrates River in chapter 17, so examining the larger context will be the key to understanding that image. 2. The secret of its drying up emerges, however, only from a careful examination of the Old Testament tradition of Babylon's fall in Jeremiah 50 and 51 and Isaiah

44-47. Understanding John's allusions to the Old Testament are often critical to correct interpretation. 3. The kings from the rising of the sun comes to clarity when one examines the phrase "rising sun" elsewhere in the New Testament. Revelation is a New Testament book, and we can grasp many aspects of the book only with reference to the other 26 books of the New Testament.

So let's take a look at how the larger structure of the book of Revelation clearly explains the significance of the Euphrates River in the text at hand. An angel holding one of the seven bowls of Revelation 16 returns to explain something to John.

"One of the seven angels who had the seven bowls came and said to me, 'Come, I will show you the punishment of the great prostitute, who sits on many waters'" (Rev 17:1, NIV).

Clearly the biblical author intended this vision and what follows to explain one of the seven bowl-plagues of chapter 16. But which one? Notice that the angel invites John to observe the punishment of "the great prostitute" who sits on *many waters*. So the bowl-plague being interpreted must have something to do with water. A quick survey of the seven last plagues in Revelation 16 reveals that three of them involve water. The second plague falls on the sea, the third plague strikes the rivers and springs of the earth, and the sixth plague touches the Euphrates River. The crucial question is, which of those three plagues is in view here? Chapter 17 will elaborate on that plague.

It helps to notice that the concept of "many waters" didn't spring out of thin air. It appears in Jeremiah 51:12, 13: "Lift up a banner against the walls of Babylon! Reinforce the guard, station the watchmen, prepare an ambush! The Lord will carry out his purpose, his decree against the people of Babylon. *You who live by many waters* and are rich in treasures, your end has come, the time for you to be cut off" (NIV).What are the many waters that Babylon lives near? The Euphrates River! Discovering the identity of the great prostitute in Revelation 17:4, 5 confirms this:

"The woman was arrayed in purple and scarlet. . . . And on her forehead was written a name of mystery: 'Babylon the great, mother of prostitutes and of earth's abominations'" (ESV).

The great prostitute is none other than Babylon the Great, the dual city on both banks of the Euphrates River! The two halves of Babylon were each about a square mile in area, looking something like the following:

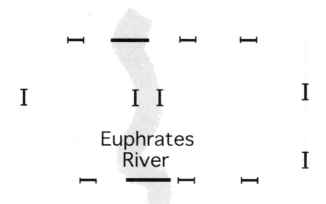

If the great prostitute is Babylon, then the "many waters" of verse 1 must be the Euphrates River. So it should be fairly obvious by now that the angel who comes to John at the beginning of Revelation 17 is the sixth angel who had poured his bowl on the great river Euphrates. The same angel has returned to elaborate on the sixth plague.

In many parts of the Middle East rainfall is minimal or nonexistent. Any place that has an abundance of water is truly worthy of notice. One such example is Egypt, where the snowcapped mountains of northeastern Africa feed the Nile's massive flow. The other such place is Mesopotamia (which means "between the rivers"), where the Tigris and Euphrates Rivers flow from the snowcapped mountains of Turkey. Dry places can have lots of fresh water if the rivers that pass through them have their origin in areas of abundant rain and snow.

But this still leaves open the question What does the Euphrates River mean in this text? Is it literally the Euphrates River in ancient Mesopotamia? Or is it a symbol of something else? Interpreters have offered a number of different answers to such questions. Some have suggested that the Euphrates River represents . . . the Euphrates River! Duh! While this is certainly a possibility in any biblical text, I don't think that is the correct interpretation here, as we will see.

Other commentators have regarded the Euphrates River as standing for the land or the territory through which the river flows. One problem with that view is that the region containing the Euphrates River seems to have changed hands frequently in the course of history. In the nineteenth century the entire length of the Euphrates River belonged to Turkey. Today most of the Euphrates River is in modern Iraq. For a time, some interpreters thought the Euphrates River represented Saddam Hussein, but that concept looks a bit dated now. Still others have branched out even further and suggested that the Euphrates River symbolizes Middle Eastern oil. The drying up of the river would then depict a shortage of fuel supplies.

All of these understandings have been convincing to some people at one time or another. But let me ask you a question. If John himself provides the meaning of the Euphrates River in his outline of the vision, does it make sense to pursue any other interpretation than the one that the biblical author himself gives us? I think the answer is obvious. So let's see what Revelation itself tells us about the Euphrates River.

The capstone of the angel's instruction to John appears in verse 15: "And the angel said to me, 'The waters that you saw, where the prostitute is seated'" (ESV). Where have we heard such language before? It is a reference back to verse 1! There the angel told John that he would be shown a great prostitute who sits on many waters. So now in verse 15 the angel is about to explain the meaning of the Euphrates River. The waters that John observed in verse 1 "are peoples and multitudes and nations and languages" (ESV).

It is now clear that the Euphrates River does not represent itself. Neither does it stand for a single nation or the leader of a nation, such as Saddam Hussein. It also does not symbolize a substance such as Middle Eastern oil. In the book of Revelation the Euphrates River represents the civil and secular powers of the entire world—all nations, all races, all ethnic groups, and all language groups. The Euphrates River depicts the political and military powers of the world that will give their support to end-time Babylon.

Babylon, by contrast, is something other than the political forces of our world. The book of Revelation describes prostitute Babylon in attire similar to that worn by the high priest of Old Testament Israel (Rev. 17:4, 5; cf. Ex. 28 and 39). She also suffers the fate of a priest's daughter for her prostitution (Rev. 17:16; cf. Lev. 21:9). So prostitute Babylon clearly represents a religious power at the end that is hostile to the Lamb and to those with Him (Rev. 17:14).

Are you beginning to see that the sixth plague must be more significant than it appeared at first glance? After all, if we are dealing with the drying up of a river that is often without water during the late summer, the plague doesn't amount to much. But if the Euphrates River symbolizes the civil, secular, and political powers of this world, the drying up of that Euphrates becomes a very major event in earth's history. The procedure we have just followed shows that the book of Revelation often interprets its own symbols, if we are patient enough to search it with care.

When modern nations are working loosely together for a common cause, we often call it an alliance (such as NATO, for example). When a particular nation is powerful enough and determined enough to dominate others by force, we label it an empire. At the end of time the Euphrates River represents the power of many nations supporting the end-time empire of Babylon. What would the drying up of the Euphrates River mean then? Probably the nations' withdrawal of support from end-time Babylon. When end-time Babylon loses its support system of nations, it will fall. How Babylon collapses at the end of time we will discover when we examine the Old Testament background of the imagery of the drying up of the Euphrates River.

The Drying Up of the Euphrates

Let me remind you, if you have read *The Deep Things of God*, that the book of Revelation parallels the Old Testament in two different ways. They are called allusions and echoes. The purpose of an allusion is to point the reader to a specific passage of the Old Testament and to apply its significance to the message of Revelation. In an allusion John intends the reader to recognize the connection between texts and to be aware of the larger context in the Old Testament. The Old Testament context thus helps to explain the meaning of Revelation. A word, a phrase, or a symbol can become a picture that replaces a thousand words. Recognizing an allusion opens fresh windows into the author's meaning. Missing the allusion leaves the author's meaning in doubt.

An echo, on the other hand, is not based on conscious intention. John may use the language of the Old Testament without being consciously aware of where in the Old Testament that phraseology came from. An echo is a usage that is "in the air"—people just pick it up from the environment in which they live. It would be particularly easy to echo the Old Testament if you grew up in a Jewish synagogue in which you constantly heard the Old Testament quoted and referred to in various ways. It would be natural for you to employ language from the Old Testament, but you would not always remember that the Old Testament was the source of the expressions you were using.

The point here is that when the author of Revelation alludes to the Old Testament, he intends for the reader to incorporate the whole context of that passage into the narrative at hand. The "drying up the river Euphrates" is about more than just a simple description of a river during dry season. That phrase connects us with an entire narrative background from the Old Testament. In order to grasp John's vision you have to understand the world in which he lived. To miss that world is to misinterpret and misuse the text.

Revelation 16-18 contains multiple allusions to the Old Testament's description of Babylon's fall. The Old Testament story occurs in three places: Jeremiah 50; 51; Isaiah 44-47; and Daniel 5. I want to call your attention particularly to Jeremiah 50 and 51. We will begin with Jeremiah 50:33, 34:

"This is what the Lord Almighty says: 'The people of Israel are oppressed, and the people of Judah as well. All their captors hold them fast, refusing to let them go.

"'Yet their Redeemer is strong; the Lord Almighty is his name. He will vigorously defend their cause so that he may bring rest to their land, but unrest to those who live in Babylon'" (NIV).

The passage makes it clear that Babylon's fall was not an accident. It was part of God's direct purpose. Babylon had become an oppressor of Israel, and the Lord desired to demonstrate His power to defend and deliver His people. At one time He had used Babylon to discipline and correct His people. But the Babylonians went too far in this role and became abusive. God may practice discipline, but He does not approve of oppression. When Israel's time of discipline was up (70 years of captivity), He intended to free them even if the Babylonians wouldn't. God continues His indictment of the Babylonians:

"'A sword against the Babylonians!' declares the Lord—'against those who live in Babylon and against her *officials* and *wise men*! A sword against her *false prophets*! They will become fools. A sword against her *warriors*! They will be filled with terror" (verses 35, 36, NIV).

The Lord declares an attack against the Babylonians. But He does not leave the language general. He specifically targets Babylon's officials, wise men, false prophets, and warriors. What are we dealing with here? It is a listing of the people who make Babylon powerful: administrators, thinkers, religious leaders, and military personnel. A nation is no stronger than the quality of those who lead and who fight for it. The prophecy continues:

"A sword against her *horses and chariots* and all the foreigners in her *ranks*! They will become women. A sword against her *treasures*! They will be plundered" (verse 37, NIV).

The previous verses talk about officials, wise men, and warriors. Now this one speaks of horses and chariots, mercenary troops and treasures. What is this all about? Again it is a listing of the resources that make Babylon strong! Horses and chariots were the battle tanks of the ancient world. Babylon's financial resources were also significant in its defense. With lots of treasure it could hire the armies of other nations to fight for it. Babylon is only as powerful as the resources of people and treasures that defend it. But we find one more resource:

"A drought on her *waters*! They will dry up. For it is a land of idols, idols that will go mad with terror" (verse 38, NIV).

What are the waters being dried up here? The waters of Babylon—the Euphrates River! You see, the Euphrates River formed part of the defenses of ancient Babylon. It provided a natural moat around the city that made an attack against the walls almost impossible to carry out. But the Euphrates River was even more than this in Jeremiah 50:38. It had become a symbol of all the resources that strengthened ancient Babylon. The Euphrates River not only represented the physical moat around the city, but all the warriors and officials and treasures that made Babylon strong. To dry up the Euphrates River meant Babylon's loss of all the resources needed to survive. Jeremiah 51:36, 37 repeat God's judgment on Babylon:

"Therefore, this is what the Lord says: 'See, I will defend your cause and avenge you; *I will dry up her sea and make her springs dry*. Babylon will be a heap of ruins, a haunt of jackals, an object of horror and scorn, a place where no one lives'" (NIV).

Once again we see that the drying up of the Euphrates River is the triggering event that results in the destruction of ancient Babylon. Thus when we encounter the drying up of the Euphrates in Revelation 16:12, we now recognize that a whole narrative history lies behind that simple statement. When Revelation 17:15 interprets the Euphrates River as a symbol of the civil and secular powers of this world in support of end-time Babylon, it is employing the symbol of the Euphrates River in a way consistent with its usage in the Old Testament. Readers familiar with the Old Testament would find that the interpretation of the Euphrates in Revelation reflects its meaning in the past.

But we need to learn a few more things about the drying up of the Euphrates River and the fall of Babylon in the Old Testament. For them we turn to Isaiah 44, another great fall of Babylon passage.

"This is what the Lord says—your Redeemer, who formed you in the womb: I am the Lord, who has made all things, . . . *who carries out the words of his servants and fulfills the predictions of his messengers, who says of Jerusalem,* 'It shall be inhabited,' of the towns of Judah, 'They shall be built,' and of their ruins, 'I will restore them,' who says to *the watery deep, 'Be dry, and I will dry up your streams,'* who says of Cyrus, 'He is my shepherd and will accomplish all that I please; *he will say of Jerusalem, "Let it be rebuilt," and of the temple, "Let its foundations be laid"* '" (verses 24-28, NIV).

The phrases "watery deep" and "I will dry up your streams" are further references to the drying up of the Euphrates River. So Isaiah 44 introduces another fall of Babylon passage. But the passage has two additional elements that we did not find in Jeremiah 50; 51. It mentions Cyrus, the king of Persia, who would actually accomplish the conquest of Babylon. Also we encounter a reference to the rebuilding of Jerusalem, God's ultimate purpose for Babylon's fall. Prophecy predicted both the fall of Babylon and the restoration of Jerusalem. Both things happened in history because God said they would.

This mention of Jerusalem shows that prophecy has a spiritual purpose. The Bible does not depict God as particularly interested in the rise and collapse of the nations as such. The ebb and flow of politics come into scriptural play only when it somehow affects the people and cause of God. Babylon's fate becomes important when it hinders what He seeks to accomplish on earth. Scripture gives prophecies not to satisfy our curiosity about political events, but to describe a just and caring God who delivers His oppressed people and rebuilds the places that matter to them. And He summons Cyrus to be His agent on earth.

"This is what the Lord says to *his anointed*, to *Cyrus*, whose right hand I take hold of to subdue nations before him and to strip kings of their armor, *to open doors before him so that gates will not be shut*" (Isa. 45:1, NIV).

I want you to notice a couple things about this verse. First of all, it tells us that the Lord Himself will see that the gates of Babylon are open when the armies of Cyrus arrive. While the Persian leader may use engineering skills to divert the flow of the river so that his soldiers can march on the dry riverbed, it still won't gain him entrance into the city unless the gates along the riverbank are open. So 100 years before it happens God assures Cyrus that He is in control of the one part of the situation that the king can't control.

The other thing you need to notice is that God calls Cyrus His "anointed." The Hebrew word for "anointed" is *meshiach*, from which we get the English word "Messiah." The Old Testament uses the word "Messiah" for a future deliverer in only two places. One of them interpreters generally understand as a prophecy of Jesus (Dan. 9:25). The other occurs here, a reference to Cyrus. God calls Cyrus, a pagan king, Messiah! This is truly amazing when you read up to verse 4 in the same chapter: "For the sake of Jacob my servant, of Israel my chosen, I summon you by name and bestow on you a title of honor, *though you do not acknowledge me*" (NIV). Messiah Cyrus is not a believer, yet God endows him with a title of honor.

What is this title of honor that God bestows on Cyrus? It is clearly the word "Messiah" in verse 1. God summons Cyrus by name 100 years in advance and calls him Messiah, even though the Persian ruler does not acknowledge Him. Although he is a pagan king—an unbeliever—God still refers to him as Messiah. The Lord is more open-minded than we are! If you and I were consulted about this decision we would object. *God has no business using such a term with regard to an unbeliever!* But He did! Why? Because Cyrus was the one He would use to deliver His people: "For the sake of Jacob my servant, of Israel my chosen." The title was appropriate because Cyrus would function as a type of the Messiah who would one day rescue God's people from the bondage of this bleak existence. And let me just note that Cyrus came to Babylon from the east! He traveled from Persia, modern-day Iran, which lies to the east of Iraq, the location of ancient Babylon.

Although the predictions came 50 to 150 years before Cyrus emerged on the scene, the historical fulfillment was exact and is confirmed by ancient historians such as Herodotus and Thucydides. The armies of Cyrus arrived from the east and camped north of Babylon. His engineers diverted the flow of the Euphrates River into a depression they had excavated, allowing Cyrus' soldiers to march under the river gates into the city. Timing the diversion to take advantage of a feast day inside the city, Cyrus' soldiers discovered that drunken guards had left open the gates along the river bank. (Some suggest that the people inside the city deliberately opened them for the invaders.) They poured into the city, conquering it and killing its ruler, Belshazzar (described in Daniel 5). In the months and years that followed Cyrus initiated a process that encouraged the scattered remnant of Israel to go back home and rebuild the Temple and the city of Jerusalem. The diagram below illustrates Cyrus' attack:

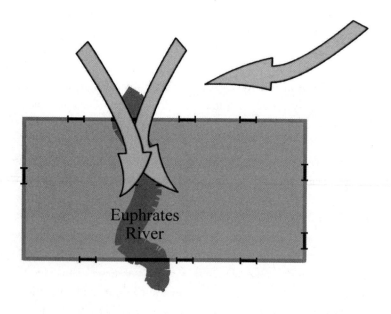

Euphrates River

Notice the total sequence once more: In Old Testament times; Cyrus, king of Persia; dried up the literal Euphrates River in order to conquer Babylon, to let Israel go free, and to rebuild Jerusalem. This narrative clearly sets the foundation for the last portion of the book of Revelation. In Revelation an end-time Cyrus (the "kings from the rising of the sun") dries up the end-time river Euphrates, then conquers end-time Babylon to deliver end-time Israel and build a New Jerusalem! The fundamental narrative substructure of the battle of Armageddon is grounded in the Old Testament story of Cyrus and Babylon's fall. The conquest of Cyrus is, so to speak, a subtext for everything that happens in Revelation 16-22. To recognize this connection is to understand what is going on in the battle of Armageddon. But to overlook it is to miss the point of these end-time events.

OT	Revelation
Cyrus	End-time Cyrus
Euphrates	End-time Euphrates
Babylon	End-time Babylon
Israel	End-time Israel
Jerusalem	New Jerusalem

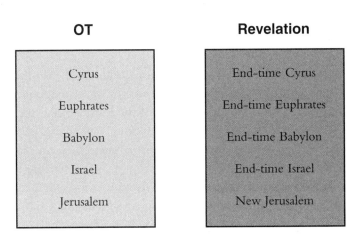

As mentioned before, Adventist interpreters and evangelists have made many helpful observations with regard to the understanding of Revelation and the final events of earth's history. But we have had a tendency to move so quickly from text to history that we often miss the fundamental story in the vision itself. It can keep us from grasping the full picture that God wants us to have. When we interpret Revelation on the basis of a full understanding of its background in the Old Testament it will clear up many things that were previously mysterious.

Kings From the Rising of the Sun

Coming back to Revelation 16:12, we have discovered from the context that the Euphrates River represents the civil and secular powers of our world (Rev. 17:15). From the Old Testament we learned how the Euphrates River functioned as a symbol of the political, economic, and military resources of Babylon (see particularly Jer. 50:33-38). In Revelation 16:12 the water of the Euphrates River dried up to prepare the way for the kings from the sunrise. To understand the "kings from the sunrise" it is helpful to look at how the New Testament uses the word "sunrise."

When you turn to the New Testament, you learn that it employs the term for "sunrise" in two different ways: (1) as a directional reference, and (2) as a symbol of Jesus Christ and the work that He is accomplishing. First of all, the term appears in the birth narratives of Matthew. The Wise Men who brought gifts to the baby Jesus came from the "east" (Matt. 2:1, 2, 9). So "sunrise" can simply mean "east."

"Which way did you go?"

"Oh, I went toward the sunrise."

Such usages are probably not theologically significant. But the second way the New Testament employs the term, the more symbolic one, is much more interesting. Around the time of the birth of John the Baptist, his father, Zechariah, sang a song of celebration, indicating that his son would prepare the way for someone greater than he: "And you, child, will be called the prophet of the Most High; for you will go before the Lord to prepare his ways, to give knowledge of salvation to his people in the forgiveness of their sins, because of the tender mercy of our God, whereby *the sunrise* shall visit us from on high" (Luke 1:76-78, ESV).

This passage contains a clear reference to the first coming of Jesus. The word "sunrise" itself seems to be a title or name for the future Messiah. Matthew 24:27 applies it to Jesus when the passage indicates the direction from which He will come the second time. Revelation 7:2 also employs it when an angel—either Christ or His agent—ascends from the rising of the sun. So the New Testament uses "sunrise" either as a directional term or as a reference to Christ and never in a negative sense. So while the kings from the "east" in Revelation 16:12 could merely indicate the direction from which the kings arrived, in light of the total picture it seems that they have some kind of relationship to Christ.

But if that is the case, why are "the kings" plural? In the original sub-text, Cyrus is "the king" and to use the singular in Revelation 16:12 would seem to make more sense. But we probably find the answer to the question in Revelation 17:14, in which the nations of the world "will make war on the Lamb, and *the Lamb will conquer them,* for he is Lord of lords and King of kings, *and those with him are called and chosen and faithful"* (ESV). In the final battle the Lamb is not alone. He is "king of kings"—there are many kings with Him. Who are these fellow kings? His called, the chosen and faithful believers. They are the very ones called "kings and priests" earlier in the book (Rev 1:5; 5:9, 10). So the "kings from the sunrise" are none other than Christ and His followers in the final battle of earth's history. The drying up of the Euphrates River prepares the way for the ultimate victory of Christ and His people at the end of time. Scripture calls God's side in the end-time battle the "kings of the east."

So the kings from the rising of the sun are actually an end-time confederacy of the saints (Rev. 14:12) from every nation, tribe, language, and people (verse 6). They go by many names in Revelation. Thus they are the remnant (Rev. 12:17), the 144,000 (Rev. 7:4-9; 14:1-5), the great multitude (Rev. 7:9-12; 19:1-6), those who keep watch and hang on to their garments (Rev. 16:15), the called, chosen, and faithful followers of Jesus (Rev. 17:14) and, of course, the kings from the rising of the sun (Rev. 16:12). The key to their victory in the final battle is the drying up of the Euphrates River.

A Battle for the Mind

In the last days of earth's history, therefore, there will emerge a worldwide confederacy of the saints. All over the world there will be people who are faithful to Jesus and on His side in the final crisis. They will worship Him and Him alone. Probably they will not be tightly organized in any institutional sense. But they are clearly defined in terms of their behavior.

But what kind of conflict is the battle of Armageddon? What kind of role will the saints have in it? My study of the New Testament tells me that the battle of Armageddon is not so much about tanks and planes and artillery as it is a struggle for the mind of every human being on earth (Rev. 14:7; 16:15). It is a battle between two trinities, each employing a trio of angels to persuade human beings to their side of the conflict (Rev. 14:6-

12; 16:13, 14). Armageddon will be the conclusion of a war that has gone on throughout Christian history. The clearest description of that conflict appears in the second letter of Paul to the Corinthians: "For though we live in the world, we do not wage war as the world does. The weapons we fight with are not the weapons of the world" (2 Cor. 10:3, 4, NIV).

What are the weapons of this world? In the Greek the phrase "weapons of the world" is literally "fleshly" weapons. But what is a fleshly weapon? It is one that tears you apart in a physical sense. AK-47 assault rifles, A-10 anti-tank aircraft, F-15 Eagles, and M1A1 tanks are fleshly weapons. Paul is telling us that the kind of warfare the followers of Christ are involved with is not waged with fleshly weapons. The weapons of our spiritual warfare are different.

"The weapons we fight with are not the weapons of the world. On the contrary, they have divine power to demolish strongholds. We demolish arguments and every pretention that sets itself up against the knowledge of God, and we take captive every thought to make it obedient to Christ" (verses 4, 5, NIV).

Have you had to struggle with your thoughts today? That's what the battle of Armageddon is all about! It is a war for the mind. A battle against false ideas, a battle against the power of the enemy, a battle for self-control. And in that conflict God will have on His side people of every nation, language, tribe, and religious background—a worldwide confederacy of the saints.

Because the language of Revelation 16 and 17 is military in nature, it has led many people to assume that the great battle at the end of time will be World War III, a military engagement among the nations of the world on a scale never before seen. But first impressions are not always accurate. While the language of the battle of Armageddon is military and the names and concepts are drawn from incidents in the Old Testament, the meaning is spiritual. The book of Revelation utilizes military language as a metaphor of the gospel.

Israel in the New Testament is a metaphor for the church—all those who take hold of the gospel and faithfully follow the path of Jesus. Cyrus becomes a symbol of Christ and His people. Babylon and the Euphrates River have become metaphors of the global enemies of God at the end of earth's history. In Revelation things are not always what they seem.

That means that the great battle at the end will have extremely personal implications. Everyone on earth will find themselves brought to a decision in favor either of the true Trinity or of the counterfeit. The most sobering aspect of the teaching of Revelation is its assertion that the decision cannot be put off forever. There will come a time that the angels will no longer hold back the winds of spiritual strife—it will be too late to get sealed (Rev. 7:1-3). It will be too late to hear the gospel mysteries proclaimed (Rev. 10:7). Intercession in the heavenly temple will cease (Rev. 15:5-8). The filthy and unjust remain filthy and unjust (Rev. 22:11). And Scripture consistently portrays the close of human probation as happening *before* the end. From the human perspective, the destiny of every person on earth will be fixed, yet life will go on for a time. Most will not know when that terrible hour takes place.

The biblical picture of the battle of Armageddon, therefore, calls us all to accountability. Our decisions and our actions matter a great deal in the ultimate scheme of things. In the small everyday battles we have with our thoughts we are practicing for the bigger battles to come. The greatest warfare for the Christian is a struggle for the mind—to focus on the real priorities of life. The battle of Armageddon is about intellectual, emotional, and spiritual allegiance. The great task that Christians face now is to discipline our minds and control our thoughts in order to prepare to be on God's side in the final conflict of earth's history.

THE AXIS OF EVIL

In the wake of September 11, 2001, President Bush came to perceive that the greatest danger to the United States was not al-Qaeda, but rogue nation states with the potential to develop weapons of mass destruction. As he approached his State of the Union address in January of 2002, he asked his speechwriters to help him articulate a case for removing Saddam Hussein from power in just a few sentences. One of those speechwriters, David Frum, decided to study the famous "Date which will live in infamy" speech given by President Roosevelt right after the attack on Pearl Harbor by Japan on December 7, 1941.

Roosevelt believed that the greatest danger to the United States at that time was not Japan but Nazi Germany. For Roosevelt, Pearl Harbor was not just a reckless attack by a relatively weak foe, but rather a warning of future, more powerful strikes from an even more dangerous enemy. He knew that Americans were ready to go to war with Japan on December 8, 1941, but he needed to persuade them to declare hostilities against the entire "Axis" of Japan, Germany, and Italy. While Germany might not be as reckless as Japan had been, its Axis alliance with Japan made the United States much more vulnerable in the future than it would have been with only Japan to worry about (Japan's industrial capacity was only a tenth of the U.S. at the time, while Germany's was about a third). So Roosevelt introduced a subtle line into his radio speech on December 8, 1941: "We will not only defend ourselves to the uttermost but will make very certain that this form of treachery shall never endanger us again."

As Frum compared the Axis powers of World War II with modern "terror states" he saw many similarities. Like the Axis powers of World

War II, Iran, Iraq, and al-Qaeda distrusted each other greatly, but were united in their resentment of the West and Israel. So they formed an "axis of hatred" against the United States. President Bush liked the analogy but made several changes in the actual speech to Congress on January 29, 2002. He added North Korea to the "axis" because of its attempts to develop nuclear weapons and because, as with Japan and Saddam Hussein, it had a history of reckless aggression.

In the speech itself President Bush stated that a goal of the war on terror was "to prevent regimes that sponsor terror from threatening America or our friends and allies with weapons of mass destruction. Some of these regimes have been pretty quiet since September 11. But we know their true nature." After briefly describing his perception of the threat capacities of North Korea, Iran and Iraq, Bush said, "States like these, and their terrorist allies, constitute an *axis of evil,* arming to threaten the peace of the world. By seeking weapons of mass destruction, these regimes pose a grave and growing danger. They could provide these arms to terrorists, giving them the means to match their hatred. They could attack our allies or attempt to blackmail the United States. In any of these cases, the price of indifference would be catastrophic" (italics supplied).

Right or wrong in this particular case, the phrase had the desired effect, leading to the invasion of Iraq about a year later. It became part of the American public consciousness and spawned many caricatures. Countries that did not support the invasion of Iraq were called an "axis of weasels." Sport utility vehicles acquired the nickname "axles of evil" for their poor fuel efficiency. The magazine *Economist* dubbed the perceived breakup of the close relationship between George Bush and Tony Blair in 2006 as the "Axis of Feeble." And a group of Middle Eastern comedians called their act the "Axis of Evil Comedy Tour."[*]

While President Bush's comparison of North Korea, Iran, and Iraq with the Axis powers of World War II has been widely questioned, the book of Revelation projects a similar situation in the last days of earth's history. An unexpected worldwide "axis of evil" will arise when the religious institutions of the world find a common cause with each other and succeed in persuading the political and economic powers of the world to support their cause. The consequences of such an alliance will, for God's people, be serious. The end-time "axis of evil" is the main focus of Revelation 16:13 through 17:18.

In the previous chapter of this book we made an extensive study of Revelation 16:12. We examined the verse in light of three extended strategies for understanding Revelation: how it fits into the structure of the book, what could be learned from its Old Testament background, and the impact on the text from the gospel orientation of the New Testament. We learned, as a result, that "the kings from the rising of the sun" represent Christ and His people in the final battle of earth's history.

While this pivotal verse does not mention Babylon, the mention of the Euphrates River brings it to our attention. The Euphrates River represents worldwide secular economic and political power united to serve end-time Babylon. Babylon and the Euphrates together represent the end-time "axis of evil." The present chapter examines the rise and fall of these enemies of God and His people.

Spiritual Struggle

But before we get deeply engrossed in the sordid details of the end-time, I want to remind you that the New Testament employs its warfare language in a spiritual sense rather than as a description of literal warfare. Christians are called to battle at the end of time, not to take up the weapons of this world, but to utilize spiritual weapons in service of spiritual goals. The battle of Armageddon is a struggle for the mind:

"The weapons we fight with are not the weapons of the world. On the contrary, they have divine power to demolish strongholds. We demolish arguments and every pretension that sets itself up against the knowledge of God, and we take captive every thought to make it obedient to Christ" (2 Cor. 10:4, 5, NIV).

But is it appropriate to apply a text from the writings of Paul to the gory battle scenes of the Apocalypse? I think so. We find a clear indication of the nature of Armageddon right in the heart of Revelation 16 itself. Notice how smoothly verses 14 and 16 fit together: "They are spirits of demons performing miraculous signs, and they go out to the kings of the whole world, to gather them for the battle on the great day of God Almighty" (Rev. 16:14, NIV). "Then they gathered the kings together to the place that in Hebrew is called Armageddon" (verse 16, NIV).

Verse 16 seems to flow quite naturally out of verse 14. Both verses speak of the demonic powers of the world trying to bring the kings of the world to the location of the final battle at the end of time. It sounds like military language. But we notice an abrupt change of pace right in the middle of a military preparation.

"Behold, I come like a thief! Blessed is he who stays awake and keeps his clothes with him, so that he may not go naked and be shamefully exposed" (verse 15, NIV).

Here in the midst of the battle of Armageddon, right in the one part that actually names the conflict, we find a call to the reader to be faithful in the troubles of the end-time. In one single verse John brings together a variety of New Testament appeals in light of the end. Both "I come like a thief" and "Blessed is he who stays awake" reflect statements of Jesus that Paul also echoed:

"Therefore, *stay awake*, for you do not know on what day your Lord is coming. But know this, that if the master of the house had known in what part of the night *the thief* was coming, he would have *stayed awake* and would not have let his house be broken into. Therefore you also must be ready, for the Son of Man is coming at an hour you do not expect" (Matt. 24:42-44, ESV).

"It will be good for those servants whose master finds them *watching* when he comes. I tell you the truth, he will dress himself to serve, will have them recline at the table and will come and wait on them. It will be good for those servants whose master finds them ready, even if he comes in the second or third watch of the night. But understand this: If the owner of the house had known at what hour *the thief* was coming, he would not have let his house be broken into" (Luke 12:37-39, NIV).

"Now concerning the times and the seasons, brothers, you have no need to have anything written to you. For you yourselves are fully aware that the day of the Lord will come *like a thief in the night*. While people are saying, 'There is peace and security,' then sudden destruction will come upon them as labor pains come upon a pregnant woman, and they will not escape. But you are not in darkness, brothers, for that day to surprise you *like a thief*. For you are all children of light, children of the day. We are not of the night or of the darkness. So then let us not sleep, as others do, but let us *keep awake* and be sober" (1 Thess. 5:1-6, ESV).

All three texts are about readiness for the coming of Jesus. By echoing these concepts in the middle of the battle of Armageddon, the book of

Revelation makes it clear that we should not take the military language of Revelation in a military sense. Early Christians reading or hearing the book of Revelation would not interpret it as some sort of end-time physical warfare. The battle of Armageddon is a struggle for the mind. The role of the righteous in the final conflict is to keep spiritually awake and to be always ready, because they do not know when their Lord will come. Armageddon is about the final proclamation of the gospel in the context of great deceptions and persecutions at the end.

Revelation 16:15 also contains an allusion to Jesus' message to the church at Laodicea (Rev. 3:14-22): "I counsel you to buy from me gold refined in the fire, so that you may be rich; and white *garments,* that you may be clothed, that the *shame* of your *nakedness* may not be revealed; and anoint your eyes with eye salve, that you may *see*" (Rev. 3:18, NKJV). The italicized words in Revelation 3:18 all appear in Revelation 16:15. In fact, Revelation 3:18 and 16:15 are the only two texts in the entire Bible that contain all four of these words. The summons to faithfulness in the middle of the battle of Armageddon echoes the plea to Laodicea to allow Christ into the life and the heart. Armageddon has a strong spiritual component. It is a battle for the mind!

So as the end of the world approaches, we find a renewed call to readiness for the Second Coming. Revelation 16:15 brings together core spiritual messages from Matthew, Luke, Paul, and Revelation's letters to the seven churches. In terms of its background and context, the verse directs its call to God's end-time confederacy of the saints.

Our spiritual task during the final battle of earth's history is to keep watch over our attitudes, thoughts, and behavior, and to remain faithful no matter the deception or the coercion we may face. We need faithful endurance and discernment, both fortified with the words of Jesus, Paul, and the letter to Laodicea. In other words, the battle of Armageddon is a struggle for the mind! When we choose to be faithful today in the midst of various temptations, we are being prepared for even greater battles at the end of time. God gave the book of Revelation not to satisfy our curiosity about the future, but to teach us how to live today in the light of things coming upon the world.

Based on what we have learned so far, we can conclude that there will be a worldwide confederacy of the "saints" (Rev. 14:12) at the end of time.

As we have already seen they receive many names in the book of Revelation. They are scattered throughout the earth. In the terrible trials at the end such saints will not necessary be organized in institutional terms. The legal and corporate structures in which the people of God have gathered themselves will be the first thing targeted by the forces of evil at the end.

But the destruction of the saints' spiritual institutions will not hinder the movement in the final crisis. Truly a remnant drawn from every nation, tribe, and religious tradition (Rev. 14:6), they will recognize each other when they meet because of a common walk with God. They will develop deep and meaningful relationships with each other, because they share a common battle to maintain a relationship with Jesus and to be ready for the events of the end. And they will be the object of much negative attention from an end-time "axis of evil." Let's take a closer look at how Revelation 16 and 17 describe that axis of evil.

Some Challenging Texts

But before we begin this study, let me point out that we are dealing with seriously challenging texts in these chapters. Commentators have struggled for centuries to understand the woman and the beast, the seven heads and the 10 horns, the five who are fallen and the one yet to come. But as we approach the last days of earth's history, we should expect greater clarity in those prophecies speaking about the end of time.

Revelation 17 has been a greater puzzle than even most texts in the book of Revelation. More than a decade ago I decided to teach a doctoral seminar on Revelation 17. Five Ph.D. students signed up. Focusing specifically on Revelation 17:7-11, we spent about 30 hours as a group, poring over the Greek text and comparing it with the Old Testament and the New (following the method presented in my book *The Deep Things of God*). Each of the five students wrote a research paper on some aspect of Revelation 17:7-11 and carefully examined what commentators in the past have said about the chapter. The whole group read and discussed each paper and drew the conclusion at the end of the class that we had raised more questions than we had answered! Revelation 17 is one of those passages in which it is much easier to see the flaws in other people's work than it is to make coherent sense of what the text is saying.

Why does the Bible contain such passages? If Scripture is God's revelation of Himself to us, should it not be perfectly clear throughout? What spiritual purpose could such a text serve? I was once on the radio with a fellow student of Revelation, Mervyn Maxwell. The topic of discussion was the seven trumpets of Revelation. As we wrestled together with the complexities of Revelation 8 and 9, Maxwell suddenly turned to me (on the air) and asked, "Why has God placed such difficult texts in the Bible? Is there anything we should learn from that?"

I had never tried to answer that question before. Since Maxwell had been one of my teachers at Andrews University a decade before, I marveled at his openness to ask such a question of his former student on the air. I felt that the Holy Spirit was with us as I shared the following with him and with our listeners.

"It seems to me that study of the Bible is our daily need. If we don't constantly feed on God's Word, we will go backwards spiritually. But if we could understand every detail of the Bible there is danger that we would grow complacent, that we wouldn't feel the need to keep studying what we think we already understand. So God has placed deep and challenging things in His Word that force us to come back to it day after day. This keeps us trying to understand. Because of these difficult texts, our curiosity grows rather than diminishes as we wrestle with Revelation. As we return to the Word each day, as we seek God in study and prayer, our hearts are nourished in its spiritual authority. So that's why I think the seven trumpets are in the Bible."

Perhaps that answer isn't completely satisfying to you, but it does make some sense to me as I continue to reflect on the issue. God cares so much about us that He does what is best for us, even if it makes us puzzled and upset. Sometimes He leaves us with questions and doubts, knowing that the struggle to understand will have positive outcomes in our lives that might not happen any other way. Raising open questions may seem a risky proposition on His part, but I have learned to trust His judgment, even when I don't understand.

Having said this, let me remind you of something I shared in some detail in the fourth chapter of *The Deep Things of God* ("Safeguards for Biblical Study"). While the difficult things of the Bible whet our appetite for scriptural study, we should spend the majority of our Bible study on those parts that are reasonably clear. It is the transparent texts of Scripture that provide a solid foundation for our spiritual lives. If we don't ground ourselves in the clear teachings of the Bible, challenging parts such as Revelation 17 can easily get twisted in ways that undermine the central things of God's Word. So while wrestling with Revelation 17 is part of God's plan for us, it should never become the center of our confidence in His will and ways.

The Forces of Evil

With that in mind, let's begin our study of the forces arrayed against the saints at the end of time. As we have seen, the vision of the bowl plagues (Rev. 16:1-21) introduces the battle of Armageddon, and then the vision of Revelation 17 elaborates on the topic. The prophet hears one of the bowl angels describing a prostitute who has relations with the kings of the earth (Rev. 17:1, 2). He then receives a short vision of a woman named Babylon, who is sitting on a scarlet beast (verses 3-6). John's reaction to the vision appears in the middle of verse 6. His interpreting angel discusses the vision, offering a number of explanations that leave us more confused than when we began (verses 7-18). That's what makes this chapter as difficult as any passage in the book of Revelation.

Let's start at the beginning of Revelation 17: "One of the seven angels who had the seven bowls came and said to me, 'Come, I will show you the punishment of the great prostitute, who sits on many waters'" (verse 1, NIV). According to this verse, the chapter that follows will offer further information about the sixth plague, in which the angel pours his bowl out on the great river Euphrates. The text introduces both of the great end-time powers that work against God and His people. The great prostitute represents one, and the waters (the Euphrates River) upon which she sits depicts the other.

As we have seen, the "many waters" symbolize the global civil and secular powers arrayed against God and His people in the end-time crisis. Here we have a civil, secular, military, and political union that dominates the world at the end of earth's history. It is truly a united nations. The prostitute represents a second worldwide union, but we have not yet explored that in detail. As we go through the chapter, we will discover that both unions receive a number of different names in the chapter. Here is a vital insight for a correct understanding of this difficult chapter.

You see, the variety of symbols in Revelation 16 and 17 do not point us to a vast array of end-time players. One could go through this part of the book and assign a nation, religion, or region of the world for each symbol. But such scenarios make this section of Revelation much more complicated than it already is. If we do this, we will miss the clarity underlying the complex symbolism of the narrative. In chapter 17 the symbols flow together and continue to focus on the same two specific powers introduced in verse 1. The key to the passage seems to be the fluidity with which the same historical entities can appear in a variety of different images, a point that becomes clear as we work our way through verses 1-9. We'll look first at verses 1-3.

"One of the seven angels who had the seven bowls came and said to me, 'Come, I will show you the punishment of *the great prostitute*, who sits on many waters. With *her* the kings of the earth committed adultery and the inhabitants of the earth were intoxicated with the wine of her adulteries.' Then the angel carried me away in the Spirit into a desert. There I saw *a woman* sitting on a scarlet beast that was covered with blasphemous names and had seven heads and ten horns" (NIV).

Revelation 17:1-3 mentions a "great prostitute," of "her," and of "a woman." Are the three one and the same, or do they represent different entities? "Her" in verse 2 clearly refers to the "great prostitute." But are the "great prostitute" of verse 1 and the "woman" of verse 3 identical, or are they different characters? Here is where we can clear up potential confusion. Verse 5 calls the "woman" of verse 3 the "mother of prostitutes." So it seems evident that the prostitute of verse 1 and the woman of verse 3 are not different—they are one and the same in the story, and they depict the same power or confederacy in the course of human history.

End-time Babylon

But what does this woman/prostitute represent at the end of time? Is she a grouping of political nations like those represented by the Euphrates River? Or does she stand for something else? Several elements of the chapter indicate that the great prostitute symbolizes worldwide religious authority in opposition to God and to His end-time people. For starters, John sees this "woman" sitting on a scarlet beast out in the desert (Rev. 17:3). It is not the first time in the book that he observes a woman in the desert. The previous occasion was in Revelation 12:14-16. There we notice the following description:

"*The woman* was given the two wings of a great eagle, so that she might fly to the place prepared for her *in the desert*, where she would be taken care of for a time, times and half a time, *out of the serpent's reach*" (verse 14, NIV).

Since the woman of chapter 12 is in opposition to the serpent/dragon, she depicts the faithful church of God in the middle period of Christian history (usually dated from A.D. 538 to A.D. 1798). In Revelation 17, on the other hand, the woman in the desert seems to have a very negative role in the last events of earth's history. So there is both similarity and contrast between the two women. In fact, scholarship has noted that the book of Revelation has four prominent women: Jezebel (Rev. 2:18, 29), the woman of chapter 12, the woman of chapter 17, and the bride of the Lamb (Rev. 19:7, 8; 21:9, 10). Two of the images are positive, and two are negative.

Jezebel is, in one sense, the forerunner of Babylon the prostitute. She depicts forces within the church that compromise and challenge the faith, something particularly true in the middle period of Christian history. The woman of Revelation 12, on the other hand, is the forerunner of the bride of the Lamb. She represents the scattered, faithful few in the middle period of church history. But there is also a cross-reference between these good and evil manifestations of womanhood. While Babylon the prostitute parallels Jezebel, corrupt leader of the church at Thyatira, she is also in contrast to the end-time bride of Christ and the faithful woman of chapter 12. So like the other three women, she is a spiritual leader. Associated in the context of Revelation with images of true Christian faith, Babylon represents an end-time global confederacy of false religion.

Are the two women the same? Does this image mean that even formerly faithful people of God will join the end-time religious opposition to God and His people? Perhaps. It would certainly explain why the sight of this woman so astonished John (Rev. 17:6). But what is clear is that the end-time religious opposition to God has a Christian face at an institutional level! Mere membership in a Christian church or institution does not guarantee faithfulness to God at the end of time. Entities that have served God and responded to his leading in the past will place their power and influence into the service of evil at the end of time. Whether or not John perceived the woman of Revelation 17 as the same woman we saw in chapter 12 (after all, Scripture calls the end-time people of God the remnant of the woman's seed, not the woman [Rev. 12:17]), the imagery of the great prostitute indicates that there will develop a Christian twist to the end-time opposition to God.

We find this Christian twist further underlined by several other observations in the text of Revelation 17. First, the prostitute's attire in verse 4 seems modeled after that of Israel's high priest in the Old Testament sanctuary. Notice the language of verse 4: "The woman was dressed in purple and scarlet, and was glittering with gold, precious stones and pearls. She held a golden cup in her hand, filled with abominable things and the filth of her adulteries" (NIV).

The high priest wore an ephod that included the colors purple, scarlet, and gold (Ex. 28:5, 6). The ephod and breastplate of the high priest also contained precious stones (verses 9-13 and 17-21). The cup in the woman's hands may represent the drink offerings of the sanctuary (Ex. 29:40, 41; 30:9; Lev. 23:13, 18, 37), and the forehead inscription (Rev. 17:4, 5) resembles the title "HOLY TO THE LORD" written on the high priest's miter (Ex. 28:36-38).

Second, the narrative of Revelation describes the prostitute's fate as to be burned with fire (Rev. 17:16). Such a punishment seems rather strange at first glance, since the regular form of execution for promiscuity or prostitution in the Old Testament was stoning (Deut. 22:20-24; cf. John 8:1-11). But there was an exception to the rule. If the prostitute turned out to be the daughter of a priest, the community burned rather than stoned her (Lev. 21:9). While the distinction is not significant in terms of its results, the biblical author carefully chose the imagery of Revelation 17 to highlight the idea that the woman of Revelation 17:1-5 is a religious power more than a secular or political one.

Prostitute Babylon, therefore, represents a worldwide religious confederacy in opposition to God and to His faithful people at the end of time. People and religious institutions once faithful to Him now join those opposed to Him and His people. While such a global ecumenical religious confederacy will likely include the major institutions of non-Christian religion, the end-time religious confederacy has a particularly Christian face.

Babylon represents God's people "gone to seed." The imagery has an undertone of apostasy. And this is not surprising. All apostasy goes back to the Tower of Babel (Gen. 11:1-9), where God scattered the rebellious people and gave them different languages to keep them apart. Such dispersed humanity became today's nations, so in the biblical view all nations that have ever opposed God go back to the Tower of Babel. Just as ancient Babel (Babylon) was the source of everything that resisted God, Babylon in Revelation 17 is the mother of prostitutes and the source of everything that defies Him today.

We have learned that a major end-time tool in Satan's arsenal is deception. And a major piece of that deception is the degree to which historic Christianity has become co-opted in Satan's service. Those who have prided themselves in fidelity to the religious institutions of the world will one day find themselves resisting the very God they thought they were worshipping! In the end Babylon masquerades before the world as the institutional representative of the true church of God. Everything is turned on its head.

No wonder John expresses astonishment at his vision of the woman (Rev. 17:6). Instead of pure and untarnished faithfulness to Christ, the woman of Revelation 17 is a prostitute drunk with the blood of the saints, the very people who in their deaths bear testimony to their faithfulness to Jesus. Although the prostitute resembles the true woman of Revelation 12 and dresses like the high priest of Israel's sanctuary, she clearly represents a power that opposes the true people of God. She is the enemy of the saints and seeks to destroy those who keep the commandments of God and have the testimony of Jesus (Rev. 12:17). Those who do not worship her eventually face a death decree and an economic boycott (Rev. 13:15-17).

An Evil United Nations

A second enemy power also comes into view in Revelation 17:1-3, which I highlight below:

"One of the seven angels who had the seven bowls came and said to me, 'Come, I will show you the punishment of the great prostitute, who sits on *many waters*. With her the *kings of the earth* committed adultery and the *inhabitants of the earth* were intoxicated with the wine of her adulteries.' Then the angel carried me away in the Spirit into a desert. There I saw a woman sitting on a *scarlet beast* that was covered with blasphemous names and had seven heads and ten horns" (NIV).

Are the "many waters," the "kings of the earth," the "inhabitants of the earth," and the "scarlet beast" symbols of separate powers or are they different ways of speaking about the same thing? This is a very important question for how we interpret here. Much confusion results if we make the text more complicated than it already is.

We have already seen that the "many waters" of verse 1 are the

127

Euphrates River (Rev. 16:12) and stand for the world's civil, military, and secular forces. So the "kings of the earth" and the "inhabitants of the earth" represent essentially the same thing as the "many waters." All three descriptors indicate a worldwide confederacy of political and military power at the end of time. While the phrase "kings of the earth" stands for leadership of the confederacy, that of "inhabitants of the earth" is a more general way of portraying the same thing.

But what about the scarlet beast? Is that also a symbol of political and military power or does it depict something else? The blasphemous names that cover the beast certainly remind us of the sea beast of Revelation 13, a counterfeit of the work of Jesus Christ. But while the scarlet beast wears the names of blasphemy, it primarily serves as another way of describing the worldwide political confederacy, a fact that becomes clear from the explanation of the vision offered in Revelation 17:7-18. The scarlet beast has seven heads and 10 horns. The seven heads represent seven kings (verses 9, 10). The 10 horns depict 10 kings (verse 12). So the beast itself is the sum total of political and military power in the world (verses 12, 13). The Euphrates River and the scarlet beast are two different ways of describing the same thing. The blasphemy in which the beast engages occurs as part of its union with the aims and activities of Babylon.

The relationship between the prostitute and the political confederacy is the central feature of verse 2: "With her the kings of the earth *committed adultery* and the inhabitants of the earth were *intoxicated* with the wine of her adulteries" (NIV). The kings of the earth do not practice adultery with the prostitute in a literal sense. Rather the relationship represents some sort of union between the worldwide religious and political confederacies at the end of time. Peace among the nations can be a good thing, but it can also be a bad thing. One example of an evil peace is the treaty signed between Hitler and Stalin in 1939. Its real purpose was to prepare the way for a war in which each sought to dominate the world.

The Old Testament employs the language of fornication and adultery for unhealthy alliances between Israel and the pagan nations around her. Ezekiel 16 portrays Jerusalem as a rejected infant that God dresses, nourishes, and raises as His own daughter. When she reaches the appropriate age, He marries her, but she scorns the marriage covenant and unites with anyone who comes by. Her lovers symbolize the pagan nations with which

Israel sought political alliance. The eagerness she displays to trust political alliances more than God causes Him to describe her as the opposite of a typical prostitute: "Every prostitute receives a fee, but you give gifts to all your lovers, bribing them to come to you from everywhere for your illicit favors. So in your prostitution you are the opposite of others; no one runs after you for your favors. You are the very opposite, for you give payment and none is given to you" (Eze. 16:33, 34, NIV).

Adultery in Revelation 17, therefore, not only symbolizes the union between Babylon and the kings of the earth—it describes the political rewards the kings of the earth receive for accepting Babylon's rule (Rev. 17:2). Through the attention that Babylon lavishes on them, she gains control of the kings of the earth. The rewards include the economic benefits that the kings of the earth will later lose when Babylon falls (Rev. 18:9, 10, 19).

The "inhabitants of the earth" represent the opponents of God in general, not just the leadership. While the leaders of the political confederacy commit adultery with the prostitute, the inhabitants of the earth go along because they are intoxicated. In other words, the leadership knowingly conducts its end-time attacks on the people of God, but the people in general are deceived. Their condition is more one of drunkenness and confusion than it is one of conscious yielding to temptation. Everyday people can commit criminal acts when it seems socially acceptable to do so (witness how easily we all blow past the speed limit when everyone else is doing it). So the people of earth will seek to harm the saints of God, even though they don't understand the issues involved.

Lust and drunkenness, therefore, are metaphors that Revelation uses to describe the people of the world at the end of time. Revelation 14:8 also combines the two metaphors: "A second angel followed and said, 'Fallen! Fallen is Babylon the Great, which made all the nations drink the maddening wine of her adulteries'" (NIV). When it comes to lust and drunkenness, people don't think clearly. They make bad decisions that don't lead to lasting relationships. After the lust ebbs or the alcoholic high is past, people usually regret what they have done. So while alcohol can be the explanation for criminal behavior, it is never an excuse for it. When a person decides to drink, they also choose to accept the consequences of the actions performed while under the influence of alcohol.

The confederacy of the saints makes no appearance in Revelation 17:1-

3. The only times the saints appear in Revelation 17 are in verses 6 and 14. Verse 6 refers to the blood of the saints and of those who "bore testimony to Jesus" (NIV). In verse 14 you find the Lamb and those with Him—His called, chosen, and faithful followers. So the saints are present in chapter 17, but they remain more in the background of the story than at the forefront.

"Then the angel carried me away in the Spirit into a desert. There I saw a woman sitting on a scarlet beast that was covered with blasphemous names and had seven heads and ten horns" (verse 3, NIV).

The woman sitting on a scarlet beast represents Babylon's end-time domination of earth's political and secular powers. Why do the nations allow Babylon to control them? People who commit adultery think that their lives will somehow be better off for it. Those who drink do so because they feel better for a while. So the union of the nations with the prostitute happens because the leaders of the nations assume that they or their nations will somehow be better off as a result. Most of the people in those nations go along with what is happening, even if they don't understand the motives of their leaders. But the account in Revelation makes it clear that such an axis of evil has a very short life span.

Verses 1-5 name the two evil confederacies in a variety of ways. The range of symbols for the same thing helps us gain deeper insight into each of them. But the relationships between them remain essentially identical throughout the passage. In verse 1 you have a prostitute sitting on many waters, the Euphrates River of the sixth plague. Verse 2 describes the same prostitute as being in union with the kings of the earth and with the inhabitants that those kings represent. And in verse 3 you have prostitute Babylon sitting on a scarlet beast.

So verses 1-5 portray a pair of confederacies united in their opposition to God and His people. We find symbols of Babylon (always female) associated with symbols of secular military and political power (beast, kings of the earth, and the Euphrates River). The woman, for a short time anyway, is in a dominant position, using the rulers of the earth and their resources to achieve her own ends of destroying the Lamb and those with Him (verse 14). That is why the beast has no crowns, unlike the dragon of chapter 12 and the sea beast of chapter 13. At the point of the vision the beast has given its authority to Babylon for a short time. The earth's political and military authorities have surrendered their power to the worldwide institutions of religion.

Three Worldwide Confederacies

In verse 6 the brief vision of the woman and the beast ends, and a confusing series of interpretations of the succeeding verses begins. But that is a subject for another chapter. Before we enter that difficult territory (verses 7-18), let me sum up what we have learned so far about the major players in the battle of Armageddon. Combining what we have discovered in this chapter with the previous one, we conclude that there will emerge three worldwide confederacies at the end of time. They will include (1) a confederacy of the saints, (2) a confederacy of the institutions of religion in opposition to God and the saints, and (3) a confederacy of civil, secular, political, economic, and military powers.

1. The confederacy of the saints will probably not be organized in institutional terms. Likely any religious institutions faithful to God will have been destroyed by this point in earth's history. Any religious institutions that survive will do so on account of being co-opted into the aims of Babylon. The confederacy of the saints will consist of kindred spirits that find each other out of every nation, tribe, language, and religious institution (they will all have "come out of Babylon" [Rev. 18:4]). The confederacy of the saints will have as its distinguishing trait its unlikeness to all other confederacies on earth. Its "kingdom is not of this world" (John 18:36) and it will not fight as the institutions of the world do (2 Cor. 10:3-5). The book of Revelation knows it by many names, such as the remnant, the 144,000, and the "saints" (Rev. 14:12).

2. The confederacy of religion is a global alliance of religious authority. While the pope is a logical one to head such a confederacy, Babylon will in fact be much bigger, as we will see (Rev. 16:13, 19). The union of religious institutions will occur out of a need to coordinate spiritual effort in the face of significant challenges. These challenges may include environmental issues (Rev. 16:1-11) and the breakdown of law and order (terrorism and crime, cf. Rev 6:3, 4), as well as spiritual opposition on the part of the true people of God. While not detailed in Revelation, such challenges must be considerable for the fractious institutions of religion to lay aside longstanding differences (just think of the barrier between the Papacy and Islam because of the Crusades!). Revelation labels this confederacy Babylon, the woman, the great prostitute, and the great city.

3. The confederacy of secular and political power will be as great a sur-

prise as the confederacy of religious institutions. For millennia, human beings have exercised corporate selfishness through their political institutions. Such groups would rather experience the loss of great numbers of people, including women and children, than give up political leverage against other political entities, a reality massively underlined in the recent events in Iraq. Yet God will so orchestrate events (Rev. 17:17) that the political powers of the world will find greater reason to work together than to fight one another. It would be a most encouraging development were it not for the opposition to God and His people that results when this political unity places itself in the service of Babylon. This political confederacy is designated by many names in Revelation. Among them we have already seen that of the Euphrates River, the kings of the earth, and the scarlet beast.

Saints	Political	Babylon
Remnant	Euphrates	Babylon
144,000	Kings of World	
Great Crowd	Many Waters	The Great City
Kings of East	Kings of Earth	
Watchful	Earth Dwellers	The Great
Clothed	Beast	Prostitute
Called	10 Horns	
Chosen	Cities of the Nations	The Unholy Trinity
Faithful	7 Mountains	Woman
	7 Kings	

All three confederacies are shocking, in light of history as we know it. That individual Protestants, Catholics, Jews, Muslims, and others might all join together in an end-time spiritual "remnant" has few examples in today's world (details of this exciting prospect await another book in this series). The idea that the religious institutions of this world might somehow put aside their differences and pursue a common cause seems ludicrous in the light of recent events. And the concept of a worldwide political unity seems equally strange in the face of the new world disorder we are experiencing as I write. Can you imagine Iran, the United States, North Korea, Pakistan, India, and Cuba all transcending their differences at the same time?

The three worldwide confederacies will be a clear indication that we have entered into the final events of earth's history. They will be so out of character with previous history that no one will mistake them when they arrive. And we are clearly not there yet.

The war on terror, however, offers a glimpse of the future. For the first time in world history the nations of the world recognize that terrorism threatens them all. Individual nations may differ on the definition of terrorism. One person's freedom fighter is the next one's terrorist. But all agree that terrorism threatens order and prosperity. And all religious institutions generally concede that they have more in common with each other than they do with the radicals in their own tradition.

So the war on terror has brought us to a new phase of things. For the first time in human history the religious and political institutions of the entire world are generally united against a small, scattered, but international group of people bound together by a spiritual purpose. Don't get me wrong. I am absolutely not suggesting that al-Qaeda is the remnant of Revelation. But the war on terror is like a dress rehearsal for Revelation's scenario of the end. It wakes us up with the realization of how close we could be. September 11 shows us how quickly the political and religious landscape in the world can change. One day, no one knows how soon, the spotlights of the world will move from al-Qaeda and other issues to the remnant. And when that time comes, the end is at hand.

When the three worldwide confederacies are in place, things will move rapidly to the end of history as we know it. Like a sports fan desperately searching for scores first thing in the morning, we all would like to know how things will turn out in the end. Who won and who lost. And Revelation will not disappoint us.

★ See "Axis of Evil," *Wikipedia.* Referenced on Aug. 3, 2007, at http://en.wikipedia.org.

THE FINAL MOVEMENTS
(WINNERS AND LOSERS)

Revelation 17 is one of the most difficult in all the Bible. But a certain hermeneutical principle will help us here. Before we get to that principle, however, we need to look at verse 6.

In verse 6 the vision ends and a confusing series of interpretations begins. Revelation 17 has opened with an "audition" (a voice speaking) that tells John about the great prostitute and the kings of the earth (Rev. 17:1, 2). In the narrative of Revelation John never actually sees the great prostitute (although he is addressed as if he did in verse 15). Rather, he is told about her. When he actually looks, he sees the woman Babylon sitting on a scarlet beast (verses 3-5).

This pattern of hearing and seeing is a common one in the book of Revelation. In chapter 1 John hears the sound of a trumpet, but when he looks, he sees Jesus speaking with him (Rev. 1:10-12). Next in Revelation 5 John hears about the Lion of the tribe of Judah, but when he looks for the Lion, he sees a slain Lamb instead (Rev. 5:5, 6). Then in Revelation 7 John hears the number of the 144,000, but he never sees them. When he does look he observes a great multitude that no one can number (Rev. 7:4, 9). What John hears and what he sees are quite different, even opposites (the 144,000 are Jews while the unnumbered multitude are from every nation), yet they are two different ways of saying the same thing (like the Lion and the Lamb of Revelation 5).

So in Revelation 17 John moves from hearing to seeing in verse 3. This is the point at which the vision begins. A short vision, it ends in the middle of verse 6. John perceives a new reality, almost in the form of a photograph, rather than a moving picture. The woman is sitting on a scarlet beast. That is as far as the action of the vision goes. Everything else in the vision, however, fills out the picture. It is somewhat similar to the vision of Revelation 1:13-16, in which Jesus is described as something of a still picture. But in Revelation 17:6 the vision ends and an angel arrives to offer John his interpretations, challenging and difficult though they have proved to be.

"But the angel said to me, 'Why do you marvel? I will tell you the mystery of the woman, and of the beast with seven heads and ten horns that carries her'" (verse 7, ESV).

Keep in mind that it is the sixth bowl angel (Rev. 16:12; 17:1) who now interprets the short vision of Revelation 17:3-6. So this difficult explanation is just as much a part of the battle of Armageddon as Revelation 16:12-16 is. Revelation 17:7 adds one additional dimension of the vision. The woman is not just sitting on a stationary beast like the photographic picture in verse 3. The angel states clearly that the beast "carries her." Here is the implication of riding, of going somewhere to accomplish a task. In fact, the Greek verb for "carry" has strong implications of "support" or "sustenance." Just as ancient Babylon's resources supported it, so end-time Babylon is aided by the scarlet beast. She "rides" the beast and controls its actions for a time.

In ancient Babylon death decrees enforced religious issues. Bow down to this image or be hurled into the fiery furnace (Dan. 3). Worship only the king or get thrown into a den of hungry lions (Dan. 6). During much of the Middle Ages the church enforced its religious dominance of Europe with torture and burning at the stake. In similar fashion, end-time Babylon will utilize the power of the state to impose its religious agenda across the entire world. It will include economic boycotts and a death decree (Rev. 13:15-17). The death decree of Revelation 13, in fact, is modeled on that of Daniel 3. Those who do not bow down to the image of the beast will be killed (Rev. 13:15).

Revelation 17:18 states the relationship between the woman and the beast in plain language: "The woman you saw is the great city that rules over the kings of the earth" (NIV). The angel clearly identifies the woman featured throughout this chapter as ruling over the "kings of the earth." That is what sitting on the waters and riding the beast are all about. The woman, who represents a global religious confederacy, assumes rule over the kings of the world for a short time at the very end of human history. But here the metaphor changes from a woman/prostitute to a great city.

Prostitute Babylon and city Babylon are the one and the same—a religious confederacy at the end of time. Thus one can describe her destruction both in terms of the execution of a prostitute (Rev. 17:16) and, from Revelation 17:18 on, as the destruction of a city (see also Rev. 18).

The shift from vision to interpretation is highly important. God always meets people where they are. In a vision the prophet can travel anywhere in the universe and to any point of time, all the way to the end of the world. But when God has the vision interpreted to the prophet afterward, the explanation must make sense in the time, place, and circumstances of the human prophet. An explanation is worthless unless it makes sense to the one receiving it.

Here we have the hermeneutical principle that we alluded to at the beginning of this section. Whenever God, an angel, or another prophet interprets a vision for the one who received it, that interpretation is grounded in the prophet's place in geography and history. If the interpreter says, "After you will come. . . ," he means after the time of the prophet, not after a particular time in the vision. This principle is especially important for the appendix of this book, and I will discuss it in more detail there. But it also affects what we will cover in this chapter. Let's continue with the angel's explanation to John.

Interpreting the Seven-headed, 10-Horned Beast

"The beast that you saw was, and is not, and is about to rise from the bottomless pit and go to destruction. And the dwellers on earth whose names have not been written in the book of life from the foundation of the world will marvel to see the beast, because it was and is not and is to come" (Rev. 17:8, ESV).

As we have seen, the beast represents the worldwide confederacy of civil and secular power. But Revelation employs an interesting twist to describe this end-time political alliance: it "was, and is not, and is about to rise." The phraseology has remarkable similarity to the description of God in Revelation 1:4 and 4:8. God is the one who "is and was and is to come." So this political beast completely serves religious ends when it allows itself to carry the great prostitute. According to the explanation to John the beast "is not." In John's day this particular manifestation of the beast did not exist—it would arise and operate only at the very end of time.

THE FINAL MOVEMENTS (WINNERS AND LOSERS)

Such political unions have happened before. The book of Daniel mentions a series of four secular empires that ruled over the ancient biblical world: Babylon, Persia, Greece, and Rome. In succession they dominated the biblical world politically for more than 1,000 years. The fourth of them—Rome—held sway in John's day. The angel was essentially telling John that the beast of worldwide political opposition to God would come back at the very end, just before its final destruction (Rev. 19; 20).

John was astonished (or "marveled") when he saw the prostitute (Rev. 17:6, 7). But according to verse 8, the inhabitants of the earth are astonished (same Greek word) when they see the beast. If what Revelation describes here takes place in our lifetimes, we also will truly be astonished. Political unity (or anything even close to it) is not a part of today's reality. We can hardly get the Democrats and the Republicans to talk to each other in a civil manner, much less work with the French, the Russians, the Chinese, the Iranians, and the like, to bring about international political unity. Many political leaders throughout history have dreamed of dominating the whole world, but it will truly happen only once—in the final stages of the battle of Armageddon, just before the end.

"This calls for a mind with wisdom. The seven heads are seven hills on which the woman sits. They are also seven kings. Five have fallen, one is, the other has not yet come; but when he does come, he must remain for a little while" (verses 9, 10, NIV).

While the last part of verse 10 is not critical to our understanding of the battle of Armageddon, nevertheless it has intrigued interpreters for many centuries, and I would be remiss if I didn't address it at all in this book. So I have written an appendix chapter on Revelation 17:10, 11. But for right now, I want to focus on the first half of the above passage.

In the original Greek the word translated "hills" could just as easily have been rendered "mountains," as is the case in the King James Version and the English Standard Version. No doubt the translator of the New International Version had the city of Rome in mind. Already in ancient times it was known as the "city of seven hills." But I suspect that John was not thinking of Rome after all, since in this explanation the seven mountains are consecutive in time rather than all present at once (verse 10).

The distinction between hills and mountains is important. In the Old Testament the word "mountains" can represent political powers, as is the case here in Revelation 17. For example, in Daniel 2 the great mountain that fills the whole earth depicts the kingdom of God, which replaces the four kingdoms of gold, silver, bronze, and iron (Dan. 2:35, 44). Jeremiah 51:24, 25 calls Babylon a destroying mountain that would one day be burned over according to God's judgment. Since the angel clearly defines the seven mountains of Revelation 17 as "seven kings," they symbolize the same secular political powers as the earlier images of Euphrates, the beast, and the kings of the earth. Since they all form a foundation upon which the woman sits, they provide the resources that give her strength in world affairs.

Just as the pedigree of the sea beast in Revelation 13 went back to the ancient kingdoms of Daniel 7, here we find the pedigree of the end-time beast in Revelation 17. The waters, the hills, and the kings are all consecutive here. They represent a series of worldwide political powers throughout history. The "fallen kings" of verse 10 simply provide the pedigree of a worldwide end-time political power that functions much as the seven previous political powers did in the course of earth's history.

We have reason to believe that John lives in the period of the sixth kingdom and looks forward to the seventh at some point in his future. But the final manifestation of this beast (the one featured in his vision) is the eighth, rather than the seventh. "As for the beast that was and is not, it is an eighth but it belongs to the seven, and it goes to destruction" (verse 11, ESV).

Revelation 17 and Armageddon

Before we move on to the slightly simpler material at the end of this chapter (Rev. 17:12-17), I'd like to briefly glance back at chapter 16 again. The same three confederacies we have identified in Revelation 17 also exist there. We see the dynamic between the religious and the political confederacies also spelled out in chapter 16:

"The sixth angel poured out his bowl on the great river Euphrates, and its water was dried up, to prepare the way for *the kings from the east.* And I saw, coming out of the mouth of the dragon and out of the mouth of the beast and out of the mouth of the false prophet, three unclean spirits like frogs. For they are demonic spirits, performing signs, who go abroad to the kings of the whole world, to assemble them for battle on the great day of God the Almighty" (Rev. 16:12-14, ESV).

The phrase "kings from the east" represents the confederacy of the saints in this passage. The term has essentially the same meaning as remnant, the 144,000, the great multitude, and the saints. In addition, we also find the confederacy of secular/political power:

"The sixth angel poured out his bowl on *the great river Euphrates,* and its water was dried up, to prepare the way for the kings from the east. And I saw, coming out of the mouth of the dragon and out of the mouth of the beast and out of the mouth of the false prophet, three unclean spirits like frogs. For they are demonic spirits, performing signs, who go abroad to *the kings of the whole world,* to assemble them for battle on the great day of God the Almighty" (verses 12-14, ESV).

As we have seen earlier, the italicized terms in the text represent the earth's political powers: the great river Euphrates and the kings of the whole world. As we would expect, the confederacy of religion also appears in the passage:

"The sixth angel poured out his bowl on the great river Euphrates, and its water was dried up, to prepare the way for the kings from the east. And I saw, coming out of the mouth of *the dragon* and out of the mouth of *the beast* and out of the mouth of *the false prophet,* three unclean spirits like frogs. For they are demonic spirits, performing signs, who go abroad to the kings of the whole world, to assemble them for battle on the great day of God the Almighty" (verses 12-14, ESV).

Thus the dragon, the beast, and the false prophet depict the religious coalition. As we will see in a moment, these three together become Babylon, the great end-time religious confederacy. They send out the three frogs—demonic spirits—to assemble the kings of the earth for the final battle. This would appear to be an earlier stage of the final events than what we saw in Revelation 17:1-10. There the woman dominates the beast and uses it for her own purposes. Here the political powers of the world have not yet come under her dominion, but her agents are moving into action with that goal in mind.

We addressed the three frogs briefly in an earlier chapter, but we still need to say a few more things about them. They come "out of the mouth of the dragon, out of the mouth of the beast and out of the mouth of the false prophet" (Rev. 16:13, NIV). The dragon, the beast, and the false prophet are the same three characters we encountered in Revelation 13. There only the sea beast's mouth was in view, but now we see all three mouths. Here the verse focuses not on the actions of these beasts but on their message. Their message turns people away from God's message in the final crisis. Historically (in the Middle Ages particularly), the sea beast did the dragon's blasphemy (Rev. 13:5-7). At an earlier stage of the final conflict the land beast acted in behalf of the sea beast (verse 12). Now in the final battle all three members act to bring the whole world under their dominion (Rev. 16:13, 14).

The three frogs are the agents or messengers of this evil trinity. Verse 14 defines them as the "spirits of demons" (NIV). To the Greeks, demons were superior to humans but inferior to the gods. For the Hebrews, angels played this role. In the New Testament demons are subordinates of Satan, serving his purposes in the same way the holy angels do those of God. The gospels use words such as "demons," "unclean spirits," and "evil spirits" interchangeably (see, for example, Mark 3:7-30).

The unclean spirits play two roles in the battle of Armageddon: persuasion and agents of miraculous signs. The land beast performed the miraculous signs in Revelation 13:13, 14, but now all three beasts instigate them. They use miracles to persuade the whole world to worship themselves rather than the true God. So the three frogs are the evil counterpart of God's three angels (Rev. 14:6-12), presenting a counterfeit gospel to the whole inhabited world.

There are, therefore, two "trinities" and two sets of messengers (three angels and three frogs) that go out into the world during the final battle. The stakes are as high as they have ever been. To the degree that God's three angels (verses 6-12) reach the world, the forces of evil will have a hard time. On the other hand, if the demonic trinity succeeds in uniting all the nations of the earth under their leadership, the final struggle of the saints will be all the more difficult. When the civil and secular powers of the world lend their powers to the demonic trinity, the stage is set for the final battle.

So end-time Babylon consists of multiple entities working together. Each evil character has a separate history and pedigree, but they unite to bring the rulers of the world under their control for the last conflict of earth's history. The counterfeit gospel of the three frogs unifies the two evil confederacies: (1) religious Babylon and (2) the secular-political unity of the nations. This "axis of evil" must be in place before the final movements occur. So in Revelation 16:12-14 all the entities we have identified in Revelation 17 are present: the three great worldwide confederacies and the agents of Babylon seeking to bring the political powers of the world under its dominion.

An abrupt change of pace occurs in the midst of this evil activity. "Behold, I come like a thief! Blessed is he who stays awake and keeps his clothes with him, so that he may not go naked and be shamefully exposed" (Rev. 16:15, NIV). As we have seen previously, in this single verse John ties together all the New Testament passages that focus on readiness for the final crisis (Matt. 24:42-44; Mark 13:37; Luke 12:37-39; 21:34-36; 1 Thess. 5:1-8). This text highlights the role of the righteous in the final battle. It even alludes to Jesus' message to the church at Laodicea (Rev. 3:17, 18). During the middle of the battle of Armageddon, therefore, we find a call to the church of Laodicea! In terms of its background and context, it is the last summons from God to His end-time confederacy of saints. God's people need to be ready for Jesus' return when the final events take place. Throughout the last battle of earth's history our spiritual task is to keep watch over our attitudes, thoughts, and behavior, and to remain faithful no matter what the deception or coercion. Armageddon is a struggle for the mind.

Here's the most confusing thing about the sixth bowl plague. The plague itself is the drying up of the Euphrates (Rev. 16:12), symbolizing Babylon's loss of political, economic, and military support at the close of the battle of Armageddon. The political powers of the world change their mind. So the events of verses 13-15 must be prior in time to the events of verse 12. In verses 13 and 14 Babylon gathers its political support for the battle, in order to attack the saints. Then in verse 15 comes the final call to the saints. Armageddon (verse 16) is the climax of the two gospels going to the world. Only after the end-time axis of evil is in place can the drying up of the Euphrates occur. So while the seven last plagues are after the close of probation, Revelation 16:13-16 present events that are earlier than the sixth plague, even before the close of probation. The events of Revelation 16 and 17 are all related to Armageddon, but the book of Revelation does not present them in chronological order.

We need to look at one final text before we summarize the climax of the battle of Armageddon: "The great city was split into three parts, and the cities of the nations fell, and God remembered Babylon the great, to make her drain the cup of the wine of the fury of his wrath" (Rev. 16:19,

ESV). This is part of the seventh bowl plague of Revelation 16. The key plague of the sixth bowl is the drying up of the Euphrates River while the key plague of the seventh bowl is the destruction of Babylon as well as of the forces that had supported and protected her, an event clearly outlined in verse 19.

As we have seen, the "great city" is Babylon (see also Rev. 17:18 and 18:10). Here we see the disintegration of the axis of evil achieved under the sixth plague. God not only separates Babylon from the political and military powers that gave it strength (Rev. 16:12)—He splits it back into its constituent units. What are the three parts of Babylon? The dragon, the beast, and the false prophet of verse 13 (and of chapter 13)!

So Babylon is not just a single entity, the way the sea beast operated in the Middle Ages. While the religious confederacy turned to the pope of that time for leadership, the religious confederacy of the very end will be bigger than any single religion. It will be a global coalition with a Christian face. In order to deceive the world regarding the claims of Jesus, it will be necessary for end-time Babylon to appear to the world as Jesus' best friend. Others will join the coalition as the deceptions of the end-time unfold.

Note also in this verse the contrast between the "great city" and the "cities of the nations." In verse 19 the "great city" falls, and then the "cities of the nations" also collapse. As we have seen, the great city is the same thing as the great prostitute (Rev. 17:18). It is the religious alliance that dominates world affairs at the end of time. Here the "cities of the nations" represent the rest of the fallen world—the civil and secular powers that serve Babylon. The verse indicates that the political powers of our world will be split off from Babylon and will be destroyed separately. How this happens becomes clearer at the end of chapter 17 (verses 12-17).

Revelation 16:19 says: "God remembered Babylon." Chapter 18 continues the theme. "For her sins are piled up to heaven, and God has remembered her crimes" (Rev. 18:5, NIV). God makes her drink the cup of His wrath. "Give back to her as she has given; pay her back double for what she has done. Mix her a double portion from her own cup" (verse 6, NIV). When God "remembers" Babylon, He carries out the final execution of judgment on Babylon and everyone who chooses to identify with her. In a nutshell, Revelation 16:19 depicts God's final action on those who have been frustrating His mission on the earth.

THE FINAL MOVEMENTS (WINNERS AND LOSERS)

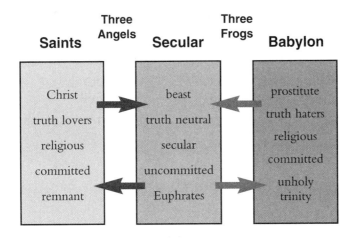

Summarizing once more: The portion of Revelation dedicated to the battle of Armageddon portrays three worldwide confederacies at the end of time. All three go by many names in Revelation. We have illustrated the three confederacies as shown above.

But the vision of Revelation 17 does not portray two opponents of God and His people at the end. There is simply one composite picture—that of the woman riding on the beast. How did things get to this place?

In Revelation 16:13, 14 we saw the three frogs (demonic angels) going out to the world with a counterfeit gospel. Their action mirrors the three angels of Revelation 14, who present the true gospel to the entire world. The end result is that those who enter the final events uncommitted or secular are forced "off the fence" into a commitment one way or the other (see 2 Thess. 2:9-12). Those who accept the true gospel join with the saints in a confederacy of kindred spirits. On the other hand, those who reject the gospel join in with the religious confederacy, some by conviction, the rest out of a desire to preserve life or income (Rev. 13:15-17). I illustrate the impact of the two contradictory gospels on the three confederacies as follows:

The end result is two short-term groupings, represented by the dragon and the remnant in Revelation 12:17. The battle lines are fully drawn and the stakes are high. The saints consist of all those who have the seal of God on their foreheads. Everyone else gets marked by the beast, either on the forehead (Babylon) or on the hand (the secular/political people). We can illustrate the outcome in the following two ways:

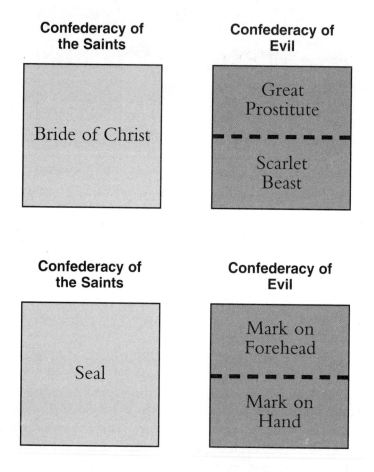

Now we come to the decisive conclusion of Revelation 17, a startling reversal that begins with more detail on how the end-time confederacy of evil develops:

"The ten horns you saw are ten kings who have not yet received a kingdom, but who for one hour will receive authority as kings along with the beast" (Rev. 17:12, NIV).

The beast that John saw in the vision of Revelation 17:3-6 had seven heads and 10 horns, but neither the heads nor the horns had crowns. This may be because the political confederacy is not ruling the world in its own right. At the point in time of the vision the beast is crownless. In this verse the interpreting angel focuses on a different portion of the beast than previously: the 10 horns (the explanation in Revelation 17:7-11 focused on the seven heads).

Because we notice a lot of kings mentioned in the battle of Armageddon, it is easy for interpreters to get confused. We find the kings of the east (Rev. 16:12), the kings of the whole inhabited world (verse 14), the kings of the earth (Rev. 17:2), the seven kings (verse 10), and now the 10 kings (verse 12—not to mention the "King of kings" in verse 14)!

The 10 kings are an end-time "character" without a pedigree. Unlike most new characters in Revelation, they have no introductory description that gives some sense of their previous history. Evidently this grouping comes into existence only at the very end of time. Their "kingdom" is very short—one hour. They emerge during the period of the eighth head (verse 11), the very last manifestation of the beast (see appendix for further information on this eighth head).

"[The 10 kings] have one purpose and will give their power and authority to the beast" (verse 13, NIV). If the beast as a whole depicts the world's combined political and economic powers, the 10 horns represent a significant subgroup of the world's nations. In order for a global political unity to happen, this powerful subgroup has to sign on. Only time will reveal the identity of the 10 kings. Those who observe this prophecy with care will watch for a move toward world unity by a major subgrouping of the world's nations, possibly in the context of the United Nations or some similar organization.

If this action should occur in the reasonably near future, we could suggest two major candidates in today's world for the role described in this passage: NATO and the G8 nations. NATO is a military alliance of the United States, Canada, and 24 European countries (including Turkey, which is partly in Europe). It was the outgrowth of the North Atlantic Treaty signed on April 4, 1949. The treaty's initial purpose was to provide a political and military counterbalance to Soviet power in Europe. With the collapse of Soviet communism, NATO has become the chief military and political power in the world. In the present situation worldwide union is inconceivable without its support.

The G8 nations, on the other hand, are more of an economic group than a political or military one. Since 1975 the leaders of the major industrial democracies have met annually to deal with economic and political issues. The six countries at the first summit were France, the United States, Britain, Germany, Japan, and Italy. Canada joined them in 1976 and Russia in 1997. While NATO is the more powerful organization on paper, the G8 countries together are capable of dominating even NATO.

Only the passage of time will give us the exact identity of the 10 kings who offer their allegiance to the end-time political confederacy. When they give their power and authority to the beast, the beast hands it over to Babylon. The end result is open and final warfare with the Lamb and those allied with Him. The 10 kings together with the beast make war with the Lamb.

"These [the 10 horns together with the beast] will make war with the Lamb, but the Lamb will overcome them, because he is Lord of lords and King of kings—and those with him are called and chosen and faithful" (verse 14, author's translation).

Whatever the makeup of the 10 kings, the handing over of their authority to the beast results in direct war with the Lamb in the person of His people (verse 14). The good news is that the end is not in doubt and the outcome is clear. The Lamb and those with Him win, and the powers of the world lose. While the narrative of Armageddon continues for a few more verses, verse 14 jumps right to the conclusion, to assure the reader of the outcome before Revelation details the final events.

This is not the first time this type of thing has happened in the book of Revelation. We find the final battle summarized in a nutshell in Revelation 12:17. There it becomes clear that the two sides in the final battle are good and evil, represented by the dragon and the remnant. But the verse does not state the outcome of the battle. Next Revelation 13 focuses on the dragon's side of the final battle—his allies and his strategy. But again we find the final outcome ignored. Revelation 14 describes the remnant's side of the final conflict, and here the author takes us all the way to the climax at the second coming of Jesus. But then in Revelation 16 we find ourselves back to the events before the end, as we explore the various players and their actions. While Revelation 16 seems to bring us close to the conclusion, at least, in the seventh bowl, Revelation 17 digresses to

THE FINAL MOVEMENTS (WINNERS AND LOSERS)

present an elaboration of the sixth bowl, which covers most of the chapter. The only reference to the ultimate end in chapter 17 is in verse 14.

So the book of Revelation exhibits a pattern of recycling, recapitulation, or flashback, however one wants to say it. It presents a big picture, sometimes mentioning the outcome; then the focus goes back to an earlier point in the series of events, elaborating on this or that detail. Revelation is certainly not a linear text. It bounces back and forth in its portrayal of the future. Probation closes in Revelation 15:5-8, yet people are still making decisions in Revelation 16:14, 15. While the sixth bowl separates Babylon from its political support (Rev. 16:12), verses 13 and 14 portray the gathering of that support. Revelation shifts back and forth in terms of time, and one must pay careful attention to the text to keep track of these movements.

So in Revelation 17:14 the end is not in doubt and the outcome is clear. The Lamb wins, and the powers of the world lose. The war of Revelation 17:14 wipes out the political confederacy, yet that confederacy appears at the height of its power again in verse 16! (And Revelation 19:11-21 brings out the destruction of the political confederacy in much greater detail.) But in Revelation 17:15 the text moves back to the fate of the prostitute, who rides the beast in the vision of Revelation 17:3-6: "Then the angel said to me, 'The waters you saw, where the prostitute sits, are peoples, multitudes, nations and languages'" (NIV).

The angel in this verse is that of the sixth bowl. The waters here are the Euphrates River, which represents the secular-political authorities of the world. These powers move into action in a surprising way in verse 16: "The beast and the ten horns you saw will hate the prostitute. They will bring her to ruin and leave her naked; they will eat her flesh and burn her with fire" (NIV).

The beast and the 10 horns together represent the unity of those political powers who saw benefit in committing adultery with the prostitute (verse 2). They let her control them for a time, but now they apparently change their minds. The Euphrates River dries up, and the political powers bring her to ruin, erasing the religious confederacy with which they had been allied. This passage seems to echo Ezekiel 16:35-41:

"Therefore, you prostitute, hear the word of the Lord! This is what the Sovereign Lord says: Because you poured out your wealth and exposed your nakedness in your promiscuity with your lovers, and because of all your detestable idols, and because you gave them your children's blood, therefore I am going to gather all your lovers, with whom you found pleasure, those you loved as well as those you hated. I will gather them against you from all around and will strip you in front of them, and they will see all your nakedness. I will sentence you to the punishment of women who commit adultery and who shed blood; I will bring upon you the blood vengeance of my wrath and jealous anger. Then I will hand you over to your lovers, and they will tear down your mounds and destroy your lofty shrines. They will strip you of your clothes and take your fine jewelry and leave you naked and bare. They will bring a mob against you, who will stone you and hack you to pieces with their swords. They will burn down your houses and inflict punishment on you in the sight of many women. I will put a stop to your prostitution, and you will no longer pay your lovers" (NIV).

Judah attempts to gain favor with the nations, but they turn on her. Note that the prostitute of Ezekiel 16 is stoned rather than burned. So Revelation does not follow its source text in every detail. Babylon, the daughter of a priest, is burned in it (see Lev. 21:9). And the agents of its destruction are the very powers that gave Babylon support earlier in the chapter.

This text seems to build somewhat on the psychology of lust. Often after lust is fulfilled, whether in rape or in "consensual sex," a changing of the mind occurs. A case in point is the story of Amnon and Tamar in 2 Samuel 13:1-19. Amnon and Tamar were both children of David, but by different mothers. Amnon "falls in love" with Tamar to such a degree that the narrative describes him as truly lovesick over her.

Upon the advice of a friend, he tricks the king into sending her to his house to nurse him in his "illness." When she arrives, he sends everyone else out, grabs hold of her, and rapes her, ignoring her protests. Then the account concludes, "The hatred with which he hated her was greater than the love with which he had loved her" (verse 15, ESV). In Revelation 17:16 we see the reaction of the kings of the earth when they come to see Babylon as the perpetrator of their defeat at the hands of the Lamb. The confederacy of political and military power destroys the religious confederacy that it had only recently supported with enthusiasm.

This "changing of the minds" is the literal counterpart of the drying up of the Euphrates River. In ancient times when the river dried up,

Babylon fell. So Revelation 17:16 is the final explanation of the sixth plague of Revelation 16. The drying up of the Euphrates once more signals Babylon's fall. When the political and military resources that had enabled Babylon to dominate the world get withdrawn, it ends up plundered by the very powers that had supported it. With Revelation 17:16 our study of the battle of Armageddon has come full circle and completes what we began in our examination of Revelation 16:12.

We need to consider an additional element here, however. Those familiar with the scenario of *The Great Controversy* will observe a great deal of similarity between that account of the end-time and the one in Revelation. But there is also one significant difference. Revelation 17 describes the final events from a global viewpoint. Ellen White portrays the final events from a local perspective.

In Revelation a worldwide political confederacy operates in behalf of a global religious confederacy. But at some point in the story the political confederacy has a change of heart and turns on the religious confederacy and destroys it. John sees all of this in the global perspective.

By way of contrast, *The Great Controversy* portrays the same events from a local perspective. The worldwide death decree of Revelation 13:15 is about to be implemented in a small town setting. The faithful people of God leave town and hide in the remotest places available. The local police, at the behest of the local religious leaders, move out at the appointed time to annihilate the people of God, perceived to be the source of all trouble in the world. The police find groups of people praying in their hideouts. But as they approach and raise their weapons, the police confront a "rainbow" of "light" that surrounds each praying company. The evident approval of God convinces the police that their local ministers and religious leaders have deceived them. Instead of carrying out the death decree, they return to town and attack the ministers. At that moment the great end-time deception stands unmasked.

"The people see that they have been deluded. They accuse one another of having led them to destruction; but all unite in heaping their bitterest condemnation upon the ministers. . . . 'We are lost!' they cry, 'and you are the cause of our ruin'; and they turn upon the false shepherds. The very ones that once admired them most will pronounce the most dreadful curses upon them. The very hands that once crowned them with laurels will be raised for their destruction. The swords which were to slay God's people are now employed to destroy their enemies" (*The Great Controversy,* pp. 655, 656).

The basic scenario is the same, but the respective venues of Revelation and *The Great Controversy* are different. The interplay of the people and their religious leaders in the latter is familiar from our study of Revelation, but the scene is localized. Rightly understood, the scenario of *The Great Controversy* is in complete harmony with the scenario of Revelation 16 and 17.

Let's finish with one last verse from Revelation 17. Still speaking of the 10 horns/kings, the text continues: "For God has put it into their hearts to accomplish his purpose by agreeing to give the beast their power to rule, until God's words are fulfilled" (verse 17, NIV).

The amazing truth at the end of the battle of Armageddon is that God is in full control of all events, even of the satanic deceptions (see also 2 Thess. 2:11). While events on earth certainly help precipitate the global confederacies, God's hand is in the shadows behind it all. The testimony of Revelation is that the temporary unity of the world's political and religious powers accomplishes God's purposes even while Satan uses the same events for his own.

In a way this makes a lot of sense. The principle of selfishness—of "every man for himself"—is the fundamental premise of Satan's kingdom. Such a principle leads not to unity but rather to chaos and anarchy. One of the hardest things Satan will ever try to do is to bring about a worldwide unity of all of his followers, whether secular or religious, whether committed or simply going along for the ride. Getting along and working together are not the kinds of things Satan has promoted through the centuries. And in the end such a unity will not occur at all without some intervention on the part of God. Even then it lasts only as long as it accomplishes God's purposes. The Lord uses the deception at the end to precipitate decisions in relation to the final proclamation of the gospel (2 Thess. 2:11).

We will conclude this book on the battle of Armageddon with some further reflections on current events and some spiritual lessons that we can draw from the battle for everyday living. You will find that material in chapter 11. But before we do that, I would like to review everything we have learned from Revelation and organize it into an organized sequence of events. My goal is that the outline in the next couple chapters will put all the pieces together in a coherent and easy-to-remember manner.

(10)

DUELING GOSPELS AND
WORLDWIDE CONFEDERACIES

I think it would be helpful to summarize briefly the order of the last events of earth's history as far as we can determine them on the basis of the book of Revelation alone. Rather than a chapter-by-chapter approach, I have grounded the order chosen in my perception of the sequence in which these events actually occur at the end of history. Since the book of Revelation does not have a linear format, but bounces back and forth in time as you work through the chapters, this outline should be a helpful way to summarize the battle of Armageddon as a whole. I will attempt to be as precise about the various events as the text allows, while taking care not to be more specific than the text permits. To overspecify the events of the end usually does more harm than good.

1. Worldwide Proclamation of the Gospel

Life has gone on for centuries since the time of the New Testament. Generation after generation has passed, many of them thinking that they were the last one of humanity. Many spectacular events occurred. Major wars have raged. Horrific storms, great earthquakes, famines, and pestilences have devastated the world. Yet none of these events has precipitated the end of the world. But one defining event will mark the shift from business as usual to the sequence of events that will truly lead to the conclusion of human history. Jesus predicted it in Matthew 24:14: "And this gospel of the kingdom will be preached in the whole world as a testimony to all nations, and then the end will come" (NIV). This text indicates that it is the worldwide proclamation of the gospel that precipitates the events of the end. While the book of Revelation is not as explicit, the global spread of the gospel is clearly central to the end-time narrative.

"Then I saw another angel flying in midair, and he had the eternal gospel to proclaim to those who live on the earth—to every nation, tribe, language and people. He said in a loud voice, 'Fear God and give him glory, because the hour of his judgment has come. Worship him who made the heavens, the earth, the sea, and the springs of water'" (Rev. 14:6, 7, NIV).

In the book of Revelation the three angels, who represent the remnant of the woman's seed (Rev. 12:17), give the eternal or everlasting gospel. The remnant comes at the end of time. The remnant of a carpet is like the rest of the roll—it is not totally new or totally different from the previous carpet. In the same way, the end-time remnant will be in continuity with the faithful people of God throughout the ages.

The remnant at the end, however, will have a unique mission and identity that will unfold in the run-up to the final events of earth's history. In the third volume of this series I intend to explore the mission, message, and identity of the end-time remnant (or the confederacy of the saints, as I have called it in this book) in more depth. While the remnant's mission will be unique, its message will be based in the New Testament gospel of the life, death, and resurrection of Jesus. It will be grounded in the gospel but uniquely packaged for the end-time.

Revelation 14:7 summarizes the end-time version of the gospel in three statements: Fear God, give Him glory, and worship Him. "*Fear God, and give glory to him; for the hour of his judgment has come: and worship him* that made heaven, and earth, and the sea, and the fountains of waters" (verse 7).

The reference to judgment is not the main point of the verse. In the Greek it is a subordinate clause ("for" or "because" the hour of His judgment has come). Rather, the final remnant presents the gospel at the end in the context of a pre-Advent judgment, giving it a unique flavor and urgency.

The Fear of God

To fear God means, above all, to take Him seriously in your life, to make Him your ultimate priority. This message is especially relevant for the times in which we live. We are so overscheduled, rushing from one activity to another, that placing God central in our lives is truly a challenge.

Because of the countless distractions we easily become casual about our relationship with Him, even though we may have all the theological knowledge we think we need. The gospel of the end-time will put God first, no matter what the cost to our personal agendas.

In the Old Testament the "fear of the Lord" was a common expression, particularly in the poetic writings of the psalms and the prophets. Hebrew poetry did not express itself in rhymes—instead it made use of rhythm and the paralleling of ideas to charm the ear. Notice the rhythm and parallel ideas of Proverbs 9:10:

"The fear of the Lord is the beginning of wisdom,

and knowledge of the Holy One is understanding" (NIV).

Even in English, the words have a beautiful rhythm, don't they? But notice the parallelism of ideas. Obviously the main verb is the same in both lines: "is." The latter part of the first line, "the beginning of wisdom," is echoed in the second line by the word "understanding." That means that "the fear of the Lord" is a parallel idea to "knowledge of the Holy One." To fear the Lord is to know Him, to have a living relationship with Him. Other texts parallel the "fear of the Lord" with "keeping the commandments" and "avoiding evil" (Ps. 111:10; Prov. 3:7; 16:6). So the Old Testament concept of the fear of the Lord has rich meaning for those who want to live by the message of Revelation 14:7. It means to know God personally, to be obedient to His will, and to avoid actions that would harm our relationship with Him or with others. We take Him seriously in everything that we do.

To take God seriously, therefore, involves an element of accountability. We live our lives in the consciousness of our relationship with Him. Aware of His presence, we constantly speak with Him and listen to Him. All our decisions in life we will make on the basis of an awareness of judgment, a consciousness that everything we do matters, even if no human on earth knows about it. God does, though, and it all matters to Him. So God's end-time people will be as faithful inside as they are outside. Always authentic, they will live with a godly sense of "fear." In the biblical sense that means awe, respect, taking God seriously in all we do.

Many people don't like accountability—they feel that it "cramps their style." They resent other people telling them what to do. But the reality is that very little of usefulness gets accomplished in this life without accountability. Let me give you an example. Suppose I decide to go jogging at 6:00 a.m. in the morning. What are the chances that I will get up without hesitation at 5:45 a.m.? Very little. But suppose I agree to meet a friend at the corner at 6:00 a.m. Now I find myself thinking, *Joe is counting on me to be there—I'd better get going.* So I climb out of bed and meet my friend to go jogging. It doesn't matter that Joe had the same thoughts. We both made it to the corner, and we both accomplished the task thanks to our accountability with each other.

The same can happen with accountability to God. We know that God is present—that He reads our hearts. So we can make a covenant with Him to do whatever challenging thing we know He wants us to get done. And the consciousness of His watching eye motivates us to get up and get doing whatever assignment we have both agreed upon. In the last days of earth's history God's people will be all the more focused on His will and His ways, and accountability to Him will be a powerful motivator toward doing what needs to be done.

I realize that the above concept of the gospel will be hard for some to accept. Your own personal history may have included physical, emotional, or sexual abuse. Abuse may even have happened in a church context or in relation to a pastor or teacher. Authority figures of any kind, even spiritual ones, can become repugnant to you in light of such a past. Accountability may be the last thing that you feel you need. My response to you would be that I fully understand. The message of accountability to God may not be what you need right now. The thought that God sees every action might drive you to unhealthy behaviors.

If the above is true in your life, let this message go for right now. Rest in the assurance of God's love. Read my book *Meet God Again for the First Time* if you are unclear in regard to how He saves people like you. The Lord is neither a tyrant nor a spiritual abuser. He cares about you more than you do about yourself. When you are ready for a deeper walk with Him, He will gently lead you there. Just don't settle for a diminished life because things have been hard for you. Study the Gospels and books such as *Steps to Christ* and *Meet God Again*. Seek out healthy mentors who can help you untangle confused and negative thoughts. Attend a small group salted with mentally healthy and stable people. Visit a counselor and pour out the things you can't even tell to God right now (see *The Desire of Ages,*

p. 297). Know that there is a higher goal for your life in these end-times and spend much time in prayer for readiness to know the truth and to follow wherever God may lead.

Give God Glory

To give God glory also requires that we put Him first in every thought and action. But the concept "glory of God" has some unique twists in Scripture worth exploring. "Glory" of course has a primary meaning of radiance or splendor. A monster fireworks display in New York City or Disney World is "glorious." Some of Ellen White's dazzling views of the throne room of God repeatedly provoked her to exclaim, "Glory."

More to the point for us, however, is a secondary meaning of the term, one having to do with such things as honor, praise, and pride. By nature all of us "glory" in ourselves. We glory in the things we possess—that new house, new car, or new surround sound system. We glory in our achievements, our Ph.D.s, our careers, our baptisms, our athletic accomplishments (even if 30 years ago!). And some of us, of course, glory a great deal in the size (or alleged size) of the fish that we have caught! We glory in whom we know, our successful children, and celebrities we may have seen or briefly spoken to. We glory in anything that makes us look better in comparison with others.

So when it comes to giving glory to God, the basic meaning is to ground our pride and joy not in ourselves and the things we have done, but in what God has done for us. To glory in our possessions, our performance, or the people we know is to lean on a broken stick. The circumstances of life can suddenly remove any of them. The one thing that nothing can take away from us is the objective reality of what God has done for us in Christ. It is a concept clearly taught in the Scriptures:

"Thus saith the Lord,
Let not the wise man *glory* in his wisdom,
neither let the mighty man *glory* in his might,
let not the rich man *glory* in his riches:
But let him that glorieth *glory* in this,
that he understandeth and knoweth me" (Jer. 9:23, 24).

Tragically, it is perfectly natural for sinful human beings to focus on their own riches, their own wisdom, their own strength. We are constantly playing "one-up" games with others to demonstrate that we are somehow smarter or stronger or have better toys than the next person. But concentrating on our own wisdom, strength, or material possessions distracts us from the only thing that will prepare us for the events of the end-time. True and lasting peace can come only when we focus outside of ourselves. Paul expressed this in one of his most powerful "sound bites": "God forbid that I should *glory*, save in the cross of our Lord Jesus Christ, by whom the world is crucified unto me, and I unto the world" (Gal. 6:14).

I have deliberately used the King James Version for these last two texts, in spite of the archaic style, because it preserves the consistent use of the original languages here. Both Greek and Hebrew use the word "glory" with reference to that in which people find their "pride and joy." The things we talk about excitedly, the things that run constantly through our minds, the things that motivate us—those are the things that we "glory" in.

According to Revelation 14:6, 7, the final proclamation of the gospel will underline the component of glory. God's end-time people will be focused on Him and what He has done, rather than on themselves and what they have or have not accomplished. The gospel—even the end-time gospel—is all about Him, not about us. We glorify God when we trust in Him for salvation, rather than in our own pitiful attempts to add something to what He has already done. And we glorify God when we believe His Word and when we rest in His finished work, as Abraham did. To glorify God is to accept the message of justification by faith in verity (see *Evangelism,* p. 90, and *Selected Messages,* book 1, p. 372).

" For if Abraham were justified by works, he hath whereof to *glory*; but not before God. For what saith the scripture? Abraham believed God, and it was counted unto him for righteousness. Now to him that worketh is the reward not reckoned of grace, but of debt. But to him that worketh not, but believeth on him that justifieth the ungodly, his faith is counted for righteousness" (Rom. 4:2-5).

But this "glory" business has an added dimension. At a couple crucial points Paul points out that we can glorify God not only with our mouths or in the things that we think about, but also with our bodies. We can glorify God (or not) with what we do and even through eating and drinking. "So whether you eat or drink or whatever you do, do it all for the *glory* of God" (1 Cor. 10:31, NIV). If we are truly conscious of Him in our lives and grateful that He has made us and has provided us with gifts and talents, then everything that we do matters, even what we put into our bodies. God's end-time people will care about what they eat and drink. They will take time for sunshine, exercise, fresh air, and adequate rest. Always they will be aware that others will judge God by the way they look and the way they behave.

"Or do you not know that your body is a temple of the Holy Spirit within you, whom you have from God? You are not your own, for you were bought with a price. So *glorify* God in your body" (1 Cor. 6:19, 20, ESV).

Paul makes his point in the context of a discussion of whether or not it is appropriate for Christians to consort with prostitutes. The apostle clearly indicates that sexual sin compounds the failure to bring glory to God, because it engages two individuals, not just one. It demonstrates spiritual confusion because it implies that the same person can glorify God with mouth or hand, yet use another part of the body to glorify self and exploit others. What we do with our bodies matters a great deal to God, and it has a powerful impact on who we are and what we become.

Whenever a minister or a TV preacher is found to be practicing the very things that he or she preaches against, it is God and His church that take the biggest hit. Secular people conclude from such things that Christian faith is ultimately a sham and that God does not really change lives and transform communities of people. When we use our sexuality for self-gratification we deny our own profession of faith and bring God's name into disrepute. What we do in response to the gospel matters a great deal. We can glorify God with our bodies.

I remember leading an Adventist tour group in a Muslim country a few years ago. The bus had on it 37 Adventists and two chain-smoking Muslims (the driver and the tour guide). On the second day of the journey the entire group got sick with some intestinal virus that also produced a high fever. The sickness rolled back and forth through the bus for nearly 10 days, while the driver and the guide remained completely unaffected. The tour group became so grumpy that the guide repeatedly threatened to abandon the tour. What impression of Adventists do you suppose the driver and guide took away from that tour?

Perfect health is certainly not an option in this life. We are beset with toxic waste, pollution, and the stress of an Internet world. Nevertheless, God's end-time people will live in such a way that others will notice a difference—a positive difference! Do you feel as though you are not there yet? I don't feel that I am either. But it is well to keep a vision of God's purpose before us—it helps to keep us focused on the goal.

Worshipping God

The end-time message of the gospel will also include a call to worship the One who created all things. In *What the Bible Says About the End-time* I show how this concept relates to the Sabbath. The gospel continues to be all about Him and not about us. We worship Him in full obedience to all His commandments with a special focus on the Sabbath as a test of the lengths to which we as God's people are willing to go in our commitment to Him. We choose to worship Him in the way that He requires because it is all about Him and not about us. Avoiding counterfeits, we will focus in detail on all that God calls us to do. And we will do so even at great cost to ourselves.

I recently returned from a speaking engagement in Guam, a beautiful island in the western Pacific. There I met Steve. Steve is the owner and manager of the best-known beach club on the island. He offers visitors such waterfront experiences as Jet Skiing, parasailing, dolphin watching, and snorkeling. When confronted with the truth about the Sabbath, he realized that Saturday was the busiest day of the week for his business. And it was also the day people signed up for Sunday, the second-busiest day. So he would be losing the two highest revenue days every week, and he was already millions of dollars in debt. It was likely that if he closed on Sabbath his business would go bankrupt and he would have to let all of his employees go. He reasoned that it was not fair to them to be so heavily affected by his own personal decision.

But under the conviction of the Spirit he decided to trust God and close his business on Sabbaths. Informing the major beach hotels of his decision, he received only derision and a complete cutoff of their business— and they had been its main source! Nevertheless, he moved ahead. That Friday night he closed the business, turned the lights out, and left the answering machine on. That Sabbath had the worst weather Guam had seen in some time! When he checked the phone on Saturday night, he was amazed to find scores of reservations for Sunday. Way above the norm! The same weather pattern continued every weekend for six months. The weather on Sabbath was terrible, and on Sunday it was beautiful. With his spirit of service and caring concern for people filtering down through his employees, his beach club not only did not fail—it became the dominant player in the local market!

I saw this with my own eyes. Every time one of his boats came to the dock, a long line of people waiting to get on quickly filled it. At the same time I noticed that the boats of his competitors were never full. They often had only two or three people on them (Steve's boats were carrying a dozen people at a time for parasailing and other water sports). It was obvious that his operation was uniquely blessed.

But what if his business had failed? What if he had gone bankrupt? Steve is still convinced that the only way to happiness and peace is through the gospel of Jesus Christ and through a response to that gospel that includes full obedience to all of God's commandments. It is better to have nothing of this world than to lose what you have in Christ. Such was the spirit of the martyrs. Steve has gotten a taste, not only of the end-time gospel commitment, but of the power of a Creator God to make something out of nothing!

Other Gospel Texts in Revelation

Revelation 14:6, 7 is not the only place in the book that makes reference to a final proclamation of the gospel. Revelation 16:15, as we have seen, echoes the message to Laodicea (Rev. 3:17, 18). At the very end of time there will be a call to authenticity and full readiness for the second coming of Jesus. The four angels of Revelation 7:1-4 hold back the winds of strife so that the final sealing message can make its way around the world. In the last moments of our world's history the "mystery of God" will be brought to completion (Rev. 10:6, 7). The two witnesses of Revelation present a message that causes people to fear God and give Him glory just before the close of probation (Rev. 11:11-13). And finally a mighty angel lights the whole world with the glory of God just before the end (Rev. 18:1).

So the concept of a final proclamation of the gospel before the close of probation is a major theme throughout the book of Revelation. One could even add Revelation 1:4-7, in which strong references to the death, resurrection, and heavenly reign of Christ precede a mention of His second coming. The whole book of Revelation is about the gospel in the context of the events just before the end.

The result of the final gospel proclamation is a worldwide confederacy of the saints, known as the remnant (Rev. 12:17); the 144,000 (Rev. 7:1-8 and 14:1-5); the great multitude (Rev. 7:9-17 and 19:1); the saints (Rev. 13:7; 14:12); the called, chosen, and faithful followers of the Lamb (Rev. 17:14); and the watchful ones who hang on to their garments (Rev. 16:15; 3:17, 18), which have been washed in the blood of the Lamb (Rev. 7:15-17; 19:7, 8). This multitude of images portray the one people of God at the end of time.

How does the gospel come to universal attention at the end? Is there some new twist, some theological detail about the gospel overlooked until then? I rather doubt it. Many people and groups claim that if only you taught it their way everything would be different. Yet those various twists haven't changed the world. If we accept the assertion of the New Testament that it presents the full and final form of the gospel (Rom. 16:25-27; Eph. 3:1-7), then it is not a new gospel that we need but one presented in the context of a new situation at the end. The decisive turn in the world's interest will occur because of God's overruling of events. He will bring things to the point where the New Testament gospel and the people who proclaim it will become the center of the world's attention (Rev. 10:11; 14:6). While it is not at the focus of the world's interest now, it will be then, and God's people need to be prepared to deliver such a message with power and clarity.

2. Worldwide Proclamation of a Counterfeit Gospel

The book of Revelation also teaches us that a worldwide proclamation of a counterfeit gospel (Rev. 9:14-16; 16:13, 14) will occur at the end. This counterfeit will be the great deception of the unholy trinity (Rev. 13). It seeks to confuse those who hear the true gospel as to just where the truth lies. The two proclamations go out to the world side by side. The preaching of the true gospel is the context in which the end-time deception functions (see Matt. 24:24-27 in the context of verse 14 and 2 Thess. 2:8-12).

We find references to Satan's counterfeit in a number of contexts besides that of Revelation 13. The counterpart of Revelation 10:7 and 11:11-13 is the fearful picture of the sixth trumpet (Rev. 9:13-21). The description of the grotesque army of the sixth trumpet is just as military as the battle of Armageddon, yet its mission is clearly in the context of faith and unfaith. This army of 200 million is the spiritual counterpart of the 144,000 (compare Rev. 9:13-16 with Rev. 7:1-4). It operates at the same point in history, attempting to draw people away from the true gospel.

As a result of its activities many perish, and the "remnant" (Rev. 9:20, 21), the "rest" of humanity, refuses to repent. The unrepentant remnant stands in clear contrast with the "remnant" of Revelation 11:13, which does repent and gives glory to God. So the double action during the sixth trumpet (which runs from Revelation 9:12 to 11:14) produces a contrasting result: people who repent and people who do not. The worldwide counterfeit of the gospel is at work in the sixth trumpet.

Revelation first identifies the counterfeit trinity. Revelation 16 specifies it as the dragon, beast, and false prophet (verse 13). They send out three unclean spirits like frogs as "gospel messengers." The spirits go out to the same world as the true gospel of the three angels (Rev. 16:13, 14; cf. 14:6). The book of Revelation signals the actions of the counterfeit gospel, therefore, by contrasting groups of angels. Four angels release the forces of evil from the Euphrates River (Rev. 9:14, 15) and four angels seek to restrain them and spread the sealing message of the true gospel (Rev. 7:1-3). Three demonic angels gather the kings of the world in Revelation 16:13, 14 and three divine angels present God's last-day message in Revelation 14:6-12.

To some degree the worldwide counterfeit of the gospel also shows up in the fornication and intoxication mentioned in Revelation 17:2. At its first appearance the false gospel has as its purpose the bringing together of a coalition of religious institutions. But even when this has occurred many institutions, nations, and groups still resist the aims of the religious confederacy. So the continued proclamation of the false gospel will seduce or at least confuse the kings and the inhabitants of the earth (a matter that we will explore shortly).

The counterfeit proclamation produces a worldwide confederacy of religion in opposition to the true God. As we have seen earlier, the book of Revelation applies many names to it: the dragon, beast, and false prophet (unholy trinity—Rev. 16:13); prostitute Babylon (Rev. 17:1-6); city Babylon (Rev. 17:18 and 18); and the great city (Rev. 11:8; 16:19; 17; 18). The promulgation of a false gospel will succeed in convincing the religious institutions of the world that they have more interests in common than they have separating them. If nothing else, they will have a common goal in thwarting the confederacy of the saints, whose gospel exposes the illegitimacy of false religion and its passion to serve God in ways that glorify human pride and power instead of God.

"There is need of a much closer study of the Word of God; especially should Daniel and the Revelation have attention as never before in the history of our work. . . . The Holy Spirit has so shaped matters, both in the giving of the prophecy and in the events portrayed, as to teach that *the human agent is to be kept out of sight, hid in Christ*, and that *the Lord God of heaven and His law are to be exalted*. Read the book of Daniel. Call up, point by point, the history of the kingdoms there represented. Behold statesmen, councils, powerful armies, and *see how God wrought to abase the pride of men, and lay human glory in the dust*" (Ellen G. White, *Testimonies to Ministers*, p. 112; italics supplied).

An interesting parallel to this concept in Revelation is that of the "mystery of iniquity" in 2 Thessalonians 2. The mystery of iniquity is the proclamation of a counterfeit gospel throughout the Christian age (cf. *The Seventh-day Adventist Bible Commentary,* vol. 7, pp. 269-271). It is restrained for a time (verses 2, 3, 6, 7), much as the angels of Revelation 7 hold back the four winds. But the restraint is removed at the end (verse 7), and the full power of the counterfeit gospel manifests itself (verses 9-12). The events surrounding the second coming of Jesus bring it to an end (verses 8, 9). Those interested in a more thorough exploration of Paul's little apocalypse (verses 1-12) should read the chapter on it in my book *What the Bible Says About the End-Time.*

Now in this order of events I have listed the proclamation of the true gospel first and that of a counterfeit second. While the texts themselves are not perfectly clear on this, it is my sense that the true revival comes first and the counterfeit follows behind it. One could argue that the counterfeit anticipates the true, but it seems to me that it is only in the context of the true gospel that the spread of the false makes any sense. You can only truly have a counterfeit when there is something genuine to counterfeit.

Even if it is not clear in Revelation, the priority of the gospel seems clearly taught in other parts of the New Testament. It is the proclamation of the gospel to the entire world (Matt. 24:14) that precipitates the deceptions of the end (verses 23-27) in Jesus' end-time sermon. The opportunity to be saved (2 Thess. 2:10) sets the context for the removal of restraint

DUELING GOSPELS AND WORLDWIDE CONFEDERACIES

and the full-blown deception of 2 Thessalonians 2:7-9. When the true gospel becomes headline news throughout the world, the evil one will marshal all of his wiles in the attempt to counteract and defeat it. His counterattack is front-row center in the battle of Armageddon.

As the two "gospels" accomplish their work two worldwide confederacies emerge into view: the confederacy of the saints and the confederacy of religion. The confederacy of the saints is the spiritual result of the true gospel working in people's hearts. Kindred spirits from every nation, tribe, language, and religion will reach out to one another, finding common cause in a world gone mad. In reaction to their loss of power and influence, the religious institutions of the world will seek to counter this development with a plausible but flawed substitute. That, along with a few threats, will provide the setting for a worldwide unity of religious institutions, something that has never truly happened before. The saints may not be visible as an organized body on earth, but God will certainly know them. The worldwide confederacy of religion, on the other hand, will be much more public and obvious.

What will this counterfeit be like, according to Revelation? Certainly it will not be teaching obedience to all of God's commandments. Obedience to the commandments of God is a defining difference between the followers of the true gospel and those of the counterfeit. In addition to such things as Sunday laws, there could be restrictions on Sabbath worship, requirements to do certain business on Saturdays, or perhaps even a spiritually sounding alternative—"keep every day as if it were a Sabbath" (but try to do that while earning a living!).

In addition, the most powerful counterfeit of the gospel has always been salvation by works. At the foundation of every pagan religion (see Ellen G. White, *The Desire of Ages*, p. 35) is the requirement to pacify a god who is, at best, needing to be persuaded that you are worth paying attention to. At their worst, pagan gods are malicious and demand constant appeasing in order for humans to survive. What a horrific way to live! And yet in many ways Christians treat God as if He cannot be trusted. No matter how clearly the gospel describes His prior actions in our behalf, we still respond as if we must earn our way into His favor. We fear that no matter what we do, He will never forgive someone as wretched as we are. So we go to church, give alms, and do good works, hoping against hope that

God might decide to be merciful and forgive our sins. And in the process, we unintentionally call Him a liar, for He has promised to forgive all who confess their condition (1 John 1:9).

So the end-time counterfeit of the gospel will include some form of works righteousness, the idea that unless you perform certain rituals or go to certain human mediators or pay a certain price, or join a particular group, you cannot receive favor with God. Human behavior becomes the condition for acceptance with Him, not the mighty power of God manifested in the life, death, and resurrection of Jesus Christ.

But isn't the Sabbath a form of works righteousness? How can the true gospel exalt both obedience to the commandments and salvation by faith alone? That is the tension that must be preserved in order for the gospel to be rightly understood. We are saved by faith alone, but saving faith is never alone. A transformed life demonstrates true saving faith. It is not the change of life, however, that delivers us—it is the work of God that saves us. The changed life is simply a grateful response to what God has already done for us.

Think about it this way: If we were saved by works in any sort of way, then all of our good deeds, all of our loving-kindness, all of our Sabbathkeeping, all of our service to God, would ultimately be self-centered acts. We would be doing all of that *in order to* become right with God. Our obedience would have a self-centered purpose. And the root of all sin is selfishness.

But when we realize that we are saved by grace through the redemption that is in Christ Jesus (Rom. 3:24, 25) and that even our best deeds will never be good enough to save us (verse 23; 4:1-5), then our acts of goodness and service become the living evidence that we *are* saved by the mighty prior action of God. Our works no longer have a selfish motive, because we realize that they themselves get us nowhere! We do good works for others because we are learning to love them the way God does. And we keep Sabbath and worship God because of an overflowing gratitude for all He has done. Our works become a reaction instead of a primary action. As a result, our salvation is no longer about us—it is about Him!

So observing the Sabbath is not necessary to win God's favor. Rather, it is the grateful reaction of one who knows the deeds that matter most have already been done in Christ. The Sabbath becomes a rest from our foolish attempts to earn favor with God—it is a resting in His works rather than in our own (Heb. 4:9-11). Furthermore, the Sabbath is no longer about what we do, but about what God has done. When we know these things, observing Sabbath becomes a delight rather than a burden.

3. Formation of a Worldwide Political Unity

The third development in the end-time sequence of events is the establishment of a worldwide secular and political unity that will create a true "united nations" for the first time in world history (Rev. 16:12; 17:1, 15, 12, 13). This parallel event to the formation of two religious confederacies goes by many names in Revelation. The book represents it by the Euphrates River (Rev. 16:12; 17:15); the kings of the whole inhabited world (Rev. 16:14); many waters (Rev. 17:1, 15); the kings of the earth (Rev. 17:2; 18:3-9); the earth dwellers or inhabitants of the earth (Rev. 13:12 and 17:2, among others); the beast (Rev. 17); the 10 horns (Rev. 17); the cities of the nations (Rev. 16:19); seven mountains (Rev. 17:9); and seven kings (verse 10). When this political confederacy is complete, the world will have three great global confederacies, each symbolized in a variety of ways in Revelation, illustrated as follows:

Saints	Political	Babylon
Remnant	Euphrates	Babylon
144,000	Kings of World	
Great Crowd	Many Waters	The Great City
Kings of East	Kings of Earth	
Watchful	Earth Dwellers	The Great
Clothed	Beast	Prostitute
Called	10 Horns	
Chosen	Cities of the Nations	The Unholy Trinity
Faithful	Seven Mountains	Woman
	Seven Kings	

The book of Revelation does not spell out the development of the political unity in much detail. The use of seven-headed, 10-horned beast imagery indicates that it stands in the heritage of the earlier world empires seen in Daniel 7 and in Revelation 12 and 13: Egypt, Assyria, Babylon, Persia, and Greece (Rev. 17:10, 11). For a more comprehensive look at the details of Revelation 17:10, 11, see the appendix at the end of this book.

The confederacy emerges in at least two stages. It is fully viable only when a significant subgroup of 10 kings decides to join and support the rest of the beast. "The ten horns you saw are ten kings who have not yet received a kingdom, but who for one hour will receive authority as kings along with the beast. They have one purpose and will give their power and authority to the beast" (verses 12, 13, NIV). Many would like to be far more specific on such topics than I have chosen to be in here, but ultraspecific applications to the present or immediate future have led to many embarrassing inaccuracies of interpretation. While texts such as Revelation 17:12, 13 do not give us enough detail to know in advance exactly how things will work out, they do provide sufficient information for us to recognize these realities when they do arrive. It is critical that God's people know the prophecies about the future even if it is difficult to apply them to specific events in advance. We are assured, however, that if we know the text, we will recognize the major movements when they surface (John 13:19; 14:29). Note the words of Jesus Himself: "I am telling you this now, before it takes place, that *when it does take place* you may believe that I am he" (John 13:19, ESV).

Jesus does not promise that prophecy (speaking specifically of His own words here) would give the disciples a detailed, unmistakable outline of events ahead of time. He did assure them, however, that when the actual events took place, they would be able to discern the times and have the kind of faith needed to survive spiritually. God sends prophecy in order, not to satisfy our curiosity about the future, but to help us develop the kind of faith we need in the present.

While the worldwide confederacy of nations certainly participates in Satan's scheme for the end, it is also part of God's plan and action. In fact, the Lord Himself precipitates this end-time version of the United Nations. "For God has put it into their hearts to accomplish his purpose by agreeing to give the beast their power to rule, until God's words are fulfilled" (Rev. 17:17, NIV).

DUELING GOSPELS AND WORLDWIDE CONFEDERACIES

God is in full control of events from beginning to end: He arranges things in such a way as to bring global attention to the gospel; He monitors Satan and His agents as they put in place the great end-time counterfeit of the gospel; and He precipitates the end-time political confederacy as well. Revelation 17:17 views events from the worldwide perspective. In 2 Thessalonians 2, on the other hand, Paul takes a more individualized approach (verses 9-12). The apostle implies that there are three groups of people: (1) those who love the truth, (2) those who hate the truth, and (3) those sitting on the fence. His three individual categories correspond to the three great worldwide confederacies of Revelation. One group loves the truth (the saints), a second hates the truth (religious institutions), and the third is reluctant to commit to one or the other (the nations). And God is in control of the whole process: "For this reason God sends them a powerful delusion so that they will believe the lie" (verse 11, NIV). It is the battle over the third category (the political-secular group that neither loves nor hates the truth) that provides the context for the final chapters of the battle of Armageddon.

The first three steps in the order of final events, therefore, are the development of three great global confederacies. It is clear that we are not now (at the time I am writing) in the process of these events, because none of the three factions are currently in place, although all three may well be in process. In a sense the first three developments of the final events will take place in parallel lines, so the sequence that I have placed these developments in is probable but not certain. Media observers may well notice the political currents before they sense the religious ones, for example, but according to the scenario of Revelation the decisive movements are the religious ones.

So it is my educated guess that the final worldwide proclamation of the gospel (under the guidance and arrangement of God) precipitates the worldwide counterfeit as a reaction. Somewhere in the course of this process an increasing collection of national alliances leads closer and closer to a global unity of nations. When all three confederacies are in place, astute observers of prophecy may well discern that the final events are in motion. But even if they do not, they will certainly realize that they are living in decisive times. Times in which people are making life-and-death decisions.

The final outcome of Armageddon will be a surprise to many.

Ω

THE CONCLUSION OF THE BATTLE

4. A Decisive Moment of Final Decision

As the two gospels advance into the world, one of them true and faithful, the other a carefully crafted counterfeit, the world finds itself brought to a moment of final decision. People must make up their minds whether to follow the comfortable traditions of Babylon or the compelling, but radical truths of the end-time remnant. We see this moment highlighted in quite a number of texts in Revelation. One of them makes it clear that life-and-death issues are at stake.

"A second angel followed and said, 'Fallen! Fallen is Babylon the Great, which made all the nations drink the maddening wine of her adulteries.' A third angel followed them and said in a loud voice: 'If anyone worships the beast and his image and receives his mark on the forehead or on the hand, he, too, will drink of the wine of God's fury, which has been poured full strength into the cup of his wrath. He will be tormented with burning sulfur in the presence of the holy angels and of the Lamb. And the smoke of their torment rises for ever and ever. There is no rest day or night for those who worship the beast and his image, or for anyone who receives the mark of his name.' This calls for patient endurance on the part of the saints who obey God's commandments and remain faithful to Jesus" (Rev. 14:8-12, NIV).

Here is very strong language, disturbing to many readers of this book. How can the Lamb, the symbol of everything good and kind and noble, the symbol of Jesus Christ, preside over such a scene of torture and anguish? How can the Lamb be, on the one hand, the victim of violence and on the other hand the one who torments and destroys?

What people often overlook is that any truly good government must at some point exercise violence in order to restrain evil. Governmental violence is not always graphic and bloody, of course. It may simply involve the kind of restraint that occurs when a policeman pulls you over at a speed trap or the IRS sends an agent to audit your tax records. You don't consider that violence? Well, let me ask you some questions. How fast would you drive if police did not exist? How much tax would you pay if it were voluntary? And how eager are most convicts to stay in jail? Good governments provide a necessary restraint so we can all live together in peace. After all, not all citizens consider what is good for others when they act.

Most people are used to this level of governmental violence. When dealing with an Adolf Hitler or a Saddam Hussein, however, just violence becomes necessarily more brutal. Oppression demands justice (Rev. 6:9-11; 16:6; 18:7, 8), but evil never gives way voluntarily. The greater the power and brutality of evil, the more force required to undo that evil.

The images of Revelation are not pretty, but they assure us that God will do whatever it takes to end violence and oppression. The fact that divine violence occurs in the presence of the Lamb does not mean He enjoys horrific images. It rather indicates that the one who has suffered much has been placed in charge of the process. While God's violence is necessary, the Lamb oversees and limits it. Only the Lamb fully understands the cost of suffering. And only the Lamb can be trusted to be merciful in the exercise of divine justice. Yes, suffering will result from divine justice, but not one iota more than necessary.

What this text brings out is that the end-time decision will not be an easy one. Those attracted to the gospel will face the threats and intimidation of Babylon (Rev. 13:15-17). On the other hand, those choosing the "easy" path will ultimately find it even harder than the first. There will be cries of anguish and songs of regret.

And the final proclamation of the gospel will affect more than just the less-religious among the nations. It will reach deep into Babylon itself and call many honest-hearted souls out of her (Rev. 18:4). The confederacy of religion will remain intact and grow even more powerful, but it will also lose many to the charms of the gospel. While the end-time Mount Carmel experience will be highly persuasive, many will find the deception too convincing, too smooth, and they will explore the gospel alternative under the conviction of the Spirit. They will yield themselves to the love of the truth and will take hold of it, no matter what the cost in earthly terms (2 Thess. 2:10-12).

But in spite of these losses, Babylon succeeds in winning over the bulk of those who live among the nations (Rev. 16:13-16). In the previous chapter we illustrated the activities of stage 4 of the final events in the following way:

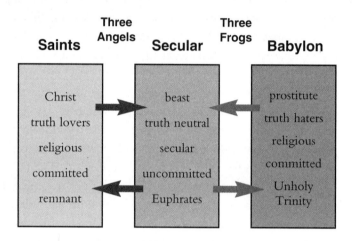

As we have seen, this decision process has been going on for a long time—all the way back to New Testament times (2 Cor. 10:3-5). Those who seek to follow Jesus have always endured a battle inside their minds, have always struggled to deal with their own pride, and have always faced the strongholds of Satan within themselves. That battle is a universal one. But the book of Revelation moves us forward to the final and most decisive spiritual battle of all time in Revelation 16 and 17. The battle of Armageddon is a struggle for the mind!

Until this moment the majority of the people on earth have not committed themselves to either side in the worldwide religious polarization. While those who present the gospel may appear weak and contemptible in human terms, God will empower their proclamation. "Come out of her, my people, so that you will not share in her sins, so that you will not receive any of her plagues" (Rev. 18:4, NIV). Revelation 11:13 makes it clear that many of those in Babylon will respond favorably. This final "remnant" could even become a majority, at least in some segments of Babylon:

"And after three days and an half the spirit of life from God entered into them, and they stood upon their feet; and great fear fell upon them which saw them. And they heard a great voice from heaven saying unto them, Come up hither. And they ascended up to heaven in a cloud; and their enemies beheld them. And the same hour was there a great earthquake, and the tenth part of the city fell, and in the earthquake were slain of men seven thousand: and *the remnant were affrighted, and gave glory to the God of heaven*" (Rev. 11:11-13).

I have chosen the King James Version once more because it rightly translates the word "remnant" here. The two witnesses of Revelation 11 are slain and then resurrected. They seem to represent Scripture on the one hand, and the proclamation of that Scripture by the people of God on the other. So the resurrection of the two witnesses and their ascension to heaven is a symbolic way to describe the final presentation of the gospel just before the close of probation (signaled by the sounding of the seventh trumpet in verse 15; cf. Rev. 10:7). Combined with powerful supporting actions by God (the great earthquake) this final work of the gospel succeeds, causing the "remnant" (90 percent of the "great city"; cf. verse 8) to become "affrighted" and give "glory to the God of heaven."

If you can get past the peculiar translation "affrighted" you will notice that it is exactly the response called for by the three angels of Revelation 14. "Fear God and give him glory" is the final call of God to the human race (Rev. 14:7, NIV). In fact, we find those who gain the victory at the very end described in exactly the same terms as those used in Revelation 11:13:

"And they sing the song of Moses, the servant of God, and the song of the Lamb, saying, 'Great and amazing are your deeds, O Lord God the Almighty! Just and true are your ways, O King of the nations! *Who will not fear, O Lord, and glorify your name?* For you alone are holy. All nations will come and worship you, for your righteous acts have been revealed'" (Rev. 15:3, 4, ESV).

So in this final moment of decision Babylon will lose large numbers, even majorities in some locations. It will greatly encourage those who proclaim the gospel in those days. No matter how hard the work seems to be, the results at the end will transcend expectation, and they will no doubt occur in places thought the most unlikely for success. We should never, therefore, limit ourselves to the parts of the world in which success comes easy. God has a plan for the hard places as well, and He longs for more people who will have the courage to press on when results are few. Prophecy does more than talk about the future—it gives us courage to do the right thing today, even if it is unpopular or seems unwise.

But while Babylon will suffer losses, it still has many tricks up its sleeve. The unholy trinity has great power: the persuasive eloquence of the three frogs, whose job it is to gather the nations; the miraculous, deceptive spectaculars of the false Mount Carmel; the great counterfeit of the Second Coming (2 Thess. 2:8, 9); the very impersonation of Jesus at one point in the conflict (verse 9; Acts 2:22); and, when all else fails, threat and coercion (Rev. 13:15-17).

At this stage of the final events, therefore, two great religious unities spread across the entire world and seek to win over the uncommitted to their side. They send out the three angels of Revelation 14 on the one hand, and the three frogs of Revelation 16 on the other. Those who receive the messages of the three angels unite with God and the true gospel. But those who respond to the three frogs join with Babylon in one of two ways—directly (by accepting its spiritual claims) or indirectly (by allowing its political control over their lives).

Again, that is the reason Revelation portrays the mark of the beast as being received on either the forehead or the hand (Rev. 13:16, 17). Many will commit to Babylon in action even though not convinced in mind and heart. Whether they go along because they fear for their lives or because they want to continue living "the good life" in this world, they are marked on the hand. Others come to believe the claims of Babylon with their whole mind and heart. Revelation depicts them as marked on the forehead. The followers of Babylon include many who do so out of conviction, but the rest acquiesce from economic rather than religious reasons. I call the latter "secular" in the sense that their primary commitments in life relate to the things of this world rather than those of the spirit. They may in fact believe in God, but that belief is not the primary motivation for their actions. In the previous chapter we illustrated the end result of stage 4 as follows:

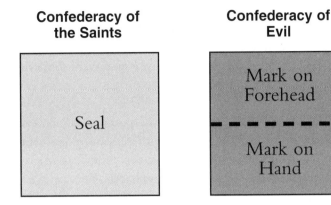

Confederacy of the Saints

Seal

Confederacy of Evil

Mark on Forehead

Mark on Hand

5. The Religious and Secular Confederacies Unite

As the final time of decision draws to a close, the world's secular and religious confederacies join together on the basis of common self-interest (Rev. 16:13, 14; 17:1-3). The result is a global unity of all public institutions, both the religious and the national. Such final institutional unity is even more dramatic than the worldwide political unity will be.

The mere thought of a unity of religious institutions in today's world is hard enough to manage. But the idea that such a religious unity could fully control all the world's nations at the same time seems utterly fantastic to human experience. Many religious and political leaders through history have imagined such global unity, but its actual fulfillment has never occurred. What kinds of events or philosophical movements could lead to such a unity? Does the book of Revelation give us any clues?

According to Revelation a number of forces will bring Satan's agencies together at the end of time. The three frogs of Revelation 16:13, 14 represent the spirits of demons going out to gather the kings of the earth. This suggests a strong role for spiritualism in unifying the world for a common cause. If there is one thing that can get the attention of secular people, it is clear evidence of the existence of supernatural powers. Popular culture has often explored such themes, frequently through such movies as *The Exorcist*. Satan will certainly use all the powers at his command to influence events in the direction he desires them to go.

End-time Babylon will certainly need to wield supernatural power in order to blend Eastern religions with Western mind-sets. Some possibilities are already evident in the development of New Age thinking in the West. New Age thinking, a subcategory of postmodernism, seems as attractive to secular people as it is to those of Eastern backgrounds. Since the "flower children" of the sixties, secular people who were formerly uninterested in religion of any kind find the open-ended spirituality of today's world quite comfortable.

In fact, the one spiritual place in which postmoderns do not seem comfortable is anything associated with the three great monotheistic religions: Judaism, Islam, and Christianity. They decry the "bashing" of other religions so common in the Christian-Muslim debate, for example, but are much more at home in the defused spirituality of southern and eastern Asia. It may not require a great deal of supernatural power (Mount Carmel-type experiences) to convince the average Westerner of God's presence today. Today, more than ever, the idea that the vast majority of earth's peoples and governments could be persuaded toward a common religious agenda is plausible.

Ecological reasons may also compel political powers to choose to join the religious confederacy. If many of the seven last plagues of Revelation 16 are taken literally (particularly the first four and the last), the world may have a total ecological breakdown at some point in the future, requiring drastic measures to maintain law and order. In the context of a revival of religious institutions, people could easily interpret such disasters as a divine judgment (which they will in fact be). In such a setting, anyone who bucks the religious confederacy might be seen as the cause of the environmental calamities. In order to save the planet, the call might go out to join Babylon and conform to its wishes.

Revelation 17:2 employs fornication as a metaphor to describe the relationship between prostitute Babylon and the kings of the world. Mutual self-interest drives the relationship. Whenever two people get together sexually outside of marriage (except in cases such as rape), they have a shared sense that the relationship will improve their lives. While this usually proves to be illusive in retrospect, such mutual self-interest initially draws them together.

People are most willing to accept coercive government into their lives when they perceive a breakdown of law and order. Submitting to restrictive authority seems a small price to pay in order to deal with crime or terrorism. As events in Iraq proved, it is easier to sow disorder than to create order. Times of serious chaos require severe measures in order to restore order. We can illustrate the end-time unity of religious institutions with the nations as follows:

At the end, therefore, the religious and political confederacies of the world will succeed in uniting for a period of time. The Euphrates River will support Babylon. The prostitute sits on the waters. The woman rides the beast. The three frogs gather the kings of the whole inhabited world. Those paying attention to these prophecies will watch for these end-time developments.

6. The Remnant Singled Out for Destruction

At this point in the final events the worldwide unity is complete, and those who resist attract notice. Since they do not conform to the requirements of the global secular and religious authority, they become perceived as a threat. So they soon get singled out for destruction. In the language of Revelation, the dragon leads the entire coalition into war with the remnant (Rev. 12:17). Those who refuse to worship the beast or his image will not be allowed to buy or sell—in other words, they will face economic and employment sanctions (Rev. 13:16, 17). Even beyond that, they will eventually face a death decree (verse 15). The 10 horns give their authority to the beast and together they make war with the Lamb and those with Him (Rev. 17:12-14).

At this point God removes the restraining influence of the four angels of Revelation 7:1-4, and all hell breaks loose, so to speak, around the world. The strongest analogies for the death decree in the Old Testament appear in the books of Esther and Daniel. Closest to home is the story of Daniel's three friends and the fiery furnace. The call for worship of an image goes out, and those who do not respond to that summons are delivered for execution.

In Daniel 3 the death decree and its execution are all on the same day. In Daniel 6, on the other hand, the authorities allow a period of 30 days for compliance; then the death decree is to be executed. The book of Esther has the death decree set several months ahead and to be fulfilled by the sword and hanging. All three events are analogies to the death decree in Revelation, yet all are somewhat different. Revelation does not by itself clarify the nature of the death decree. The description in *The Great Controversy* (pp. 613-636; cf. *Prophets and Kings*, pp. 605, 606) seems most similar to that of Esther.

Will the saints be martyred or delivered at the end? The three Old Testament accounts just mentioned are encouraging. In all three cases God rescues His people in the midst of the death decree. Daniel's three friends get thrown into the furnace, but they are not consumed—they receive promotions! Daniel is thrown into the lions' den, but the lions do not hurt him, and he is also promoted. Esther and her people are allowed to defend themselves and they succeed, with the result that Mordecai is further promoted. So the three Old Testament parallels suggest that the people of God will escape the final death decree and will be promoted into the kingdom of God!

On the other hand, certain texts in Revelation suggest that some, at least, of the saints will suffer the ultimate earthly penalty: "If anyone is to be taken captive, to captivity he goes; if anyone is to be slain with the sword, with the sword must he be slain. Here is a call for the endurance and faith of the saints" (Rev. 13:10, ESV).

According to this verse, some of the saints will become captives and some of them will be slain, requiring the rest to exercise endurance and faith. Revelation 20:4 speaks of those who were "beheaded" on account of the Word of God and the testimony of Jesus. The individuals here are not just any Christian martyrs, but specifically those who faced the economic boycott and death decree of Revelation 13:15-17. So the picture seems to be one of a general deliverance that will not, however, be universal. Some will lose their lives in the final events, but the rest will be delivered, as we will see shortly.

This is not the most pleasant message imaginable. Many Adventists have lived in fear of the end-time and the persecutions anticipated there. How should you and I relate to the possibility that we might experience such a fate personally? I have come to believe that one of the spiritual gifts that the Holy Spirit delivers to God's people (see 1 Cor. 13; Rom. 12; and Eph. 4) is that of martyrdom. In the ultimate sense, it is a gift that can be exercised only once. If you have ever read accounts of the martyrs during the Middle Ages and the Reformation period, you will notice that they often did not seem to feel the flames consuming them. It is as if God intervened to give them what they needed in the time of ultimate decision and crisis.

God will not allow us to experience more than we can possibly bear (1 Cor. 10:13). To invest a lot of time worrying about the persecutions of the future is not spiritually productive. Should God allow us to go through hard times, He will give us everything we need to honor Him during it. If we are faithful in the little things today, He will see us through the big things tomorrow (Luke 19:17).

7. The Close of Probation

At some point in the course of these events probation closes for everyone on earth. Revelation indicates that it occurs in the lead up to the sounding of the seventh trumpet (Rev. 10:7), just before the seven bowls are poured out (Rev. 15:5-8). It is sometime just before the second coming of Jesus (Rev. 22:11, 12). Not an arbitrary decree on God's part, it is rather a point in time when everyone on earth has reached a settled relationship with one or the other of the two worldwide gospels (Rev. 14:6-12). After it people can no longer change sides, nor would they truly wish to. This reminds me of an Ellen White statement about people "settling into the truth, both intellectually and spiritually, so they cannot be moved" (*The Seventh-day Adventist Bible Commentary,* Ellen G. White Comments, vol. 4, p. 1161) Minds will no longer alter. Firm decisions are being made on earth and fully ratified in heaven.

What is not clear from the book of Revelation is whether we should list the close of human probation as stage 6, 7, or 8. I have placed it as point 7 but without a great deal of conviction. It seems to me that the declaration of a death decree against the people of God represents a significant hardening against the gospel (stage 6). All human institutions have become set in their opposition to God and the gospel. But in the context of the death decree some individuals will still be making their last moves (stage 7). The execution of the decree represents the actions of people and institutions that are fully hardened in their opposition (stage 8). The exact timing of the close of probation in relation to stages 6 and 8 is not explicit in Revelation.

The gospel continues to go forth as Babylon gathers the nations, unites with the beast, and begins to focus on destroying the saints. There comes a time that everybody on earth has made their decision and the heavenly temple is empty (Rev. 15:5-8). The righteous will still be righteous and the filthy will still be filthy (Rev. 22:11). From that point on, people will remain the same spiritually. If anything changes, it will involve further growth in the same direction. The good are getting better and the bad are getting worse.

8. The Remnant Under Attack

At some point along the way the religious and political powers of the world conduct a final attack on the remnant/saints. The powers of the world use their economic, military, and law enforcement resources in an attempt to destroy God's faithful people. Initially it will probably be more of an economic matter, seeking to persuade the saints by threatening their ability to earn a living (Rev. 13:16, 17). But eventually the political, military, intelligence, and police forces all combine together to seek out and destroy the people of God (verse 15). The oppression will be of such a severe nature that for a time, at least, all may appear lost for the faithful. As mentioned earlier, the war on terror has provided an idea of the kinds of resources that the nations can bring against groups and individuals who have a different agenda from that of the approved majority.

The book of Revelation describes this police action in global terms. The nations of the world make war against the Lamb and His called, chosen, and faithful followers (verse 14). Revelation also portrays it in terms of the rising waters of the Euphrates River (Rev. 16:12; 17:1). Babylon sets in motion all the economic, military, and law enforcement resources available to it. We have seen how the drying up of the Euphrates is a major theme in at least two Old Testament books (Jer. 50; 51; and Isa. 44-47). They describe how Babylon loses the support of its political, economic, and military resources. Note the following interesting text:

"The Lord spoke to me again:

"'Because this people has rejected the gently flowing waters of Shiloah and rejoices over Rezin and the son of Remaliah, therefore the Lord is about to bring against them the mighty floodwaters of the River—the king of Assyria with all his pomp. It [the Euphrates River] will overflow all its channels, run over all its banks and sweep on into Judah, swirling over it, passing through it and reaching up to the neck. Its outspread wings will cover the breadth of your land, O Immanuel!'" (Isa. 8:5-8, NIV).

This Old Testament narrative describes the armies of Assyria as the overflowing waters of the Euphrates River. The Assyrians conquered every city of Judah except Jerusalem, the capital. The Lord depicts their attack as a flood that overflows the entire land up to the neck. The walls of Jerusalem provide the neck, and the surviving city is the head. So the flooding Euphrates becomes a metaphor of an overwhelming military attack that carried all the way to the capital city of Jerusalem. The end-time Euphrates will pose a similar threat to the people of God at the close of human history.

Such imagery supports the idea that some, perhaps many, of God's people will lose their lives before the close of probation. The combined religious/political confederacy will shed the blood of the saints (Rev. 13:10; 17:14; 18:5-8; 20:4). The good news is that after the close of probation no such event will happen. The martyrdom of the saints, which through history often became like seed, drawing many new converts to the faith, will no longer have any purpose. In the ninth stage of the final events God puts an end to persecution and slaughter.

9. God Intervenes on Behalf of the Saints

As the attack of stage 8 reaches its climax, Revelation makes it clear that God intervenes in behalf of the saints. Withdrawing His permission for a worldwide unity of satanic power (Rev. 17:17), He dries up the Euphrates River by sowing distrust and enmity between the political and the religious confederacies (Rev. 16:12). As a result, the powers that oppose the people of God fragment once more. The political unity comes to hate Babylon more than they do the remnant, resulting in the miraculous deliverance of the saints.

Again, the book of Revelation describes this development on a worldwide basis. But the same change of direction occurs at the local level throughout the world. Christ intervenes at the very moment that the two worldwide confederacies are doing their best to crush the lives of the saints. As a result, the political and military powers (and the police forces at the local level) of the world withdraw their support from Babylon and turn on it, leading to its utter collapse (Rev. 17:16; 18:9-19; 19:1, 2). The people of the world see that they have been deceived, stop focusing on the saints, and start directing their hostility against those who had tricked them.

179

10. Babylon Destroyed by the Nations That Supported It

This stage is fairly brief, and there is not much more to say about it. The secular powers of the world turn on those responsible for the great deception. When Babylon stands exposed as a spiritual fraud, the very powers it depended on to extend its spiritual reach now annihilate it. "The beast and the ten horns you saw will hate the prostitute. They will bring her to ruin and leave her naked; they will eat her flesh and burn her with fire" (Rev. 17:16, NIV). But while the nations are the ones that actually carry out the destruction of Babylon, we should briefly note two further dynamics at work.

First, the nations themselves will come to regret the action almost as soon as they conduct it (Rev. 18:9-19). The mourning of Revelation 18 involves both those deeply involved with Babylon as well as those with a more superficial relationship. They all mourn because all the wicked lose when Babylon falls. Great wealth and prosperity come to an end with its destruction. The world order will never recover from Babylon's destruction.

Second, in the end it turns out that the nations were not acting entirely on their own accord. God remains in control of the process all the way (Rev. 17:17; 16:19). No political or religious union can long endure unless He supports it. So in Revelation 17:16 the nations fulfill His intent against their own will. Their momentary rage results in their own ultimate hurt.

The fall of Babylon not only splits it off from the nations, but it shatters from within as well. Revelation 16:19 tells us that Babylon fragments into three parts: the dragon, the beast, and the false prophet (Rev. 16:13, 19). So even the unity of Babylon itself does not last for long. The various religious entities that make up Babylon at the end also go their separate ways after the exposure of their deception. The total worldwide unity of evil quickly collapses.

11. Christ Finishes the Destruction at His Second Coming

Revelation makes it clear that the nations of the world do not just crumble or kill each other off. At the end there is need for a proactive execution on God's part. And God the Father does not take over at that point, but continues to allow Jesus Christ to be the visible agent of divine activity on the planet. The Lamb Himself finishes the job of destroying evil at His second coming (Rev. 14:9-11). It is the Lamb and His followers who overcome the 10 horns and the beast (Rev. 17:14). The rider on the white horse and those with him who vanquish the beast and the false prophet at the very end (Rev. 19:11-21).

While Revelation does not call the rider on the white horse the Lamb, his description recalls the son of man in chapter 1 (Rev. 1:13-16) and the Lamb of Revelation 17:14. At this stage of the final conflict anything left of the unholy trinity and the secular-political confederacy perishes. Among the means used in the divine execution are great hailstones (Rev. 16:17-21), fire (Rev. 14:9-11; 19:20; 20:7-10), the sword of the rider's mouth (Rev. 19:21), and military action (Rev. 17:14).

It is none other than Jesus Christ, the lowly one, the meek and mild, who executes destruction on the nations at the end. It is safely left in the hands of one who has suffered much Himself, for whom execution is a "strange work."

"The Lord will rise up as he did at Mount Perazim, he will rouse himself as in the Valley of Gibeon—to do his work, *his strange work,* and perform his task, *his alien task.* Now stop your mocking, or your chains will become heavier; the Lord, the Lord Almighty, has told me of the destruction decreed against the whole land" (Isa. 28:21, 22, NIV).

12. The Lamb Gathers the Saints to Be With Him

Several passages in Revelation indicate that the final act of the drama is the Lamb gathering the saints to be with Him forever. The book of Revelation does not tell us explicitly that it includes the righteous dead, although certain texts support that idea in at least a limited sense (Rev. 1:7; 14:13; 20:4-6). The resurrection of the righteous dead at the Second Coming, however, is a clear teaching in other parts of the New Testament.

"For this we declare to you by a word from the Lord, that we who are alive, who are left until the coming of the Lord, will not precede those who have fallen asleep. For the Lord himself will descend from heaven with a cry of command, with the voice of an archangel, and with the sound of the trumpet of God. And the dead in Christ will rise first. Then we who are alive, who are *left,* will be caught up together with them in the clouds to meet the Lord in the air, and so we will always be with the Lord" (1 Thess. 4:15-17, ESV).

Notice that Paul has a "remnant" here ("we . . . who are *left*"). Just as in Revelation, the remnant consists of those who pass through the final crisis and are alive to meet Jesus when He returns. They find themselves caught up to meet Jesus in the air, along with the righteous dead raised in the context of Jesus' return to earth.

Revelation also does not explicitly tell us where Jesus takes the righteous at His second advent. It tells us only that they are gathered to Him as a wheat crop is gathered to the farmer at harvesttime (Rev. 14:14-16). The saints find themselves swept up to meet Jesus in the air, just as Paul said to the Thessalonians. But neither text tells us whether Jesus leads the righteous to heaven with Him or brings them back to earth. John 14:1-3, however, clears up this matter:

"Let not your hearts be troubled. Believe in God; believe also in me. In my Father's house are many rooms. If it were not so, would I have told you that I go to prepare a place for you? And *if I go and prepare a place for you, I will come again and will take you to myself, that where I am you may be also*" (ESV).

The key element here appears in the third verse. Jesus goes away to prepare a place for His disciples. When He returns, He does not come to be with them where they are. Instead He will take them to be with Him where He is. At the Second Coming Jesus gathers the righteous, both living and dead, to Himself and escorts them all to heaven with Him to live there for 1,000 years. Then at the end of that 1,000 years they return with Him in the New Jerusalem back to earth, to live there with Him forever (Rev. 21:2, 3). So while Revelation does not tell us explicitly that the righteous are in heaven during the 1,000 years, the transfer of the New Jerusalem at the end of that period is consistent with what Jesus said to His disciples in John 14.

Summary

I have organized the final events of the battle of Armageddon into 12 major movements. I don't doubt that you or others could organize these events in a slightly different way. You could perhaps make a list of 10 or 14 (in my first attempt I had 10). And you might choose to put different titles on them. Perhaps you might even disagree on the order in a place or two. But I believe the basic outline is clear.

God's people need to have a basic sense of what is coming, but they don't have to know all the details today. As I said before, God gives us prophecy not to satisfy our curiosity about the future, but to motivate and instruct us to do the right thing today. For the sake of those readers who learn best by visual demonstration, I offer the following attempt to chart the above sequence:

THE ORDER OF FINAL EVENTS IN REVELATION

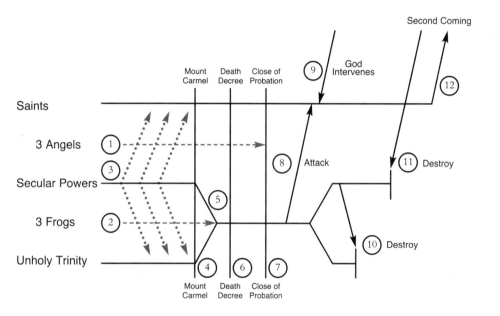

FINAL REFLECTIONS ON ARMAGEDDON

The War Against Al-Qaeda and the Battle of Armageddon

Are the events since September 11 some sort of dress rehearsal for the end of time? It certainly seems so to me. It is the first time in all of history that the mainstream political and religious bodies in the world have to a large extent united in a common cause against an international, underground movement held together by a common faith. While Europe in the Middle Ages was a powerful union of church and state, the Islamic world provided a significant counterbalance to papal ambitions at that time. Today no nation or combination of nations is fully able to block the political and economic agenda of the United States. More and more the world has one single superpower, and every other nation has to take that fact into account in every political and economic decision.

Many nations, such as Russia, China, India, and most governments in the Middle East, would like to find ways to offset American power, but they have been unable to do so. At the time of the Iraqi invasion, France sought to use the European Union as a counterweight against the American position, but the majority of European nations did not go along. A combination of Russia, China, and India would be significant, but competing self-interests seem likely to prevent such an alliance. While nationalism and ethnic centrism are stronger than ever, there is an underlying reality that we are closer to a single world system than ever before in history.

And this single world system finds itself threatened, not by a nation or a combination of nations, but by a small international collection of individuals bound together by religious ideology, hiding in "the rocks and the mountains" and in chaotic cities such as Baghdad, Kandahar, Jakarta, and even London and Madrid. It sounds very much like the scenario laid out in the battle of Armageddon. Worldwide religious and political unity against a scattered spiritual group from every nation, tribe, language, and people. Now al-Qaeda is not the end-time remnant of Revelation! But the echoes of Revelation in the current world situation are remarkable and bear watching as we approach the end of the history. Let me briefly outline a few scenarios of how the war on terror could prove to be the earliest stages of the battle of Armageddon.

1. From Chaos to Tyranny

The war in Iraq has clarified one thing. It is a lot easier to create chaos than it is to produce peace and order. In a context in which people are willing to blow themselves up in order to destabilize society for everyone else, it is very hard to establish and maintain security. And it is too easy to harm the innocent in the process of protecting them, which exacerbates the chaos. Chaos tends to breed more chaos. Over time, as people become more and more frustrated by the violence and disorder around them, they become nostalgic for the "good old days," when strong dictators such as Saddam Hussein and Josef Stalin made sure the "bad guys" left the average citizen alone.

The Great Controversy seems to support just such a scenario. Ellen White projects a situation in which worldwide chaos leads to a drive for security and strong government. In her scenario, one of the measures for restoring order is a renewed commitment to Sunday observance. Those who observe the Sabbath stand out in their opposition. In spite of their loyalty to divine law and order, they are perceived as enemies of earthly law and order, supporters of the very chaos that society now seeks to avoid. Society denounces them as in rebellion against legitimately constituted authority (*The Great Controversy*, p. 592). People feel that it would be better to eliminate the dissenters than allow the world to fall back into chaos (*ibid.*, p. 615).

It is not hard to imagine the cry for peace and security combining with nostalgia for the religious traditions of the past. People sense that one of the reasons for the chaos is the lack of God's favor. They come to believe that a worldwide religion taking up the best of all the religions can bring the human race back into divine approval. In the context of Islamic terrorism the scenario of Revelation and *The Great Controversy* becomes quite believable.

2. A Rebirth of Institutional Ecumenism

Adventists have always feared the kinds of ecumenical attempts associated with the World Council of Churches in Geneva. There skilled negotiators from the mainstream Protestant denominations around the world explore ways in which such churches can gain deeper respect for each other and the things they have in common. Although the Roman Catholic Church is not a direct member of the Council, it has observer status and often participates in substantive talks.

While such institutional efforts had quite a bit of traction 100 years ago, in many ways the traditional ecumenical efforts have fallen on hard times. The general breakdown of civil discourse around the world has had an impact on them. But the scenario of Revelation suggests that ecumenical efforts such as the World Council of Churches will somehow become center stage again. In the next wave, however, non-Christian religions will also play a significant role, so the past is only a small foretaste of the massive worldwide institutional unity that Revelation projects for the final events of earth's history. We have probably not heard the last regarding traditional forms of ecumenical unification.

3. The Role of Postmodernism

Readers may wonder if a worldwide confederacy of institutional religion is impossible in the light of developing postmodernism. Postmodern thought marginalizes religion in favor of a more diffused kind of spirituality. Its proponents view religion as the cause of wars and strife, and the call goes out to worship God in ways that minimize differences.

But while postmodernism may seem to portend the death of institutional religion, one aspect of it could lead to an end-time religious confederacy. It is the criticism of strong religious convictions. In postmodernism anything goes as long as one does not hold one's faith in ways that can make others uncomfortable. The power and conviction with which the end-time gospel spreads through the world could trigger a postmodern reaction. Postmoderns regard many of the world's problems as caused by people with strong convictions. During a crisis it may seem that the saints have to be eliminated in order for the world to reach the spiritual harmony that appeals to the postmodern consciousness. Postmodernism tends to be tolerant of anything except what it perceives as intolerant.

FINAL REFLECTIONS ON ARMAGEDDON

The end-time religious confederacy will certainly have to be very tolerant of differences. On the one hand will be an "anything goes" kind of spirituality. On the other hand, the proclamation of the true gospel will be so threatening that its "intolerance" will stand in clear contrast with the major world religions. Lessons learned in the war on terror could be applied against anyone who resists the global religious confederacy for whatever reasons.

Postmodernism, therefore, is not the barrier to the end-time scenario of Revelation that it appears at first glance. If the concept of postmodernism is new or unclear to you, see my forth-coming analysis of how it affects Adventist faith.

4. The Islamic Side of Adventism

Most Adventists that I know have the general Western perception of Islam as a hateful and corrupt religion that perverts the truth of Scripture. On the other hand is the testimony of a Muslim doctor I have met. "Muslims know that Seventh-day Adventism is the closest to Islam of all the other religions," he commented to me. Muslims may *know* this, but to Adventists this may seem like quite a stretch.

But it should be no surprise to any Adventist who has spent time among Muslims in the Middle East. I have never spent an hour with a Muslim in the Middle East without the question "If you are from America, how come you are not a Christian?" When I first asked why they thought I was a Muslim rather than a Christian, I made an important discovery. In their minds the defining marks of a Christian are: (1) drinking alcohol, (2) eating pork, (3) dressing immodestly, (4) following the pope, (5) idolizing America and Hollywood, and (6) laxness in obedience to God.

I came to realize that on all the practical issues that define a Muslim from his or her Christian counterparts in the Middle East, Adventists track with Muslims rather than Christians. And once I accepted that the label "Christian" was a gross misrepresentation of who I was in the Middle East, I had no further barriers in engaging Muslims on spiritual themes. In fact, the Adventist context may be the ideal place that Muslims, Christians, and Jews can find common ground as we approach the end of the world.

Now consider with me a scenario in which the current world situation rapidly moves toward the confederacies of Armageddon. Imagine (and I know this is hard) that one or more of the jihadist leaders becomes convicted by the claims of Jesus and announces a unilateral truce. They point out that Allah is all-powerful and does not need human intervention to accomplish His purpose for the world. It is true faith that will bring about the triumph of Islam, not bombs, hatred, and anger. Imagine also that this conviction becomes associated with the work of the biblical remnant.

Almost overnight there would be a million new jihadist suspects in North America, and millions more around the world! The searchlights of "homeland security" in every nation could focus on those who keep the commandments of God and have the faith of Jesus, setting the situation portrayed in *The Great Controversy* in motion. God's faithful people would become the object of international scorn and calumny. Intelligence agencies and police forces around the world, goaded on by religious entities that feel threatened by this spiritual movement, would shift into action against the faithful people of God.

Sound far-fetched? Not if it is compatible with the scenario painted by inspiration in Bible prophecy. We have studied those parts of Revelation that clearly describe the last days of earth's history and the events leading up to them. As we have explored the meaning of the word "Armageddon" and its use in the context of Revelation 12-18 we have come to realize that in the end the entire world will find itself at war with an international movement of kindred spirits, seeking God's will and ways rather than those of the world. This end-time movement will be broader than we may have realized. The very breadth of the movement will one day prove to be an overwhelming threat to the great and powerful of our world.

5. The Role of America in Prophecy

Adventist study of Revelation focused early on the identification of the United States with the land beast of Revelation 13. It paid particular attention to the idea that the land beast has lamblike features when it first appears but comes to speak as a dragon (Rev. 13:11). In other words, America emerges on the historical scene as a relatively positive power, a haven for the oppressed, particularly the religious minorities of Europe. Unlike most nations, whose political position rests on corporate self-interest, America arises with a corporate vision of its responsibility to feed the hungry, help the weak, and rescue the oppressed. When America goes to war, it's for a just and noble cause, not out of national selfishness.

FINAL REFLECTIONS ON ARMAGEDDON

By God's design, America's geographical location is fairly unique. Sheltered by oceans on the east and on the west, it is so rich in natural resources that, except for the recent need for foreign oil, America is self-sufficient in most raw materials. Its abundance of rich farmland means it does not need to fight wars for basic survival resources such as food. From the mid-nineteenth century on, the only nations that border the United States— Canada and Mexico—have not been hostile and are, in any case, relatively weak militarily. (The recent bout of insecurity regarding the border with Mexico is a largely new thing for the United States.) The last invasion of the "lower 48 states" was during the war of 1812, unless you count brief forays such as the raid into New Mexico by Pancho Villa in 1916. America's borders have not been a major concern for some time until recently.

The United States, therefore, has been blessed with the luxury of living without significant threat to its existence from potentially hostile neighbors. Because of its abundant natural resources, it has not needed to be an aggressor power such as Japan, dependent for its survival on imports of food and raw materials. Japan has to be obsessed with the good or bad intentions of its neighbors (including the United States), as there are so many ways that external forces can threaten the country's survival. The United States has had few such concerns until the present.

Compare the United States with China, for example, a country of similar physical size. China has always felt itself under threat from hostile neighbors. The great bear of Russia lurked in the north, and central Asia had its host of unpredictable tribes. India lies to the southwest and Vietnam to the south (China has fought brief wars with both since World War II). To the east are Korea, Japan, and Taiwan. Wars have raged with all three during the past 100 years. And then there is the unlimited reach of the United States navy to worry about. So the Chinese must be constantly thinking of their own political and economic self-interest. The very survival of its people demands it.

Turkey offers another example. Historically it has many economic interests in the Balkans, but has tangled often with Greece in the process (most recently in 1974). It has many interests in the Caucasus, but faces the ethnic and religious hostility of Armenia. To the east is Iran and to the south Syria and Iraq. An increasing danger to the east are the Kurds, a unique people group that has no nation of its own but is in the majority in several provinces of Turkey, Iran, and Iraq. While Turkey has become a relatively prosperous country, it feels continually under threat from the military, ethnic, and economic potential of its neighbors.

As the examples of China and Turkey suggest, most nations naturally find themselves driven to a political stance of corporate selfishness. When people feel cornered, they defend themselves vigorously. Their full attention is on their own needs and interests. America was no different at the time of its founding. Both native peoples nearby and European powers such as Britain, France, and, for a time, Spain all loomed as dangers. But by the mid-nineteenth century America felt secure from outside threat and began to develop the sense that God had placed it on the earth to be a blessing to the world. It was not to operate from selfish ambition. Freeing the slaves was, to some degree, motivated by the desire to be a nation not tainted by the kind of selfish ambition so characteristic in traditional geopolitics.

But all of that began to go by the wayside with World War II. Japan's attack on Pearl Harbor shattered the sense of security that had once been complete. The cold war also made it clear that in today's world, a nation does not have to be near to be threatening. America came to realize that its security and even its survival depended to a large degree on events in the Eurasian land mass (from Great Britain to Singapore). The population and resources of Eurasia are so great that any power that can completely control the Eurasian landmass will rule the world. So the continuing worldwide reach of the American navy and air force is not an accident. Contented isolation is no longer an American option. It is very much in the national interest of the United States to act in ways that keep the nations of Eurasia divided.

Such pressures have transformed the United States from a benevolent power that intercedes in world affairs to protect the weak to one that aggressively acts to ensure its own interests. Many regard the invasion of Iraq in 2003 as a major turning point. Whatever motives of rescuing the Shiites or the Kurds there might have been, the overwhelming purpose of the invasion was America's own political self-interest. In the eyes of the world America is now perceived more as a neighborhood bully (dragon?) than as an understanding partner.

And there is no turning back. Al-Qaeda and its allies will not go away quietly. The threat of weapons of mass destruction in the hands of terrorists is an ongoing danger. In order to ensure its own survival America must act as an empire, intruding into the affairs of its neighbors around the world in the hunt for those who desire to harm it. It does not matter if a Democrat or a Republican is president. America's leader cannot ignore the geopolitical realities of today's world. The same President Carter who sought to slow down the development of the "dragon" set in motion events that led ultimately to the invasion of Iraq. America now speaks as a dragon. A major aspect of the stage is set for the events of the end.

Conspiracy Theories

I suppose I should not try to write on this topic without saying a word about various conspiracy theories afloat in regard to September 11. It is widely held in places such as the Middle East and South America that the Bush administration orchestrated the events of September 11 to compel the American people to go along with his dream of an American empire. Some have suggested that Osama bin Laden was either a willing accomplice in this process or that al-Qaeda's involvement was fabricated to justify the actions against the Taliban in Afghanistan and Saddam Hussein in Iraq.

The film documentary *Loose Change* sought to make the case that instead of an exploding aircraft bringing down the towers of the World Trade Center a controlled demolition collapsed the floors of the towers inwardly. A retired professor from Claremont named David Griffin outlined the most convincing of such theories. The documentation and argumentation of the book is downright brilliant.* Yet I just don't buy it.

It is conceivable that in a tightly controlled dictatorship, such as that of Saddam Hussein, brutal and self-serving actions on a massive scale could be done and no one would hold the leadership accountable. But in a nation such as America, with a fractious and divided free press, with a powerful opposition party, with an Internet that exposes everything from the details of Paris Hilton's intimate life to what Condoleezza Rice had for breakfast, it is hard to imagine anyone thinking that they could get away with such a plot, much less actually carrying it out.

For me the decisive problem with the conspiracy theories is the great difficulty of keeping secrets in an Internet world. For Osama bin Laden to pull off September 11, it only required a few dozen operatives and a few million dollars. To accomplish the kind of thing the conspiracy theories suggest would have demanded a massive operation, with hundreds, per- haps thousands, of people each playing their part and then keeping it se- cret for the rest of their lives. In my humble opinion that just wouldn't happen in today's world. Merely setting the charges for a controlled demo- lition of the World Trade Center (during a fire drill) would have involved hundreds of skilled but ordinary workers who would have no compelling reason to remain silent about their actions in a world in which almost everyone longs for a moment of fame.

Why is it that no one at the center of American government or media accepts any of the conspiracy theories? The Clintons, Gores, and Obamas of this world would have every reason to expose the plot if they believed such a thing had occurred. They are more than convinced that President Bush has acted in a perverse way, yet they place no stock in the conspir- acy theories regarding September 11. Why is there no credible historian or media outlet exploring the possibility? Conspiracy theories always make the most sense to those who are not at the center of events. They are not aware of the holes in their evidence and the flaws in their logic. And those who are at the center may know these flaws but don't consider the theo- ries worthy of response.

Some will think me a fool for taking this position. So be it. I have to be honest with the evidence I know. Criticism is the price of putting one's opin- ions onto the public stage. At the beginning of this book I have outlined an analysis of events that makes sense to me. History will one day be the judge.

Having said this, however, I still want to make one thing clear. Even if the Bush administration has not stooped as low as Griffin and others sug- gest, the natural consequence of American actions during the past 50 years is moving toward empire and away from the Bible-based sense of respon- sibility to make the whole world a better place. It doesn't require question- able conspiracy theories to see that America is speaking more and more "like a dragon."

What concerns me most from a spiritual perspective is that chasing after conspiracy theories can distract us from the real plot that Revelation brings out into the open. It is the great satanic deception at the end of time. Behind the actions of presidents and prime ministers there is a more uni- versal battle going on. Christ and Satan are battling for the control of the whole universe as well as this earth. Satan's grand conspiracy is the primary focus of this book. The political and military details are only illustrations of how the larger conspiracy could work out. It is well to be as detailed as Scripture in laying out the events foretold in prophecy. But, as I observed earlier, it is dangerous to be more detailed than Scripture is. When we mingle our own hopes and dreams with the prophecies of Scripture, we can lose sight of where the text actually wants to take us. Once again I emphasize that the primary purpose of prophecy is not to satisfy our curiosity about the future, but to teach us how to live today.

How to Live Today

In several places in the battle of Armageddon narrative the hideous creatures and the ugly events take the back stage for a moment and a glimpse of more personal truth appears. As we have seen, one of them is Revelation 16:15: "Behold, I come like a thief! Blessed is he who stays awake and keeps his clothes with him, so that he may not go naked and be shamefully exposed" (NIV). This text, coming right in the middle of the one place in the Bible that actually names Armageddon, echoes many New Testament passages about personal preparation for the return of Jesus and the events of the end.

Another such text is Revelation 17:14: "These will make war with the Lamb, but the Lamb will overcome them, because he is Lord of lords and King of kings—and those with him are called and chosen and faithful" (author's translation). Here the great war at the end engages an army of people whose primary purpose is not to destroy others with weapons, but to be faithful to their divine calling and election. This is a very different kind of battle from the ones that nations and insurgent operations still fight today. As I have said repeatedly, the battle of Armageddon is a struggle for the mind. It is also a battle for the heart—a call to heartfelt allegiance to the Lamb that was slain (Rev. 5:9, 10, 12; 13:8).

We need to look at one further text in Revelation 16 and 17 whose spiritual implications we have not yet noted. "The woman you saw is the great city that rules over the kings of the earth" (Rev. 17:18, NIV). We have seen how this verse underlines in plain language the role that Babylon plays in the final conflict against the political powers of the world. Babylon's riding of the beast is a symbolic way of saying that it "rules over the kings of the earth."

But we find an interesting twist on this global perspective in verse 18. The concept of Babylon is not limited here just to end-time Babylon. Through the "great city" Babylon symbolizes, to a degree, all the satanic powers that have ever ruled on the earth. In the Greek the phrase translated "that rules over" is a present participle. The present participle is one of the most continuous expressions possible in the Greek. It means that, in a sense, "Babylon" is a principle that constantly rules over the kings of the earth. Thus it lies behind all the political powers that have ever tried to coerce and/or deceive people.

This reminds us that the great battle at the end of history is one fought more at a personal level than in the movements of great armies and political powers. The principle of Babylon is self-centered religion, something that tempts us all. Whenever we are tempted to put self ahead of others in our spiritual work, we are, on a small scale, taking the wrong side in the cosmic conflict. And whenever we try to coerce the minds of others to our own spiritual viewpoint, we are taking the wrong side in our personal conflict. For me personally, the most dangerous Babylon of all is the one that lurks in my own heart.

This personal view (which seems to be the primary focus of *The Great Controversy*) is not in contradiction to the global view that occupies such a large part of the book of Revelation. It would not be wise to turn Revelation into just another treatise on salvation and personal godliness. On the other hand, it is possible to become so focused on global events that we sidetrack ourselves from the crucial task of preparing our own hearts for the conflict. We allow ourselves to become distracted by speculations and time setting, and thus avoid the decisive spiritual work that is our first task. So a book like this would not be complete unless it gives some consideration to the personal, spiritual side of the material we have covered. As always, the purpose of prophecy is to motivate right living today. To do the right thing, we need to understand first what the right thing is and then be motivated to do it. A spiritual understanding of prophecy is a powerful motivator to right action.

1. God Will Make Things Right

The first spiritual lesson I would like to underline is the idea that God will make things right in the end no matter how much opposition He may face. In the book of Revelation it becomes clear that He is well able to orchestrate events and work around human choices in order to serve His ultimate purpose. Even when things seem totally out of control from our own perspective, God is still in charge. He can use the confederacies of His opponents ultimately to destroy them. And He can employ the deceptions of the enemy to provoke faith among the faithless. While the process may be confusing and uncertain at times, the outcome is not in doubt! God wins! And those who have aligned themselves with God win when He does!

Let me personalize this truth. As I write these words, I must confess that I'm a little worried these days. I live in a house that's completely paid for and also provides some income from an apartment on the lower floor. If something were to happen to me, my wife could probably survive quite well on less than $1,000 a month if she had to. But this secure picture has a problem. My house is in southwestern Michigan, where housing is relatively cheap. But I've just accepted the position of dean of the School of Religion at Loma Linda University in southern California. The sale of our comfortable Michigan home will barely provide a down payment on a similar house in southern California. And while Loma Linda is being very fair with us in light of this reality, the change has introduced a large element of financial risk for us. We will need a huge mortgage in order to get by. It is as if our family were starting all over again financially.

This situation has reinforced for me the reason that I worry. I don't worry a whole lot about the past. It's over, and I can't do anything about it (I respect the fact that some readers, because of abuse or trauma, may find the past a lot harder to shake). Also I don't worry too much about the present. God has been good to me and my family, and I've learned to trust that He will take care of us from day to day. When I worry, though, it is because I don't know the future. I find it harder to trust in God when I don't have immediate evidence of how things will turn out. For me, worry is grounded in my inability to know the future.

The core message of the battle of Armageddon, however, is that God is in control, even when things seem out of control. But this truth is not just a past or a present reality in my life. According to Revelation, God is in control not only of the past and the present, but also of the future. And if He is in control of the future of the nations, then He is also in control of my future. I can trust my home, my family, and my job to His care.

I guess that's what I love about the book of Revelation. Despite all of its weirdness and challenging symbols, it has an underlying sense of confidence that God can be trusted in everything, even in the future. I'm not sure that any other Bible book (except perhaps Daniel) is nearly so effective in making this point. To ignore these apocalyptic books is to miss the blessing that comes from knowing that God is in control. As my family makes this major move in response to His leading, I can trust Him to manage the risk.

2. Unmasking Evil

A critical point that the book of Revelation makes is a warning against the attractions of evil. Paul says that Satan sometimes presents himself as an angel of light (2 Cor. 11:14). While he has no love for the things of God, no love for purity and goodness, Satan is the greatest actor of all time. He is well able to present himself in whatever form will accomplish his purpose with any particular individual. So while he sometimes seeks to control people with frightening displays (as is parodied in the many "fun houses" that spring up around the Halloween season in the United States), he more often tries to show evil as a beautiful and beneficial thing.

His tactic is quite evident in the movie industry, for example. It portrays adultery, theft, and even murder as good things provided they are done with the "right" motives (according to the needs and concerns of the script). Such motion pictures subtly lead the viewer to consider unrighteous actions as admirable. And make no mistake about it—the perpetrators of such behavior are invariably attractive in both physical form and in personality. The actor may not even be that good-looking in real life, but the magic of makeup and camera angles heals all, and the viewer comes to see evil in a positive light, without even realizing that he or she has been manipulated in that direction.

The book of Revelation pulls the mask off of such charades. Behind the faces of the beautiful people who act wickedly we encounter the hideous countenances of vicious meat-eating beasts. Instead of a loving, sculpted form, these creatures are misshapen, with abnormal quantities of heads and strange amalgams of features (Rev. 13:2; 9:7-9, 17-19). Revelation is, in many ways, an ugly book, for it does not gloss over evil, but presents its darkest side in the full light of day (see Rev. 17:16, for example). Our fallen world presents evil as an attractive option, and it is a real and present danger that honest people of God will be drawn away from their faithfulness by misperceptions of spiritual reality. Therefore, Revelation jolts us with R-rated force to get our attention and prevent us from slipping down the slope into seemingly pleasant addictions. Sin may seem to be fun, but it is guaranteed to ruin one's tomorrows. Revelation shocks us back into reality. Behind every attractive sin lurks a demonic force ready to take advantage of one's lapse (Rev. 16:13, 14).

It is a message I need to hear every day. If the book of Revelation did not exist, we would not have as clear a perception of reality as we do. Every day I am faced with choices that seem innocuous, thoughts that go neither here nor there, attractive temptations that "will do no harm"—or so it would seem. As I surf the Internet many directions may seem neutral at first, but then quickly bring one in contact with options that are attractive yet destructive. When I'm shopping I notice opportunities to depart from the "list" and waste money on that which will not make my life better in the long term. Driving down the road, I encounter billboards that call me to "let go" of my mind and wander into places that God doesn't want me to enter. Today's world affords so many subtle and attractive options that at best distract us from our mission and at worst burden us with horrible addictions.

The plain reality is that in today's world I need a slap in the face every day, a reminder that things are not always what they seem and that the wages of sin is truly death, not only for all time, but, in a spiritual sense, already in this life. Unless I am constantly plugged into a higher reality, I will find myself easily shifted into directions that I would regret one day. The battle of Armageddon is truly a struggle for the mind. It is a conflict that for us has already begun and that we must wage every day. The terrible consequences of attractive sins are things that we must never forget, and Revelation is a powerful reminder of those truths.

3. The Need for Discernment

The book of Revelation makes it clear that as we face the terrible deceptions and other challenges of the end-time, the only safe place will be a clear knowledge of the gospel and of the prophecies that give us advance intelligence about the challenges we will face. The spiritual subterfuges of the end are of such severity that the only way to survive them is with clear discernment based on a comprehensive knowledge of God's will as outlined in the Scriptures.

God has called the Seventh-day Adventist Church to be a people of prophecy, a people who have been trained to discern the signs of the times and to apply the Word of God to every situation in life. He has summoned us to warn the world that at the end of time things will not be as they seem. Safety does not exist in mere human discernment, science, or any other application of the five senses. The deceptions of the end will be of such a nature that the only safeguard will be total reliance on the clear teachings of God's Word. But in order to obey the Word of God, we need to know the Word. And we cannot afford to know it secondhand, through the teachings of others (like me), however dedicated they may be. For our own personal safety we need to experience the teachings of the Word for ourselves.

This suggests a couple courses of action that we need to take as we approach the final events. 1. First of all, clear-minded discernment is one of the chief qualities of God's end-time people. But in order to exercise it, we need to study the Bible as we've never done before. We need to pray as never before. We need to stand for truth like a rock yet exercise a considerable amount of self-distrust regarding our opinions. If the only way out of the deception dilemma is a clear knowledge of God's Word, we will want our study to be as accurate and as safe as possible. That means studying in groups whenever possible, since they are more intelligent than an individual person. It means employing broad reading of the Scriptures along with a focus on the relatively clear texts rather than the unclear ones. For a great deal more detail on the above methodology, see *The Deep Things of God*, chapter 4, which elaborates on these safeguards to Bible study.

2. Clear-minded discernment is also the product of good physical and mental health. When we practice natural remedies, we are enhancing our ability to grasp spiritual truths. Physical exercise, lots of fresh air, good nutrition, proper amounts of rest at the right times—these are principles that enhance the mind's ability to discern the meaning of the Scriptures and the difference between truth and error. Not only that, the very study of the Scriptures themselves is another way to stretch the mind and increase its capacity to understand spiritual truth. In addition, psychological health is an underemphasized health principle. Many of the weird and aberrant po-

sitions people take on spiritual matters are the result of unhealthy psychological and emotional dynamics. As people deal with their own personal demons they become better able to recognize the real demons that lurk in the spiritual realm.

4. The Role of Obedience

No matter how you read the apocalyptic portions of Revelation, the key and ultimate issue is: Who is God and on which side of the final crisis can He be found (I refer here particularly to the end-time Mount Carmel experience of Revelation 13:13, 14 and 16:16). The deceptions will be severe, and even the elect of God will tremble at their severity (Matt. 24:24). So it is imperative that God's Word provide His end-time people with some markers or indicators by which they can detect the workings of the true God from the deceptions of the counterfeit.

The primary indicator differentiating the saints from the religious confederacy is obedience to the Ten Commandments, with particular emphasis on the first four. Since the enemies of God and His people at the end will, no doubt, observe some or many of the commandments, the truly faithful will be distinguished by their observance of *all* the commandments of God, including the Sabbath. The enemies of God's people, in other words, will be noticeable by their selective disregard of one or more of the Ten Commandments.

In this context, the allusion in Revelation 14:7 to the fourth commandment is highly significant. It identifies one commandment in particular that the unholy trinity and those from all nations that adhere to the unholy trinity will all disregard. This underlines the end-time importance of faithful and continual observance of God's commandments, including the often-neglected fourth. Such honoring of the commandments is not the basis for salvation, but is the grateful response of those who have overcome (Rev. 12:11) and have "washed their robes. . . in the blood of the Lamb" (Rev. 7:14; cf. the interesting textual options in a modern translation of Rev. 22:14). The people of God throughout history have responded to His mighty acts by rehearsing those acts through word, festival, obedience, and ethical behavior. Thus a natural response to the mighty act of God at the cross is obedience to all of His requirements, including the seemingly arbitrary one of a specific day of rest and worship.

5. Grounded in the Word

Don't be too quick to trust your senses or your opinions. It is not difficult to put Bible texts together in such a way as to lead to an erroneous conclusion. I know that it is natural to accept what your eyes see, your ears hear, and your hands handle. And most of the time our senses offer a fairly accurate rendition of the reality that lies around us. But we can all recall times when we completely misinterpreted reality on the basis of our perceptions. And at the end of time the wave of deception unleashed by end-time Babylon will render the five senses unreliable indeed. At that time we will be able to trust our senses only to the extent that they reflect what is accurately taught in the scriptures.

It is imperative as we approach the end, therefore, that we seek to go more deeply into God's Word. Many distractions surround us today, and we find many good excuses for not taking extra time for Scripture. But in the light of what we have learned about the battle of Armageddon, we need to make Bible study and prayer higher priorities than ever before. If you are not sure how to study the Bible to dig out its challenging features, get hold of a copy of the first book in this series, *The Deep Things of God: An Insider's Guide to the Book of Revelation*. It contains a complete plan of study for the book of Revelation along with important safeguards to prevent unwitting misinterpretation. Trust me, if you will invest 20-50 hours of study along the lines suggested in *Deep Things* (over a month or more, of course), you will discover amazing things and you will find deep Bible study to be one of the most exciting and deeply fulfillment activities that you have ever tried. I highly recommend the process.

6. The Secret Things Belong to God

It is intuitive to assume that if God took the trouble to reveal Himself in Scripture, every detail should be understandable, given enough research and the guidance of the Holy Spirit. But neither Scripture nor reality seem to support that assumption. In Deuteronomy 29:29 the Bible says: "The secret things belong to the Lord our God, but the things that are revealed belong to us and to our children forever, that we may do all the words of this law" (ESV). This text clearly distinguishes between things that we can know and those that only God can know.

That the "secret things" include some parts of the Bible is well illustrated in the appendix to this book. Significant portions of Scripture have resisted all attempts at a full understanding, and Revelation 17 does not seem to be an exception. While some aspects of the chapter seem reasonably clear, much continues to defy our best efforts. Why would God put things in the Bible that we cannot grasp, in spite of diligent effort?

Earlier I mentioned a time I was on the radio with Mervyn Maxwell, a seminary colleague and fellow student of Revelation. The subject of discussion was the seven trumpets. As I spoke about the difficulty of finding one's way through the trumpets, he turned to me and said, "Why would God put things in the Bible that we can't understand?" As I said before, for an instant I was floored (being on the radio can do that to you), not knowing what to say. Then an idea came into my mind that seemed compelling at the time (it satisfied Maxwell and me, at least) and still makes sense to me today.

Let me repeat it. "To keep us coming back to the Bible," I responded. "Reading the Bible is as essential to us spiritually as food is essential to our bodies. We must 'eat' the Word every day to survive spiritually. But if we could come to the place at which we had figured out all there was to know about the Bible, we wouldn't feel we needed to study it anymore. We would 'lose a taste for it.' God has placed many difficult things in the Bible so that we would be motivated to keep coming back, keep learning, keep growing in our understanding. It is curiosity about what we don't know that motivates us to continue feeding ourselves and growing in the Lord."

The difficult texts of the Bible are fruitful tools in God's hands that bring us back for more. So a certain amount of curiosity about the problem texts of the Bible and about the future is healthy. But we must not allow the difficult parts of the Bible to fascinate us so much that we miss the clear teachings that are critical to our salvation.

Whenever I present to Adventist audiences overseas, I am intrigued by how much the audience questions at the end focus on these difficult texts. No matter where I go, people are fascinated with the 144,000, the seven heads of the beast, and similar details. I wish they had more questions about faith and salvation or about how to get along within the family and how to become a better person. It almost seems that an infatuation with the details of prophecy can be a way of avoiding the most vital issues of everyday life.

One time a man stood up and asked about Deuteronomy 29:29. "The

Bible teaches us that the secret things belong to God," he said. "What are those secret things?"

How would you answer such a question? I responded simply, "I don't know—that's why they are called secret things!" Was that an unscholarly response? I don't think so. A true scholar will always come upon questions that he or she cannot answer. And certainly the secret things of God—and a few verses in Revelation, no doubt, fall into that category. A mature Adventist is one who is able to rejoice in the things that are clear in Scripture and to be content that some things may always be unclear.

It is appropriate at this point, I think, to remind you of the fourth chapter of the previous book in this series (see *The Deep Things of God*, pp. 79-92). There I shared five "safeguards" for the study of the Bible. They are like five keys to a lifelong relationship with Scripture. If you pursue your Bible study along these five lines, you are not likely to go far wrong. I list the five keys briefly here, but would encourage you to go back to that chapter for the details.

1. Approach the Bible with much prayer for the Spirit's guidance and from a distrust in your own understanding up to that point.

2. Use the original languages or a variety of translations in your native language.

3. Spend the majority of your time in the clear texts of the Bible.

4. Spend the majority of your time reading the fuller text of the Bible itself, rather searching with a concordance or a computer program.

5. Listen much to the criticism of your peers.

For Adventists, a sixth principle would be to apply the five principles also to the writings of Ellen White. As is the case with the Bible, many have missed her central messages by speculative studies based on selected statements. When we consistently approach the Bible and her writings along these lines, we will find them life-changing powers in our lives. The "secret things" provide a flavor that keeps us coming back, but they must never become the center of our focus. Great power resides in the things that are clear.

Conclusion

I find myself awed by the amazing picture of truth that we find in the chapters of Revelation that focus on the battle of Armageddon. The decades-long process that led up to the writing of this book was a deep privilege. I feel challenged to put God first in my life as never before. I want to have clear discernment as I approach the future. And my deepest desire is that all those who read this book will find in it something that sustains them in the challenges that lie ahead.

The best news of all is that the end of the Bible is not an "abyss of meaninglessness," administered by random fate through an asteroid or a madman with a doomsday machine. History does not end with a hopeless and terrified whimper, but rather with a Person, a Person that can be known and appreciated now, and is capable of taking care of those who love Him then (Rev. 14:13). The Bible pictures the end of the world as a series of terrifying events, but they are under the control of one who cares deeply for the human race, one who loves humanity so much that He was willing to die for it (Rev. 5:5-12). When He returns, He will overcome the oppressors and bring justice and peace to all who are with Him, the "called, and chosen, and faithful" (see Rev. 17:14; 19:11-21). He is King of kings and Lord of lords (Rev. 19:16, ESV).

---

* David Ray Griffin, *Christian Faith and the Truth Behind 9/11: A Call to Reflection and Action* (Philadelphia: Westminster/John Knox Press, 2006).

APPENDIX

THE SEVEN HEADS OF REVELATION 17

The death of Pope John Paul II and the election of his successor triggered a great deal of interest among Adventists in the seven-headed beast of Revelation 17. A flurry of e-mails from pastors, friends, and former students indicated considerable buzz about the possible implications of the chapter for current events. And it was not the first time that I have experienced a flurry of interest in chapter 17. So I would be remiss if I said nothing at all about the issues in the chapter.

The focus of greatest interest is verse 10, which describes the seven heads of the beast as consecutive. "Five have fallen, one is now, the other has not yet come, and when he comes he must remain for a short time." Adventist lay interpreters have, for several decades, sought to connect the heads with the series of popes who have held office since the reestablishment of the Vatican as a recognized nation in 1929. Most studies through the years saw John Paul II as the last or next to last in the sequence. Thus his death, and the age of his successor, rekindled speculation regarding the nearness of the end, especially since Benedict XVI is the seventh pope since 1929.

The Position of Mainstream Scholarship

In the wider world of mainstream scholarship, research on Revelation 17 limits itself largely to a preterist approach, which regards the book of Revelation as a symbolic reflection on the situation of John's day. According to this view, the seven churches of Revelation faced threats from both inside and outside the church. The "Nicolaitans" and the followers of "Jezebel" (presumed to be a church leader at variance with John late in the first century) challenge the churches from the inside. The Jews and the Roman authorities confront the churches from outside. The symbolism of John's vision, therefore, would address how the church should respond to these threats in the first-century context, particularly that from the Roman authorities.

When it comes to Revelation 17, the preterist position notes that the "seven mountains" of verse 9 could also be translated "seven hills." (The biblical "Mount" of Olives, for example, is a mere hill, rising just several hundred feet above the site of ancient Jerusalem.) Several first-century writers referred to Rome as the "city of seven hills."[1] The bulk of preterist scholars, therefore, see in the seven heads references to seven specific emperors of the first century.

This perspective is flawed, however, in the sense that there exists no consensus regarding the emperors intended.[2] David Aune, author of the most detailed commentary on Revelation ever written,[3] summarizes no less than nine contradictory lists of emperors found in the scholarly literature.[4] So even if the preterist interpretation were John's intention, it is not at all clear what he had in mind here. And recent discoveries raise doubts that there occurred extensive persecution against Christians during the time of Domitian.[5] So the Roman emperor hypothesis is shaky at best.[6]

A number of preterist scholars such as Aune, therefore, see the seven heads of Revelation 17 in more symbolic terms, although here too we observe a lack of consensus on their meaning.[7] So for mainstream scholarship Revelation 17:10 remains an unclear text, one of the most vexing in all of the Bible. This fact should caution anyone who seeks to find meaning for today in a superficial reading of the passage.[8]

Major Adventist Interpretations

Turning to Adventist interpretation of the passage, Ellen White, the most authoritative Adventist interpreter, does not seem to address the issue of Revelation 17:10 at all. In fact, she has extremely little to say even about Revelation 17 as a whole.[9]

Uriah Smith also commented relatively little about the seven heads of Revelation 17:7-11. Although he does seem to believe that the "one is now" head of verse 10 is the Rome of John's day[10] he makes no attempt to interpret the "five have fallen."

In his revision and update of Smith's work,[11] Mervyn Maxwell appears to move away from Smith's position that the "one is now" head must be understood as reigning in John's day (although he is not perfectly clear on this). Instead he suggests the "one is now" could be the time of the wounded head of Revelation 13:3, which he understands as "Christian Rome in its wounded state." In this scheme the seven heads are Babylon, Persia, Greece, pagan Rome, Christian Rome, Christian Rome (wounded) and Christian Rome (revived).[12] Jacques Doukhan has endorsed Maxwell's position in some detail.[13]

Kenneth Strand, in an article submitted to the Daniel and Revelation Committee of the General Conference, agreed with Smith that the standpoint of the "one now is" is John's day.[14] But like Smith, he merely asserted that view and did not make a case for it. He also argued that we should translate the "hills" of Revelation 17:9 as "mountains"[15] and that mountains in Bible prophecy never represent individuals but always kingdoms or empires. Strand goes on to list the five "that have fallen" as Egypt, Assyria, Babylon, Persia, and Greece, and the "one now is" as the Rome of John's day.[16] One can infer from Strand's comments elsewhere that he understood the seventh head to be papal Rome of the Middle Ages.[17] His presentation, unfortunately (for our purposes), was more of an attack on preterism than an outline of what Adventists could or should make of the text.

Ranko Stefanovic, in his recent commentary, seems to take up the view of Strand, but without detailed argument.[18]

In conclusion, I would note that neither the scholars nor the administrators of the church have put major effort into the interpretation of Revelation 17:7-11. It may reflect Ellen White's seeming disinterest, the difficulty of the passage, and the sense that it is not crucial to Adventist faith and identity. The current interest in the passage, however, calls for a more careful analysis of the text from an Adventist perspective.

The Exegetical Process

What follows is not an exhaustive study of the possibilities in the text or the conclusions in the secondary literature about the passage. But I trust that it will be a helpful starting point and guide for future work. All who wish to contribute to the church's understanding of this text will want to consider the methodology offered in my book *The Deep Things of God*, pages 93-176. If anyone is aware of a more thorough method for approaching the text of Revelation, I would welcome learning about it. But until then I have grounded the following in that methodology.

A brief note on the role of scholarly exegesis in the church's exploration of the Bible is warranted. Many people feel that if we could only examine all the scholarly evidence in the Greek and other sources, every Bible text would become clear. Others regard the disagreements among scholars as an indication that the whole process of biblical scholarship is a waste of time. Both extreme positions fall short of reality. The process of exegesis will sometimes clarify things that were poorly understood. But at other times it will muddy waters that we previously thought were clear.

In simple terms, exegesis helps us discern which texts of the Bible are clear and which are not. "In a multitude of counselors there is safety." When exegetes from a wide variety of backgrounds and perspectives all agree on a text, we can safely conclude that the passage is reasonably clear. When the same exegetes find little to agree about in a text, it is usually a "problem text" or a "difficult passage." My playful description of an unclear text is one "in which it is much easier to see the flaws in someone else's interpretation than to build a convincing interpretation of your own." Revelation 17:10 is one of those unclear texts.

Texts can be ambiguous for a lot of reasons. We may not be familiar with the exact meaning of certain words in the text. The grammar and syntax of the Greek may allow more than one interpretation of a construction. Perhaps we may not know the intended audience to which a work is addressed. The viewpoint that a biblical author is contradicting or responding to may have been lost or the setting or the time in which a revelation was presented. An author may be alluding to some earlier and now-vanished literary text. Or an author may be echoing an oral tradition that we do not have access to. God meets people where they are. And when we are not where the original readers were, the chances of misunderstanding can be great.

But God is in control of His revelations. The Spirit is available to help us understand what is of ongoing validity and importance. Certain tools of exegesis will open our eyes to evidence and unlock possibilities that we would otherwise miss. So there is hope that careful exegesis can shed some light on Revelation 17:7-11, bringing at least pockets of clarity to what has been previously foggy. At the least it can help us see what is clear and what is not and why. This can help us avoid overstating our case for a particular interpretation of the text.

ARMAGEDDON AT THE DOOR

A Brief Analysis of the Context
Relation to Chapters 16 and 18

As we have seen, Revelation 17 builds on the earlier vision of the seven bowl plagues in Revelation 15 and 16. Since the woman of Revelation 17:1 is named Babylon (verse 5), and the "many waters" of Babylon are the Euphrates River (Jer. 51:7, 13), Revelation 17 is particularly an exegesis of Revelation 16:12-16 (which includes reference to Armageddon), the sixth bowl plague. Thus Revelation 17 is about the final battle of earth's history (Rev. 17:12-17).

After John's initial encounter with the bowl angel (Rev 17:1, 2), he goes into vision "in the spirit" (verse 3). He sees a woman (presumably the prostitute of verses 1, 2) sitting on a scarlet beast with seven heads and 10 horns (verse 3). The woman is dressed in spectacular, royal fashion (verse 4), reminiscent of the city Babylon (Rev. 18:16) and, perhaps, of Israel's high priest (Ex. 28).[19] Upon her forehead is a miter, naming her "Babylon the Great, Mother of Prostitutes" (Rev. 17:5, ESV). John sees that the woman is drunk with the blood of the saints and the martyrs of Jesus (verse 6). The sight amazes him (verse 6). The rest of the chapter is an angelic explanation of the vision of verses 3-6. So we could structure chapter 17 as follows:

1, 2: angelic introduction to the vision
3-6: vision of the woman riding the beast and John's reaction
7-11: angelic explanation of the beast and its seven heads
12-14: angelic explanation of the 10 horns and the Lamb's war
15-18: angelic explanation of the woman's destruction

The crucial distinction here is between the vision (verses 3-6), in which John sees images without explanation, and the angelic explanation, in which the angel explains and sometimes expands various details of the vision (verses 1, 2, 7-18). This distinction between vision and explanation will prove helpful at a later stage of our study.

Revelation 18 is, in some ways, a mirror image of Revelation 17—two sides of the same coin. Revelation 17 portrays Babylon in terms of a prostitute, while Revelation 18 symbolizes it as the great city. Revelation 17:18 links the two images into one: "And the woman that you saw is the great city that has dominion [Greek: "kingship"] over the kings of the earth" (ESV). Since Revelation 18 clearly portrays some of the final events of earth's history, Revelation 17 is a description of end-time realities as well.

APPENDIX

Relation to Earlier Beasts

A second aspect of the context is that both woman and beast have interesting antecedents in chapters 12 and 13. The seven-headed, 10-horned beast is preceded by the dragon in Revelation 12 and the beast from the sea in Revelation 13. The seven heads in Revelation 17 are clearly consecutive (Rev. 17:10). In Revelation 12, on the other hand, we find no indication whether the heads of the dragon function all at once or in sequence. Revelation 13, however, states about the beast from the sea that "one of his heads was, as it were, wounded to death" (verse 3). So we should also see the seven heads of Revelation 13 as consecutive.[20]

If this is so, the dragon of chapter 12, the sea beast of chapter 13, and the scarlet beast of chapter 17 manifest three different stages of one and the same beast. The dragon of chapter 12 is best associated with the actions of the Roman Empire (in the person of Herod the Great) against the Christ child (Rev. 12:5).[21] The activities of the sea beast are later.[22] Evidently the sea beast operates under two separate heads. The first is wounded to death, but then the sea beast returns with a new head at a later time (Rev. 13:3, 12). Adventists have been fairly unanimous in seeing the actions of the sea beast before its wounding as a forecast of the medieval church.

The scarlet beast of Revelation 17 clearly functions in the context of the seven last plagues, so it is the final form of the beast, presumably under the "eighth" head. It is the very last manifestation before the beast joins the false prophet in the lake of fire (Rev. 19:17-21). The seven heads of the beast in Revelation 17:7-11 would, therefore, seem to include the actions of the dragon and the sea beast, actions that are manifestations of the beast under earlier heads.

Relation to the Woman of Revelation 12

The woman of Revelation 17 recalls the faithful woman of Revelation 12. John's last view of the faithful woman was in the desert. There the earth rescued her from the flood of water spewed out of the dragon's mouth (Rev. 12:15, 16). When he again sees a woman out in the desert, it is the harlot Babylon! No wonder John is astonished (John 17:6). Clearly the Babylon of Revelation 17 has a Christian face. She represents the end-time religious counterfeit of God's faithful remnant, the seed of the woman (Rev. 12:17).

The Context of Daniel 7

An additional context of the three beasts is its background in Daniel 7. When you look carefully at that vision, you realize that the four beasts of Daniel 7 total seven heads and 10 horns! The connection with Daniel 7 is clearest in the beast from the sea (Rev. 13:1-10). It has characteristics of the lion, the bear, the leopard, and the fourth beast (cf. Rev. 13:1, 2). It, like the beasts of Daniel 7, emerges from the sea (Rev. 13:1; Dan. 7:2). All three beasts are designed to recall the vision of Daniel 7. The prophecy of Revelation 17 is modeled, therefore, on the beasts of Daniel 7. The various heads there symbolize more than individual kings or religious leaders—they represent whole nations or empires that rule for extended periods. Thus the seven heads of Revelation 17 probably symbolize whole nations or empires rather than individuals.

Revelation 17:7-11

The passage begins innocently enough. The angel tells John that he will explain the mystery of the woman and the seven-headed, 10-horned beast that the prophet had seen in the vision (Rev. 17:7). But things quickly get confusing after that. In verse 8 the beast "was, now is not, and will come up out of the Abyss and go to his destruction" (NIV). Then the angel describes the amazement of the wicked ("those that dwell on the earth") when they see the beast who "was, and is not, and will become present" (see verse 8).

In verse 9 the mind that has wisdom learns that the seven heads are actually seven mountains, "on which the woman sits. These are also seven kings" (verses 9, 10, NKJV). So the woman is not only sitting on a beast, but on seven mountains (which are the same as the seven heads). And the seven mountains are also seven "kings" (likely "kingdoms" as in Daniel 2:36-45, the last kingdom being represented by a mountain).

Then in verse 10 John learns that five of the heads/mountains/kings "have fallen, one is [now], and the other has not yet come; but when he does come, he must remain for a little while" (NIV). The crucial question of this verse is as to when we should understand the "now." Is it the time of John, as Strand and Stefanovic have suggested? Perhaps is it the time of the vision, when the woman sits on the beast? Or is it the time of the deadly wound in Revelation 13:3, as Maxwell has offered? Some who have seen in the seven heads seven recent popes have proposed that the "deadly wound" was actually the wounding of John Paul II in St. Peter's Square more than 20 years ago. But John Paul did not die on that occasion, and the force of the Greek in Revelation 13:3 is "wound of his death." John Paul's eventual death was not connected to the injury he suffered 24 years earlier.

In Revelation 17:11 things get even more complicated. "And the beast who was and is not, the same is an eighth [head] and is one of the seven, and he will go to [his] destruction." The passage does not mention the word "head," leaving ambiguous whether beast or head or both are intended by "eighth." The fact that "eighth" appears connects this verse with the seven heads of Revelation 17:9, 10. But it is the "beast" that is the "eighth," and the "eighth" is described in the same language as the beast itself in verse 8: "he will go to [his] destruction." So is the eighth head the same thing as the beast? What about the other heads, then? Are they "the beast," or are they separate from it?

The more carefully you look at the passage, the more things you find that don't seem to hold together. The best explanation of verse 11 would seem to be that the beast exists itself in seven (or eight) consecutive phases, each of which has its own head. When John views the beast in the vision (Rev. 17:3), it is in its eighth phase. But the seven heads he sees are echoes of the seven earlier phases.[23] So while the beast appears with seven heads in the vision, the image of a seven-headed beast represents a beast that lives, dies, and is resurrected seven or eight times.[24] Is your head spinning yet? Mine too.

What We Know for Sure So Far

A few things are clear so far. 1. Revelation 17 is sandwiched between two end-time passages: the bowl plagues of Revelation 16 and the fall of Babylon in Revelation 18. So the primary focus of the vision is on the end-time battle of Armageddon and the fall of Babylon. 2. In terms of the reality to which the symbols point, the seven heads of the beast are consecutive or sequential—they are not all on the beast at the same time. 3. The detailed description of the seven heads is part of an angelic explanation (Rev. 17:7-18) and is thus not part of the vision proper (verses 3-6).

Earlier in this book I show how the woman who sits on the beast represents worldwide religious authority in opposition to the end-time remnant. The beast itself symbolizes the civil and secular powers of the world united against God's people and in support of prostitute Babylon. To save space, I will not repeat the biblical evidence for these conclusions. The beast itself is not, therefore, to be confused with the end-time Papacy, the potential head of worldwide religious authority. The beast depicts the civil powers of the world who end up turning on Babylon and destroying it (verse 16). So a fourth thing is reasonably certain: 4. The beast of Revelation 17 represents political and military power rather than religious authority.

The Time of the "Now"

A major unresolved question is exactly when the seven heads function. Are they all at the end of time? Or were at least five of them already in the past when John wrote his book? Or is the time of the head that "is now" somewhere in between, as Maxwell has suggested? Are there some patterns in Bible prophecy that can guide us to a solid answer to our questions? I believe that we need to keep two basic principles in mind.

God Meets People Where They Are

A generally accepted principle of biblical interpretation is that God meets people where they are. In other words, He gives Scripture in the time, place, language, and culture of specific human beings.[25] He respected the knowledge, experience, and background of the biblical writers. Paul, with his "Ph.D.," expresses God's revelation to him in a different way than does Peter, the fisherman. John writes in simple, clear, almost childlike Greek. On the other hand, the author of Hebrews has the most complex and literary Greek in all the New Testament with the exception of the first four verses of Luke. In Matthew you have someone who understands the Jewish mind.[26] Mark, on the other hand, reaches out to the Gentile mind.[27] So the revelations recorded in the Bible came in a way comprehensible to each audience.

Ellen White clearly articulates this principle in *Selected Messages*:

"The writers of the Bible had to express their ideas in human language. It was written by human men. These men were inspired of the Holy Spirit. . . .

"The Scriptures were given to men, not in a continuous chain of unbroken utterances, but piece by piece through successive generations, as God in His providence saw *a fitting opportunity* to impress man at sundry times and divers places. . . .

APPENDIX

"The Bible, perfect as it is in its simplicity, does not answer to the great ideas of God; for infinite ideas cannot be perfectly embodied in finite vehicles of thought" (book 1, pp. 19-22; italics supplied).[28]

While this principle is true for the Bible in general, does it apply to the sweeping historical sequences of apocalyptic? Did God consider the language, time, and place of Daniel and John when He provided the visions they record in their books? Indeed He did. Biblical apocalyptic also met God's people where they were. The book of Revelation is firmly grounded in the experience of seven churches in Asia Minor (Rev. 1:11, 19; 22:16). God intended it to make sense to the one who reads and those who hear (Rev. 1:3).[29] The vision of Christ utilized the language of John's past, the Old Testament, as the primary source for its symbolism.

And God meets people where they are in Daniel as well. While Adventists tend to distinguish between Nebuchadnezzar's "dream" and Daniel's "vision,"[30] the biblical text does not make that distinction. The experience of the two "prophets" was the same.[31] In Daniel 2:28 the prophet tells Nebuchadnezzar, "Your dream and the visions that passed through your mind as you lay on your bed are these" (NIV). Daniel 7:1 explains that "Daniel had a dream, and visions passed through his mind as he was lying on his bed" (NIV). The Aramaic of Daniel 7:1 is essentially identical with that of Daniel 2:28.[32] In both cases God chose to reveal Himself in visionary form. He was in full control of the revelation.[33]

To Nebuchadnezzar in Daniel 2 God portrays the future world empires by means of an idol.[34] Such imagery makes sense in that time and place because, to the pagan king, the nations of the world were bright and shining counterparts of the gods they worshipped. For Daniel the Hebrew prophet, on the other hand, the nations of the world were like vicious, ravenous beasts who were hurting his people. So in the vision of Daniel 7 God again draws on the prophet's knowledge and setting. This time, instead of symbolism drawn from the Babylonian world, He shapes the vision along the lines of the Creation story in Genesis 1 and 2.[35] God describes Daniel's future in terms of a new creation.

The sequence of history in both visions is roughly the same (Dan. 2:45; 7:17) as is the primary message: God is in control of history (Dan. 2:37, 38; 7:26, 27). But in his choice of imagery, God meets apocalyptic writers where they are![36] The above summary leads me to a couple conclusions:

1. God speaks to the prophets in the context of their own time, place, and circumstances. He communicates in language they can understand and appreciate, even when He employs apocalyptic terms. The Lord uses the language of the prophet's past to paint a picture of the prophet's future. God meets people where they are. In our study of Bible prophecies such as Revelation 17, therefore, it is imperative that we seek to understand them in terms of the original time, place, language, and circumstances, as well as the content of the whole of Scripture. Thus God's meaning for today will not contradict the message that He placed in the vision in the first place.

We should not confuse this with the preterist position. The preterist viewpoint argues that Daniel and Revelation offer no insight into the far future of their prophets. Apocalyptic books speak instead to the immediate situation, and that situation only. An Adventist approach, on the other hand, believes that God places in the apocalyptic visions accurate information about the far future, but that He describes that future in the language of the prophet's time and place. If we want to understand what God was telling John about the future, we need to first understand what the prophet himself grasped.

2. The purpose of apocalyptic visions is not simply to satisfy human curiosity about the future (although that may have played a role in the first instance, according to Daniel 2:29). They are a message about divine character and workings. God is not only communicating something about the future course of history—He is revealing Himself as the one who is in control of that history. To study apocalyptic only as a key to unlock details of the future is to miss its message about a Deity who seeks to be known by His people. From a Christian perspective, apocalyptic is never rightly understood unless its central focus is on the "son of man," Jesus Christ.

The Difference Between Vision and Interpretation

In light of the previous section, however, we must distinguish between the time of apocalyptic visions and the time of their interpretation. In a vision the prophet can travel anywhere in the universe and to any point of time, including all the way to the end of the world. The events of the vision are not necessarily located in the prophet's time and place. But when the prophet receives an explanation afterward, it always comes in the time, place, and circumstances of the visionary.

We can clearly see this principle in Daniel 2. While the vision of the statue carries Nebuchadnezzar to the end of earth's history, the explanation of the vision by Daniel is firmly grounded in Nebuchadnezzar's time and place. The interpretation begins with a straightforward, unambiguous assertion, "You are that head of gold" (Dan. 2:38, NIV). The prophet then tells the king that the series of kingdoms that follow are "after you" (verse 39, NKJV) in point of time.

As was the case with Daniel 2, the apocalyptic prophecy of Daniel 7 divides into two parts: a description of the vision, which transports the prophet through time and space (Dan. 7:2-14), and an explanation of the vision, given in the language, time, and place of the prophet (verses 15-27). Even though Daniel experienced all elements of the vision, including the final events, the explanation clarifies that the vision is essentially about the future experience of Daniel's people (verses 17, 18, 23-27). The explanation comes for the benefit of Daniel first. It, therefore, interprets things in terms of his location in the world and history, that is, in terms he can understand.[37] The same pattern appears in Daniel 8 and Zechariah 4.[38]

So whenever vision moves to interpretation, the principle of "God meets people where they are" must be applied to the explanations given. Prophets don't usually seem to grasp the revelation from the visions alone.[39] An explanation is necessary for the revelation to be understood.[40] Since that explanation occurs for the benefit of the prophet, it derives from the time, place, and circumstances in which the seer lives. Present, past, and future are not grounded in visionary time, but in terms of the prophet's physical location and timeframe. This principle has profound implications for the interpretation of difficult apocalyptic texts such as Revelation 17:7-11.

Implications for the Seven Popes View

Popular views that tie the heads of Revelation 17 to specific recent popes run counter to a number of aspects of the text. First, their proponents usually consider the seven heads as beginning with Pope Pius XI in 1929. Why they should do so at all cannot be established from the text of Revelation. Normally, as we have seen, prophetic explanations are given in the time and place of the prophet (I am not aware of a *clear* exception to this rule). That would make the sixth head the time of John, A.D. 95.

If that is the case, seeing the seven heads as consisting entirely of end-time characters is not an option.

A further problem for this view is that the seven heads are based on Daniel 7, in which the heads do not represent individual kings or religious leaders but major nations and/or empires,[41] a fact further underlined by the equation of the heads and the kings with seven mountains. "Mountains" in Bible prophecy (such as in Daniel 2 and Jeremiah 51) symbolize major kingdoms as well. So an interpretation that requires the seven heads to represent seven individual popes stretches the imagery to unrecognizable proportions.

Furthermore, we find evidence within the book of Revelation itself that the three beasts of Revelation can be equated with the sixth head (Rev. 12—pagan Rome of John's day), the seventh head (Rev. 13—the papal Rome that succeeded pagan Rome), and the eighth head (Rev. 17 itself—the final worldwide political unity).[42] While not at the compelling level of "clear texts" in my mind, these connections move the weight of evidence strongly against seeing all seven heads as end-time individuals. If the final manifestation of the beast is political and military in nature, rather than religious, associating the heads of the beast with popes is not helpful in understanding. The Papacy is better associated with the woman of Revelation 17 rather than with the beast.

A further peril in such viewpoints as the seven popes theory is that they incline those who hold them to a species of date setting. It may be "soft" date setting (in the lifetime of this pope, or the next, rather than a specific day or year), yet it places the focus not on the spiritual message of the biblical revelation but on the speculative issue of when Jesus will return (or other end-time events will occur). I have written at length on the dangers of date setting of all kinds in *The Millennium Bug*. The desire to know the "times" and the "seasons" (Acts 1:6, 7) is natural for human beings, but it drives us to erroneous interpretations of Scripture. It is best avoided.

Seventh-day Adventists have long believed that the Papacy will play a major role in the final events of earth's history, and nothing in Revelation 17 would contradict such a view. But we find in the chapter no significant evidence that the sequence of popes at the end of time is the focus of the passage. At best such a view is the sum total of a series of questionable assumptions. It cannot, therefore, offer compelling guidance to the larger body of the church. Rather it convinces only those who need it to be so.

Implications for the Maxwell/Doukhan View

The view outlined by Maxwell and detailed by Doukhan comes closer to the evidence of Revelation 17 in its larger context than the seven popes theory. Since Doukhan argues this position in the most detail, I will outline his argument briefly.[43]

Doukhan would agree with me that the seven heads of Revelation 17 are based on Revelation 13 and Daniel 7 and that we need to see them as major empires or nations.[44] From his perspective the Daniel 7 connection becomes determinative of the beginning of the seven heads. The beast from the sea (Rev. 13) incorporates all five major entities of Daniel 7: the lion of Babylon, the bear of Persia, the leopard of Greece, the indescribable beast of Rome, and the little horn that follows the fourth beast. For Doukhan this articulates the five that "have fallen." Since the list derives from Daniel 7, it must begin with the first beast of Daniel 7—the lion of Babylon.[45]

Next Doukhan argues in impressive fashion that the three sequences of four parts each in Revelation 17:8-11 are parallel to each other.[46] He feels that we should see these four-part sequences as four phases of the beast as it approaches its final destruction in Revelation 17-19:

Rev. 17:8	Rev. 17:10	Rev. 17:11
once was	five have fallen	once was
now is not	one is	now is not
comes up out of the Abyss	other has not yet come	eighth king
goes to destruction	remains a little while	goes to destruction

That the three sequences are completely parallel is the key to Doukhan's argument, but it does not strike me as self-evident. For one thing, the first sequence seems to relate to the beast in its end-time phase. The second sequence speaks specifically to the heads (which in Doukhan's scheme begin in the time of Daniel). The last, as we have seen, seems to blend language related to the beast in verse 8 with language related to the head sequence in verse 10. Its primary focus appears to be on the final phase of the beast.

Doukhan argues that the time of the sixth head is the period of papal wounding, that is, from 1798 to 1929. The seventh and eighth heads are one and the same, reflecting the resurgent Papacy after 1929. His argument is impressive and worth careful consideration. Its major tension with the biblical evidence, however, is in its assumption that John would be given an explanation rooted in a time frame so far into his future. The sixth head that "now is" is best understood in terms of John's time and place, and in light of its location in the angelic explanation portion of the chapter rather than the vision proper. The evidence Doukhan draws from Revelation 13 and Daniel 7 is important, but it is not enough, I believe, to argue that we should overturn the basic biblical pattern of vision and explanation.

What Do I Think?

Obviously, what I think is ultimately not the issue, but I owe it to you, in light of years of wrestling with these texts, at least to give the position that makes the most sense to me at this point. The cornerstone to my position is again the basic conviction that in revelation God meets people where they are. When God explains Himself to a prophet (whether directly or through an angel), His intention is to make things as clear as that person can handle (John 16:12). God's explanations have extended meanings beyond what the original prophet could understand, but those extended meanings will never contradict the original revelation. They will be natural expansions or outgrowth of what the prophet received and understood (see *The Deep Things of God*, pages 33-78 for much more on this principle).

This means that the natural way to understand the "five have fallen, one is now, and one is yet to come" is in terms of John's time and place. The seven heads represent a series of empires or major national movements in the course of human history. If the "one is now" is the Roman Empire of John's day (clearly portrayed in Rev. 12), what are the five empires that have fallen? I agree with Strand and Stefanovic that they would be the five great nations/empires that functioned as superpower enemies of God's people throughout the Old Testament. Thus they would be Egypt, which held the people of God in captivity for hundreds of years; Assyria, which subjugated Judah and destroyed Israel; plus the three powers mentioned in Daniel 2, 7, and 8: Babylon, Persia, and Greece.

The seventh empire, future from John's day, would be the beast from the sea (Rev. 13), the great papal power that dominated the world spiritually and politically for more than 1,000 years. I understand the "eighth head" to be the beast of Revelation 17 itself, a worldwide political and military unity yet to occur.

Such a view coheres with what we have learned about the battle of Armageddon in this book. In the final days of earth's history a worldwide political confederacy functions in support of a global religious unity (dragon, beast, and false prophet—Rev. 16:13-19) for a period of time (Rev. 17:1-3). The two great powers seek to destroy God's faithful remnant (Rev. 12:17; 14:1; 16:15; 17:14), but they get turned aside by God's intervention (Rev. 17:17). In fury at being deceived by end-time Babylon (Rev. 13:13, 14; 16:13, 14), the worldwide political unity turns on Babylon and destroys it (Rev. 17:16). This political unity is the eighth head, the final manifestation of the beast. It goes to its destruction (Rev. 17:8, 11) in the final conflict at the second coming of Jesus itself (Rev. 19:11-21).

A feature of the text I still wrestle with is the intriguing phrase "the same is an eighth [head] and is one of the seven" (see Rev. 17:11). The eighth and last phase of the beast's manifestations is, in a sense, the rebirth or reincarnation of one of the seven earlier ones. Which of the seven? Babylon? That would be supported by the name of the prostitute, but it is not the name of the beast. The Roman Empire? The connections with the beast of Revelation 12 suggest that. Papal Rome? Here we note the connections with Revelation 13, and the concept of the "image of the beast" that would play a major role at the end of time (Rev. 13:15). If one goes this way, I prefer the latter viewpoint, but Beale may be correct when he says that "one of the seven" simply means that the eighth is of the same character as the seven.[47] Like those that precede it, the eighth head is evil, rules on the earth, and is part of a succession of historical events.

Conclusion

Does my view explain every detail of the text? Obviously not. In spite of our best efforts Revelation 17 remains, and may always be, something of a problem text. While the above is how I make sense of this text, I am open to the possibility that I have missed some things that might prove my position inadequate in one way or the other. But those who wish to counter my view must not think that such a refutation can come from a superficial reading of the text. There is much information that I have not been able to share here, but in spite of all my studies I remain in awe of the complexity of this text.

To me the safest conclusion we can make is to avoid basing a major spiritual or theological insight on the twists and turns of this fascinating vision. While none of the above views may ultimately prove correct, the evidential base for a "seven popes" view is too problematic to accept as fact. At best it is the hopeful suggestion of some who long for Jesus to come soon. I share with them in that longing, and I respect the anticipation that drives them and also their desire to trigger revival and reform in the church. We must not forget, however, that when Jesus does in fact come, most of us will still be surprised at His timing (1 Thess. 5:1-3), no matter how hard we have tried to sniff it out in advance. According to both Matthew and Ellen White, God will reveal the day and the hour only when the approaching cloud is already visible to our sight![48]

Satan will use any means he can to distract us from our double mission of character development and gospel outreach. The great spiritual messages of Adventist faith are compelling in their own right. The clear message of Scripture is the everlasting gospel in the end-time context of God's final judgment (Rev. 14:6, 7). That message does not need an artificial boost from speculative exegesis of difficult passages.

---

[1] David E. Aune, *Revelation 17-22*, Word Biblical Commentary (Nashville: Thomas Nelson, 1998), vol. 52c, pp. 944, 945.

[2] See the analysis of this position by Kenneth A. Strand, "The Seven Heads: Do They Represent Roman Emperors?" in *Symposium on Revelation—Book 2*, ed. Frank B. Holbrook, Daniel and Revelation Committee Series (Silver Spring, Md.: Biblical Research Institute, 1992), vol. 7, pp. 178-206.

[3] David E. Aune, *Revelation*, Word Biblical Commentary (Waco, Tex.: Word Publishers, and Nashville: Thomas Nelson, 1997-1998), 3 vols.. The commentary contains more than 1,800 pages of relatively small print.

[4] Aune, *Revelation 17-22*, pp. 946-948.

[5] Adela Yarbro Collins, *Crisis and Catharsis: The Power of the Apocalypse* (Philadelphia: Westminster Press, 1984), pp. 69-76; Leonard Thompson, *The Book of Revelation: Apocalypse and Empire* (New York: Oxford University Press, 1990), pp. 174-185.

[6] Note also Strand's observation (p. 186, note 18) that elsewhere in Revelation the word for "hill" used in Revelation 17:9 is translated "mountain," and nowhere else does Scripture apply this word to an individual. In addition, Strand notes (p. 187) that Rome's seven hills are not sequential, as are the "hills" of Revelation 17:9.

[7] Aune, *Revelation 17-22,* p. 948.

[8] I have not analyzed the viewpoints of dispensational futurists regarding the seven heads of Revelation 17 (the position portrayed in the *Left Behind* series of novels). The reason for this is that the viewpoint, while wildly popular among evangelical Christians, is, for sound ex-

egetical reasons, not taken seriously by mainstream scholars of Revelation. I do not feel, therefore, that this approach to Revelation will be helpful to Adventist students of Revelation 17, even though careful study of the chapter may lead to the conclusion (as I currently hold) that the vision focuses on the final events of earth's history. My dismissal rests on quality of exegesis issues, not merely disagreement with dispensational futurist conclusions.

[9] A quick look at standard references offers the following comments on Revelation 17 as a whole: *The Great Controversy,* pp. 382, 440, 536; and *The Seventh-day Adventist Bible Commentary,* Ellen G. White Comments, vol. 7, p. 983 (letter 232, 1899; manuscript 24, 1891; *Review and Herald,* Nov. 29, 1892). If there are any further clear comments on Revelation 17 in published or unpublished works, I would be delighted to hear about them.

[10] Uriah Smith, *Daniel and the Revelation,* rev. ed. (Nashville: Southern Pub. Assn., 1944), p. 711.

[11] C. Mervyn Maxwell, *God Cares: The Message of Revelation for You and Your Family* (Boise, Idaho: Pacific Press, 1985).

[12] *Ibid.,* pp. 471-475.

[13] Jacques B. Doukhan, *Secrets of Revelation: The Apocalypse Through Hebrew Eyes* (Hagerstown, Md.: Review and Herald, 2002), pp. 161-164. Though his little book has gone relatively unnoticed, Doukhan in these pages offers the single most extensive exegesis of this difficult passage by any church leader or scholar. I will share his view as a significant alternative to mine at the end of this appendix.

[14] Strand, p. 191.

[15] *Ibid.,* p. 186.

[16] *Ibid.,* p. 191.

[17] *Ibid.*

[18] Ranko Stefanovic, *Revelation of Jesus Christ: Commentary on the Book of Revelation* (Berrien Springs, Mich.: Andrews University Press, 2002), p. 515.

[19] J. Massyngberde Ford, *Revelation, Anchor Bible* (Garden City, N.Y.: Doubleday, 1975), vol. 38, pp. 287, 288; cf. G. K. Beale, *The Book of Revelation,* The New International Greek Testament Commentary (Grand Rapids: Eerdmans, 1999), p. 857.

[20] The fact that the beast of Revelation 13 is grounded in the consecutive beast/kingdoms of Daniel 7 offers further evidence that the seven heads of the sea beast occur in consecutive order.

[21] Beale, p. 639; J. Ramsey Michaels, *Revelation,* The IVP New Testament Commentary Series, ed. Grant R. Osborne (Downer's Grove, Ill.: InterVarsity Press, 1997), p. 147; James Moffatt, *The Revelation of St. John the Divine,* The Expositor's Greek Testament (Grand Rapids: Eerdmans, 1956), vol. 5, p. 425; J.P.M. Sweet, *Revelation,* Westminster Pelican Commentaries (Philadelphia: Westminster Press, 1979), pp. 196, 197.

[22] The crowns shift from the heads (on the dragon in Revelation 12) to the horns (on the sea beast in Revelation 13). This mirrors the move from the head of the fourth beast to the 10 horns in Daniel 7. Just as the 10 horns are later than the fourth beast in Daniel 7, the shift of crowns from heads to horns indicates that the sea beast (which receives its authority from the dragon [Rev. 13:2]) is later than the dragon in point of history.

[23] Beale seems to have come to the same conclusion on the basis of the Greek (p. 875).

[24] Some have suggested a connection between this beast and the Hydra of ancient Greek mythology. The Hydra was a many-headed monster eventually destroyed by Hercules. But every time a head got chopped off, two grew in its place, and the monster became more fearsome than before. So the analogy is limited.

[25] *Problems in Bible Translation,* (Washington, D.C.: General Conference of SDAs, 1954), pp. 95, 96.

ARMAGEDDON AT THE DOOR

DOOR

26 Matthew continually shows how the life of Jesus fulfills the Old Testament Scriptures, with which the Jews were familiar (see, for example, Matt. 1:22, 23; 2:5, 6, 15, 17, 18). He uses Jewish terms without explanation.

27 Mark explains Jewish terms to his non-Jewish audience (compare, for example, Mark 14:12 with Matt. 26:17).

28 We find perhaps no clearer illustration of this than the Ten Commandments, which come directly from the mouth of God (Ex. 20:1-19), yet include significant elements of the cultural milieu within which they were received (slavery, idolatry, and neighbors who possess oxen and donkeys).

29 The Greek construction in Revelation 1:3 means to "hear with understanding." The language assumes that the original readers of the book would have grasped its basic message.

30 Leslie Hardinge, *Jesus Is My Judge: Meditations on the Book of Daniel* (Harrisburg, Pa.: American Cassette Ministries Book Division, 1996), pp. 27, 28, 134; Roy Allan Anderson, *Unfolding Daniel's Prophecies* (Mountain View, Calif.: Pacific Press Pub. Assn., 1975), pp. 42, 87.

31 While William Shea does not address this wording directly, he does comment, "The mode of revelation in these two cases was the same. The recipients, however, were quite different. The dream of chapter 2 was given to a pagan king initially for his own personal benefit; the dream of Daniel 7 was given directly to the prophet Daniel to communicate to God's people" (William H. Shea, *Daniel 1-7*, ed. George R. Knight, The Abundant Life Bible Amplifier [Boise, Idaho: Pacific Press Pub. Assn., 1996], p. 155.

32 Daniel L. Smith-Christopher, *The Book of Daniel: Introduction, Commentary, and Reflections*, The New Interpreter's Bible, ed. Leander E. Keck (Nashville: Abingdon Press, 1996), vol. 7, p. 100.

33 John J. Collins notes that the "vision formula" also appears in Daniel 4:13, regarding Nebuchadnezzar's dream of the great tree. John J. Collins, *Daniel With an Introduction to Apocalyptic Literature*, ed. Rolf Knierim and Gene M. Tucker, The Forms of the Old Testament Literature (Grand Rapids: William B. Eerdmans Pub. Co., 1984), vol. 20, p. 76; John J. Collins, *Daniel, A Commentary on the Book of Daniel*, ed. Frank Moore Cross, Hermeneia: A Critical and Historical Commentary on the Bible (Minneapolis: Fortress Press, 1993), p. 294.

34 I call the image an "idol" in part because of how the Old Testament uses the term elsewhere: 2 Kings 11:18; 2 Chron. 23:17; Amos 5:26, etc. But Nebuchnezzar's own reaction is instructive. In Daniel 3 he knows exactly what to do with the "image"—set it up so that people can worship it!

35 In both Genesis and Daniel things begin with a stormy sea (Gen. 1:2; Dan. 7:2). And in both cases a "son of man" receives dominion over the animals.

36 Which of the two visions reflects a perspective closer to the mind of God? I would suggest Daniel's in chapter 7. To the human mind the nations of the world are glorious things worthy of the utmost in human devotion (idolatry). While Daniel 2 has no critique of idolatry, God meets Nebuchadnezzar at his point of view to help him understand who really controls history. From God's perspective the nations are ugly, misshapen, bizarre-looking beasts who tear and destroy. His plans will never be fully accomplished through them. For the people of God devotion to country must always take second place to their devotion to God.

37 One could argue that in the midst of the explanation of Daniel 7:15-27 comes an addition to the vision. Verses 21, 22 affirm: "As I watched, this horn was waging war against the saints and defeating them, until the Ancient of Days came and pronounced judgment in favor of the saints of the Most High, and the time came when they possessed the king-

222

dom" (NIV). This seems to be a visionary extension of verse 8 and of the judgment interlude in verses 9-14. Daniel goes on to record the answer to his request for further information on the fourth beast and the little horn. "He gave me this explanation: 'The fourth beast is a fourth kingdom that will appear on earth. It will be different" (verse 23, NIV). Thus vision and interpretation is not rigidly separated, but they must nevertheless be clearly distinguished in point of time. It seems also to be the case in Revelation 17, in which the chapter begins with a short explanatory introduction (following up on the vision of the bowl plagues—Rev. 17:1, 2), followed by a short vision (verses 3-6), accompanied by a lengthy explanation of elements of the vision, including some expansions (verses 6-18).

[38] Klaus Koch divides Daniel 8 into "vision" (*Schauung*–2-14) and "meaning" (*Deutung*–15-26). Klaus Koch, "Vom Prophetischen zum apokalyptischen Visionsbericht," in *Apocalypticism in the Mediterranean World and the Near East*, ed. David Hellholm, Proceedings of the International Colloquium on Apocalypticism, Uppsala, August 12-17, 1979 (Tübingen: J.C.B. Mohr [Paul Siebeck], 1983), pp. 415-421.

Another Old Testament example of vision followed by interpretation occurs in Zechariah 4, which has a pattern similar to Daniel 7. In Zechariah 4, however, the vision is extremely brief (verse 2, 3), and is introduced by the interpreting angel (verses 1, 2). The interpretation of the vision involves a lengthy back-and-forth dialogue between the prophet and the angel (verses 1, 2, 4-14).

[39] Ellen White's son described her visions as "flashlight pictures," something like a silent movie. Sometimes an angel came to explain aspects of the vision; at other times Ellen White had to do research in commentaries and history books to gain an understanding of what God was trying to communicate to her.

[40] Susan Niditch, *The Symbolic Vision in Biblical Tradition* (Chico, Calif.: Scholars Press, 1983), p. 185.

[41] This is true also of the four heads of the leopard. Interpreters widely recognize them as representing the four divisions of Alexander's empire, three of which unquestionably survived as major nations for several hundred years. It is possible that heads may equate to specific Roman emperors in the apocryphal book of 4 Ezra (2 Esdras in the Apocrypha). Ezra sees a vision of an eagle with 12 wings and three heads (4 Ezra 11:1-12:9). The eagle is a reinterpretation of the fourth beast of Daniel 7 (4 Ezra 12:10-12). Some scholars feel that the three heads of the eagle (4 Ezra 11:29-35; 12:22-30) depict Vespasian, Titus, and Domitian. See D. S. Russell, *The Method and Message of Jewish Apocalyptic* (Philadelphia: Westminster Press, 1964), p. 194.

[42] Note the discussion under "Implications for the Maxwell/Doukhan View." See also Doukhan, pp. 161-164.

[43] Doukhan, pp. 161-164.

[44] *Ibid.*, p. 163.

[45] *Ibid.*

[46] *Ibid.*, pp. 161-163.

[47] Beale, p. 876.

[48] Matthew 24:30, 31. The only "sign" of Jesus' coming explicitly given in Matthew 24 is Jesus coming with the clouds. Cf. GThe Great Controversy, pp. 640, 641.

THE DEEP THINGS OF GOD